Winning the College Admission Game

STRATEGIES FOR PARENTS

Peter Van Buskirk

Donna —
Thanks for all
you do to help young people
achieve their educational
dreams!

Peter Van Buskirk

PETERSON'S

A ⓝelnet. COMPANY

PETERSON'S

A ⓝelnet. COMPANY

About Peterson's, a Nelnet company

Peterson's (www.petersons.com) is a leading provider of education information and advice, with books and online resources focusing on education search, test preparation, and financial aid. Its Web site offers searchable databases and interactive tools for contacting educational institutions, online practice tests and instruction, and planning tools for securing financial aid. Peterson's serves 110 million education consumers annually.

For more information, contact Peterson's, 2000 Lenox Drive, Lawrenceville, NJ 08648; 800-338-3282; or find us on the World Wide Web at www.petersons.com/about.

Editor: Wallie Walker Hammond; Production Editor: Susan W. Dilts; Manufacturing Manager: Ivona Skibicki; Composition Manager: Linda M. Williams; Interior Design: Greg Wuttke

ISBN-13: 978-0-7689-2491-6
ISBN-10: 0-7689-2491-X

Printed in the United States of America

10 9 8 7 6 5 4 3   09 08

First Edition

"Peter Van Buskirk speaks with the wisdom of both a veteran admissions officer and a loving parent. *Winning the College Admission Game* offers valuable insight on the college search for students and parents alike."

—Edward B. Fiske, author, *Fiske Guide to Colleges*

"Finally, a student-centered approach to getting into college! Peter goes inside the process and tells it like it is. His ability to engage both the parents and the students with meaningful solutions makes this a 'must read' for families getting started in the college admission process. I am sure that college access professionals engaged in the work of the National Council for Community and Education Partnerships (NCCEP) will find this resource guide helpful in guiding more low-income and minority students to gain access to postsecondary education."

—Hector Garza, Ed.D., MPH, President, NCCEP

"This book is a must-have for all parents. Read it when your child is young and continue to read it to remind yourself of all that is involved as a parent in helping your student make the best decision—the first time. The contrast of the Pyramid of Selectivity with the Admission Funnel provides visual images that truly clarify the process of admission to college."

—Alicia Roy, high school principal

"This high-quality book takes you through the process of getting into college. It is easy to understand, explains what families should be doing—from the beginning of the process of looking for the right school(s) and what those schools look for, to applying for financial help and handling acceptance or rejection."

—Ralph Langham, parent/Adjunct Professor, Stetson University

"*Winning the College Admission Game* is fun to read and filled with insider information. Peter Van Buskirk provides insights to assist you in helping your son or daughter make that important decision about college. In particular, don't miss 'The Hidden Agenda,' 'Behind the Scenes with the Admission Committee,' and 'Engaged Parenting.'"

—William Bushaw, Executive Director, Phi Delta Kappa International

"Through thoughtful analysis and lively anecdotes, the author welcomes the reader into the complicated and seemingly capricious world of college admission. Like a trusty guide in a foreign country, Van Buskirk orients teens and parents to the language and culture of college admission and provides valuable context and advice for their own unique journeys."

—Susan Kastner Tree, Director of College Counseling, Westtown School

"Amid the clutter of books telling students 'how to get in,' this book poses the far more important question of 'where do I belong?' Peter Van Buskirk makes it clear that 'winning' occurs when a student thrives socially, academically, and personally. This rule book will make that kind of 'winning' more likely."

—Mark Sklarow, Executive Director, Independent Educational Consultants Association

"*Winning the College Admission Game* takes you through the steps necessary to select a college based on reason, not stress; confidence, not uncertainty; and academic quality, not merely 'big name.' With extensive experience in the system, Van Buskirk can be trusted to help you find a good match college. Check out this book. You'll save both tears and dollars."

—Steven R. Antonoff, Ph.D., author, *College Match and College Finder*

Dedication

More than 30 years ago, I embarked on my own path to college. In the days before college rankings, Web sites, and glossy recruitment materials, the "pick it and go" approach seemed to work pretty well. I don't know that I made all the right decisions or that I took advantage of all the information I had at my disposal, but things worked out just fine. And for that, I owe my parents a debt of gratitude.

Born of a generation that believed it was important to work hard and sacrifice so that their children could experience more and better opportunities, my parents gave me—and each of my 4 siblings—the gift of a college education. They also gave us the freedom and encouragement to find our direction, to step out of their shadows, and become whomever and whatever we might be. This generosity came without question or condition. It was their choice—their gift to each of us.

I would like to dedicate this book to my parents, Mary and Max Van Buskirk, and to all other parents—past, present, and future—who, seeing the power of the potential in their children, sacrifice to give them the gifts of opportunity and encouragement. Without your belief in your children, this book would be neither possible nor necessary.

Contents

Contents

Acknowledgments

I would like to thank the editorial staff at Peterson's and, especially, my developmental editor, Wallie Hammond, for their belief in this concept and their support in bringing it to fruition. Other critical contributors who deserve recognition for their creative insights and editorial reflections are Sam Barnett, Francine Block, Varo Duffins, Don Heider, Moira McKinnon, and my sister, Margaret Van Buskirk. My children, Jennifer, Heidi, and Kyle, deserve credit for keeping me humble and making me wiser about colleges, parenting, and life in general. Finally, my wife Mischelle has been the backbone of this project. I am forever grateful for the patience and unconditional love and support she extended during the long hours and late nights of drafting and editing when it seemed this project could go on forever! This book is as much hers as it is mine.

Introduction

Dear Parent,

I am humbled and flattered to be able to share with you *Winning the College Admission Game: Strategies for Parents and Students*, a book that is dedicated to helping young people find success in the college selection process. For more than twenty-five years, I had the privilege of working in higher education as an admission officer, enrollment strategist, athletic director, and executive officer to the Provost. I have also served three tours of duty with my own children as they found their respective ways to college. If nothing else, my experience tells me two things: 1) the college-going process has become increasingly complex and 2) the wealth of available information on the topic does little to add clarity to the understanding of how young people can get from where they are to where they want to be educationally.

My first objective with this book is to unveil the mystique that enshrouds the admission process in a manner that is clear and logical regardless of the intended college destination. As consumers, we tend to become absorbed in the detail of the opportunity that stands before us in such a way that we lose our ability to see it *or ourselves* objectively. This is manifest in the college-going culture by the tendency to focus on specific destinations or colleges, rather than appropriate pathways. As a result, we have become college- or end-oriented at the expense of good decision making on behalf of our young people.

This book is an attempt to sort through the rubble and noise of the process for solutions that refocus on the student. You will note that these pages do not reference by name any schools or group of schools. That is intentional. Obsessions with names and places can be distracting to young people who need to better understand who they are and why they want to go to college. You can infer a lot about schools by what I have written and from the tools I provide you for teasing the reality from the rhetoric. I just don't believe anyone is served by holding up one school or group of schools over another at a time when kids are struggling with self-actualization.

I do believe your student will make good decisions about her future when in the possession of good information about herself and the options that lie before her. Her ability to recognize her strengths and to make smart choices in the classroom and in life will stand her in good stead as she contemplates her college options.

This brings me to my second objective for the book. Your student needs help—your help—in making these decisions. The college-going process requires teamwork between parents and their children at precisely that time in their lives when collaboration on anything may seem like a remote possibility! The concept of the "flip-book" is intended to address that dynamic. In the pages that follow, I will lend insight into the college admission process *and* provide guidance with regard to how you might engage your student in related conversations and/or activities. On the "flip" side of the book, I will do the same with your student. If this works, a common understanding will emerge of the roles and expectations that should serve the two of you well in the college planning process.

That said, the title of the book is a bit of a misnomer. The college-going process isn't a game in the sense that we traditionally think about games with rules, playing fields, and scoring opportunities. It is, however, a competition in which participants put forth their best efforts as they vie for cherished places in classes at colleges and universities around the country. There are indeed rules for this competition and "scoring opportunities" abound. One might further argue that the college applicant pools into which these young people cast their lots are, in effect, the competitive playing fields, and winning—gaining advantage on that playing field—is tantamount to "getting in." Consequently, the competition metaphor is applied consistently throughout the book.

You will discover quickly, though, that *Winning the College Admission Game: Strategies for Parents and Students* is not an answer book. It is not a guide to getting into the most elite and competitive institutions. Rather than providing "one-size-fits-all" answers, this book helps students develop a method for discovering their own answers. By revealing the logic of the selective college admission process, it enables students to make critical assessments about colleges and to find the right "fit" so that they are successful in their searches and in college itself.

As you work your way through this book, you will learn how to help your student while respecting that this important rite of passage belongs to her. So breathe deeply. You *will* survive this process. With *Winning the College Admission Game: Strategies for Parents and Students,* you have a reliable guide to a system that works—and that can make the entire experience as enjoyable as your son's or daughter's success.

—Peter Van Buskirk

Chapter 1

Adjusting to Life in the Passenger Seat

Just WHO Is Going to College?

I am often struck by the eagerness of parents as they approach the college admission process. Whether rooted in years of anticipation and planning or simply a matter of excited impulse, this eagerness is revealed whenever parents compare notes about their kids. You hear it in the stands at ball-games, at the morning coffee break, and across the backyard fence:

"*We* can't wait to get started!"

"When do you think *we* should go interview?"

"When will *we* hear as to whether *we* got in?"

Sound familiar? It makes me wonder: "Just who is really going to college?"

Ownership and the way you establish that ownership with your child will be vital to his success in the college process. In order for him to fully grasp what it takes to compete and be a good candidate, he must first own the process *and* the outcome. After all, he is the one going to college. You may be picking up the tab, but in order for this process to work—for him to embrace the opportunity with confidence—you need to discreetly slip into a supporting role.

Slide Over

Do you remember the first time you slid over and let your child take the wheel of the car—*your* car, no less? As soon as he put the car into gear, you had to summon every ounce of patience and calm you could muster. No matter how much you prepared yourself, as the car lurched forward you realized just how little control you had over the situation. With every jarring movement and casual near-miss (i.e., "*Sorry. I didn't see him coming.*"), you questioned your sanity and vowed that, if the two of you survived, you would be happy to drive him everywhere for the rest of his life!

Harrowing as that experience might have been, you were able to somehow work together to keep the car on the road. And you did go out again and again until he became adept behind the wheel. Now, he is not only comfortable driving the car, you are increasingly confident in his ability to do it well. The next step: his first road trip—with just a few of his best friends. Have fun!

Giving up control goes against the grain of just about every parenting principle by which you have attempted to live. Oh, you'll eventually do it just like thousands of parents before you, but it still won't feel natural. If you want your student to find happiness in his own space, though, you've got to give it up. The college years are his. He needs to use them to figure out who and what he will be as he enters the rest of his life.

Ownership Personified

"Dad," my daughter Heidi asked nervously, "would it be okay if I decided not to go to college right away? You know, maybe I could travel a little bit or get a job. What do you think?"

These were not exactly the words a twenty-year veteran of higher education expected to hear from one of his own! After all, that was my job—recruiting students into the "sacred pursuit" of a college degree. Of all the kids in the world, mine were supposed to "get it." This should have been part of their programming since day one. But this was my daughter. Where had I failed? What would I say?

Then it hit me. I was responding to what was going on inside me—to my disappointment—rather than her confusion. Would it really matter if she didn't go to college right away? I knew it wouldn't, even though my first thought was, "If you don't go now, I'm worried that you won't go at all—and I'm not keeping you on the payroll forever!" Then I got a grip and realized that she would be fine. She just had to figure things out her way.

To her credit, Heidi was gently trying to find her own voice in the conversation with her dad regarding her future. She had some ideas of her own that she wanted to try out and was trying her darnedest to get me to work with her. Prior to that moment, she had felt obliged to follow *my* script. Now she wanted to change the lines, if not the script. Even though I knew better, I hated to think that she might deviate from the plan, *my plan*. That's what she was asking, though. She wanted to know if she could look at the future from the perspective of her dreams and desires, not mine. It was nothing personal, just a matter of ownership. She was right on task. If there were a problem, it rested with me.

"That's okay," I said, surprised that I was able to smile and sound so confident. "What I want most for you in life is happiness and success, however you find them. I've always assumed that you would go right to college after high school. But that's my vision. What do you have in mind?"

"I don't know exactly," she said as she brightened and smiled. "I was just thinking about some things." That was it. It had been a short but powerful exchange. She now felt free to chart her own course and I had come to a clearer realization of my evolving role as a parent.

Such experiences can be humbling whatever your position in life or your relationship with your kids. I don't pretend to know what the right words are for such a conversation or that they will magically trip off our tongues as though scripted. The real wisdom in dealing with young adults in situations such as this, though, is found in knowing *when* to stop directing and *how* to start guiding. When this happens, you extend one of the greatest gifts you can give your child—the freedom to step out of your shadow, to find her own voice, and to become an adult.

Heidi now realized that she was no longer being directed. She could choose, with confidence, the path she wanted. She could travel or she could work. If she chose college, it would be on her terms. Regardless, she knew that the options were indeed hers—and she had her father's support as she figured them out.

Too often we assume that college follows immediately after high school—that it's the "thing to do." The first year of college is not just "grade 13." It is the start of a new way of learning and of your student taking control of his life. A college education, then, should be purposefully embraced and not merely accepted as the next step after high school. Perhaps taking a year or so off before college can be just the right solution for a young person. Volunteering at a homeless shelter, working in a bookshop, or finding immersion in a cross-cultural experience can be very educational.

If the time is spent productively, the focus and maturity gained through "gap year" experiences can add immeasurably to the subsequent college experience—they certainly won't diminish the strength of his application to college! I have seen marked growth and maturity in many of the young people who applied for admission after a year or so away from the classroom.

Final Thoughts for the Rider in the Passenger Seat

As your child prepares to strike out on his own, you need to make sure that his sense of self is not diminished by the "ups and downs" of the college selection process. He must proceed with the confidence that his worth is not determined by the realization of a dream, especially yours. Success or failure as an applicant to a given college will not change the course of human events! It certainly doesn't lessen the power of his potential.

As you move forward, make sure your student's needs and interests are central to the process. Know *who* you are dealing with and help him find the post–high school options that fit his aptitude, talent, and learning style. By lessening the fear of failure (that he will not meet your expectations), you increase the chance of success.

Happy outcomes are achieved when parents and their children share a healthy, student-centered perspective regarding the future and the role that college will play in defining a young person's growth and success. Wide and rich with opportunity, the educational "playing field" holds places of value for everyone. My objective is to teach you and your child how to think about the college process so that he will have the best chance possible of gaining admission and finding success.

Finding that success will require a special kind of teamwork. In order for your child to compete effectively and emerge successfully from the challenges that lie ahead, the two of you need to find a common language and a shared perspective. You also need to slide over and let him take the wheel.

Chapter 2

The Pyramid of Selectivity

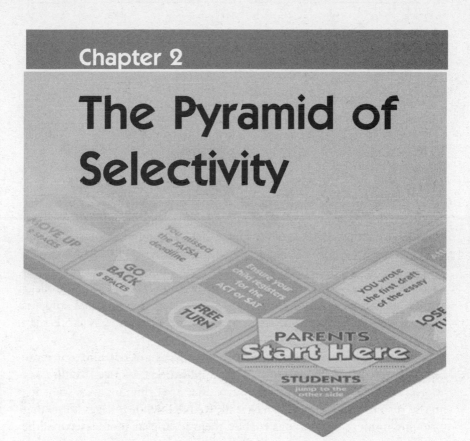

That Was Then, This Is Now!

Have you ever wondered how you would fare if you were to apply to college today? I can't tell you how often I hear parents utter, with certain relief in their voices, that they are glad to have gone to college when they did—"there's no way that I would get in if I had to apply now!" You are not alone if you are comforted in the knowledge that you don't have to do it all over again.

The truth is, you would probably do just fine. Yes, the process of going to college is different now than it was then. If nothing else, it was simpler then. You got an application and a catalog. If you lived close to the campus, maybe you sat for an interview. You applied and you got in.

The rules of the game have changed, however, and the whole process is commercialized beyond belief. Now, colleges market themselves to kids—and kids are being marketed to colleges. The media have gotten involved—often sensationalizing the process—and dozens of cottage industries have sprung up to help students find an advantage in the process. You can no longer draw exclusively on your own experiences as a college applicant to guide your child. Different times require different approaches.

In order to give your child the right kind of support, you need to become oriented to the dynamics of the process she is about to encounter. This chapter will look at why the competitive landscape has changed and lay the groundwork for what should become a successful college search.

New Behaviors

If you are the parent of a high school junior or senior, you may have gone to college in the 1970s or 80s. Since then, the number of college-age students has grown, as has the percentage of college-eligible students who are applying to four-year colleges. In particular, more women and members of ethnic minority groups have found seats in the college classroom than ever before. And the number of international students pursuing undergraduate education in the United States has more than tripled since 1990.

To complicate matters even further, colleges are reaching out more aggressively than ever to attract more applications. Notice, I didn't say more students. Most colleges and universities are brimming with students. In the rush to win the fame game (read: RANKINGS), colleges know that bringing in more applications enables them to appear more selective (the choosier the better!) while giving them more opportunities to increase their yield (percent of admitted students who enroll) on offers of admission—a sure sign of popularity.

You have probably begun to see evidence of this push for applications as your mailbox at home is stuffed—daily—with viewbooks and flyers from dozens of colleges. Initially, the rush of attention was exciting. After all, your child is wanted by . . . all . . . these . . . colleges! Then, reality sets in and you begin to look for a box large enough to stash the goods—just in case she decides to read them one day.

It is no wonder that today's students are applying to a greater number of colleges given the increasingly aggressive recruitment tactics of most schools. Not long ago, a friend called with a question about a letter his daughter, a high school senior, had received from a highly selective university. It seemed this institution was encouraging her application—after the deadline! While the young woman possessed superb credentials, her dad knew that she was not likely to be admitted at this university, a place she had not even considered previously. While he was interested in my reaction, he already had a good read on the situation. "They just want to count her application, don't they?" he asserted. He was right. There could be no other reason for such a gratuitous solicitation.

Selectivity

The concept of selectivity will be central to our thinking going forward. As you have gathered, selectivity is derived in part from the premise of demand over supply. Also known as "admit ratio," it refers to the relationship between the numbers of applicants and acceptances at a given institution. Whenever an institution can turn away applicants, it is selective.

A vast majority of the 3,000+ undergraduate schools in the United States can exercise some

Between the Lines

Find the Level of Selectivity Within Institutions
Be careful in interpreting selectivity at universities that admit by college or degree program. In such cases, the college of engineering might experience a much different level of selectivity from, say, the college of arts and sciences or the college of nursing. The admit rate for the biology program might be different from the admit rate for the history program or the education program. Make sure the admit ratio you use as a point of reference for your student is the one that speaks specifically to the college or program of interest.

degree of selectivity. The concept will be a useful tool in assessing the relative importance of different elements in your child's application. The more selective the college, the greater the importance of—you name it—SAT results, senior year grades, essay preparation, and so on.

Focusing on selectivity also helps us avoid the trap of having to talk about any one institution or type of institution. (Singling out institutions by name becomes distracting when the emphasis should be on the student.) The beauty of selectivity is that it can be easily discovered. Simply refer to the admission profiles of the schools in which your student is interested for the necessary data. How many applications were received and how many of those applicants were admitted? This information should be available on institutional Web sites and in college literature as well as in most guidebooks.

Factors That Drive Selectivity

As you research selectivity across institutions, be careful not to arbitrarily equate selectivity with *quality*. While many of the highly selective colleges and universities are indeed places that provide superb undergraduate experiences—they are places of quality—not all places can point to academic quality as the driving factor behind their levels of selectivity. Rather, the size of their applicant pools, as well as the degree to which they are selective, is directly attributable to their popularity. Factors such as climate, location, social life, and successful athletic programs are known to drive popularity at many institutions.

I watched with real interest as my eldest daughter, Jennifer, sorted through the recruitment materials that began to arrive at our house in her junior year. The early sorting seemed straightforward. She had established two piles of literature. Every brochure on the first pile featured a picture of a palm tree, a pool, or a sandy beach on the cover. All other literature went on the second pile. Curious about her thought process, I inquired about her sorting criteria. She responded simply and without hesitation, "Well, Dad, you know I'm a warm weather person!"

I had just been reminded that popular locations can be powerful drivers of selectivity! Locations in exotic climates, and not academic quality, are the drawing cards for thousands of students who apply to colleges that, as a result, become increasingly selective. The same is true of schools in "hot" urban environments. How often do you hear kids assert that they want to go to Boston? It almost doesn't matter which school just as long as it is in Boston! Now, Boston is a great "college town," but many of its resident institutions have enjoyed far more popularity (and selectivity) than they might have were they to be located in just about any other city.

Successful athletic programs can boost popularity. More than one university can point to basketball championships or football heroics that have pushed their selectivity through the roof. The same can be said of colleges with robust social environments (party schools?!) or lists of famous alumni.

So far, we have touched on some of the variables that contribute to an institution's selectivity—variables that drive an institution's applicant total upward. Next, we will take a look at how relative selectivity can be expressed in graphic terms.

The Pyramid of Selectivity

Imagine that all the colleges in the United States can be located some-where on a pyramid according to their levels of selectivity—or how hard it is to get into each. The farther up the pyramid you go, institutions become increasingly selective and fewer in number. The most selective are at the top of the pyramid; those that are easier to get into are at the bottom of the pyramid.

The Pyramid of Selectivity

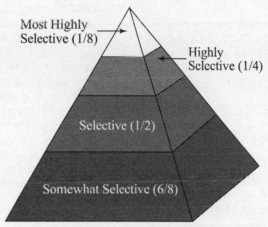

(Fractions approximate the odds of getting in at each level of selectivity.)

It is important to note that there are excellent schools all over the Pyramid of Selectivity—at the top, at the middle, and at the lower levels. You do your child a disservice if you allow her to believe that she should not settle for anything less than a college at the top of the Pyramid—especially when such a place might not be the best place for her. In reality, the biggest differences among most colleges are not qualitative. Quite simply, some are just harder to get into than others for reasons that have nothing to do with quality.

The Pyramid of Selectivity will be instructive throughout this book as it provides context for the discussion of a whole range of factors in the admission process. For example, you may be curious to know how the "C" your daughter got in chemistry will affect her chances. Or how the slow start she experienced in her freshman year will affect her competitiveness. In each case, the answer will be: "it depends."

It depends on where she aspires on the Pyramid. If her grades have improved since and she is looking at a university that will admit two out of three (middle of the Pyramid), she may be in luck as that place can afford to be more forgiving of irregularities on her record. The university that admits one out of eight, however, will be a long shot as the depth of the competition among its candidates forces it to make fine distinctions *among the students who submit "straight A" records*. A random "C" can lead to an early exit from the competition at such "hard to get into" schools.

In fact, the same record that is rewarded with admission and a scholarship at one level of selectivity might not even be admitted at another level. That is not a reflection on the student as much as it is a factor of the extraordinary competition at some institutions. Each will make decisions to admit and, in many cases, provide financial support to students in a manner that is reflective of its institutional values.

Between the Lines

The Choices They Make
Determination and attentiveness to detail are critical elements for young people as they *prepare* to compete for admission to college. Much of their ultimate success rests in the pattern of choices they make academically, the decisions to spend extra effort in learning, and the investment in those special interests and talents that set them apart from their peers. The choices they make speak volumes about who they are and what they want to become—key points of distinction as they compete for admission.

The "Yes" Letter

Most colleges on the Pyramid are selective to some degree—they can say "no" to at least some of their applicants. As a college applicant, then, it is not enough to be the best—to simply show up and expect to be admitted based simply on absolute merit. Rather, your student must put forth her best effort in all phases of the competition whether she is considering colleges at the top, middle, or bottom of the Pyramid.

The fact that she is bright and talented is a good start. Our objective is to give her a formula for a strong finish. Make no mistake about it. Applying to a college—wherever it might fall on the Pyramid—places your child squarely in the middle of a competition that does not lack for highly qualified candidates. The winners receive the "Yes" letters.

Preparation

The "winners" in the college admission game are typically the competitors who have done the most to prepare themselves. Here, "the devil is in the details." Coaches preach attentiveness to the little things. And they insist that such attentiveness comes through earnest practice and preparation. They are never willing to concede anything to a competitor with seemingly superior talent.

The real competition for entrance into college, then, begins long before any applications are submitted—long before most students actually begin to think about life after high school. College may be on *your* radar screen as an objective for your teenager, but it remains a distant thought for her even on a good day! She has too many other and more important things to think about. Here's the scary thing: *It is precisely the stuff that happens during the months and years of youthful oblivion before a credential is submitted that will have a bearing on the outcome of her college applications.*

Revelations such as this about the college entrance process are often unsettling to parents whose high school students have already progressed beyond the point at which they could have been counseled in different directions. The "if only" laments begin to emerge. "If only we had known about the importance of course selections . . ." "If only we had understood the importance of visiting college campuses . . ." "If only we had known about what colleges consider two or three years ago."

The intent of the following chapters is to put you "in the know." Gaining this insight now, however, puts you in the awkward position of seeing the future but not being able to act on it directly. Instead, you get to watch as events unfold in slow motion. Your parental instincts want to draw you into action, but *you can't do the things that need to be done* in order for your student to be well prepared for the competition. You might want to take care of everything, but this one is on her.

Your Role

You *do* need to be prepared, though, to guide and support. You need to see the road ahead so you can help your student avoid the dead-ends and pitfalls. You need to be in a position to coach your student and help her make informed choices when she may not be immediately inclined to connect the dots on her own. (I will do what I can to lend a hand in the other half of the book!) Finally, you need to summon every ounce of patience and develop a sense of humor.

As she draws closer to the application process, your child *will* benefit from your insight and support with regard to preparation. You may not think that she will listen to you, but the chances are that she really does value your experience and perspective. Besides, this is going to be your best chance to make a difference. She is the one who's going to college. She is the one who must compete.

In moving forward, remember to guide rather direct. Ask rhetorical questions that require reflection and a focus on "why" rather than "what, when, and where." In doing so, you will help her find the answers and direction she needs. Put the development of her talents and interests—and not college entrance requirements—at the center of your conversations. Encourage her to be true to her passions, to be passionate about her work, and to keep her expectations reasonable while striving to do her best.

Getting into college is a big deal. Regardless of your child's aspirations as they relate to the Pyramid, the stakes are high as the participants compete on an academic and intellectual proving ground. It is an intense competition among worthy contestants at the top of their respective games. As a result, the whole process—the gauntlet of essays, interviews, tests, and more tests—can take on Olympic dimensions for your student. The outcome determines who moves on to which college.

The stakes are also high because your child is trying to prove herself to you. Be alert to the fact that a lot of her self-esteem is wrapped up in both the process and the outcomes. The further up the Pyramid she aspires, the stiffer the competition. The odds of success may be against her—in some cases, very long against her—even though she is a "qualified" applicant. By collaborating, we will try to give her the best chance of finding success.

Nonetheless, there can be no guarantees. The outcome will rest less on absolute merit—high scores, grades, and extracurricular activities that are common among most applicants—and more on preparation, passion, and good fortune. Whatever the outcome, your child must feel your unconditional love and support. Applications may fall short, but the young people who stand behind them must not be allowed to feel as though they have failed.

Chapter 3

Beginning the Conversation About College

MOVE UP 3 SPACES

GO BACK 3 SPACES

FREE TURN

Because you child registers for the ACT or SAT

YOU wrote the first draft of the essay

LOSE TURN

PARENTS **Start Here**

STUDENTS jump to the other side

Special Instructions

One of the most daunting tasks facing a young person in the college search is determining the colleges to which he will apply. Unless he is one of the rare individuals who has had his whole life figured out from a very young age, he probably shudders at the thought of getting started. How? When? With over 3,000 colleges and universities from which to choose, where should he apply?

Adding to the dilemma is the fact that not all kids are alike. There are no cookie-cutter solutions. If you have more than one, you know what I am talking about. Each young person holds a different understanding of his circumstance and is motivated by expectations that arise from it. Each views the world from a different place. While the process might seem like it should be straightforward, the teenager with whom you are dealing does come with special instructions.

I am reminded of this every time I am with my three kids. They are very different human beings or, as they would suggest, "wonderfully unique individuals." The routes they took to college, as well as their interests and strengths and commitments to the process, varied widely. Happily, the process—however we ended up defining it—worked. We managed to survive each other and they all found passage into wonderful college homes. Along the way, I discovered that the very process itself can be as humbling as it is revealing and rewarding. I also found that the trick to engaging a student in the college process involves listening more and doing less.

Planning for Quality Options

Before you even start to talk with your child about places and programs, you need to establish a roadmap or a string of guideposts that will guide him logically through his decision making. Kids like to know why things are happening in their lives. While college may be the assumed next step in life, make sure he begins to internalize *why* that is the case—or, for that matter, *if* it is the case. Trying to figure out where to go or how to get in may be premature if he doesn't have a good grasp on why he is going.

Such a roadmap might resemble what can be referred to as "the decision tree." The basic premise is that, faced with options, one can weigh the consequences of each before taking action. Upon achieving an objective, another set of options can be considered. You have probably employed this "if then" tactic in other aspects of parenting as well. In doing so, you have helped your student understand that his options are a direct result of the choices he makes.

Apply the decision tree to the discussion of your child's future. What kind of options would he like to be able to consider in life? What does he need to do in order to achieve these options? Where does college fit *for him*? Why? Encourage him to be expansive in his thinking. The decision tree can project well beyond college as he begins to imagine the possibilities that could grow out of the various options or paths he might choose in the future. As he imagines his goals, he will begin to see more clearly the importance of managing his decision making.

Specifically, your student needs to understand that the choices he makes on a daily basis will have a direct bearing on the options he might consider upon graduating from high school. Quality options rarely materialize out of thin air. If he aspires to colleges (options) that can be very selective—and you might reference the Pyramid of Selectivity here—he will need to make good choices when confronted with options in his daily life. The opportunity for him to choose his direction, whether it relates to colleges, jobs, or places to live, can be incredibly motivating. It is certainly preferable to the sense of hopelessness that comes with feeling stuck on a track with limited options.

You have seen this in your own life and understand the accountability that is involved. Your child needs to understand that—he needs you to speak to him from your experience. This conversation will be the beginning of an important period of reflection for both of you. As he comes to grips with the answers, he will begin to look forward to the college process and his future with a clearer focus and a deeper sense of ownership.

Between the Lines

The Quality Option
College is among the most important options that your child will consider in his young life. It competes with other options such as travel, employment, and even unemployment. The opportunity to pursue a college education is your gift to him. You know that choosing that option will have a bearing on the quality of life he experiences, and you want him to have the best. His decision to act upon the opportunity is his gift to himself.

Understanding Priorities

If college is an established option, then you can begin to focus on priorities—his priorities. While your child may demonstrate an outward eagerness to get started with the next chapter in his life, the odds are that he is privately uneasy about getting from point A to point B. There is a big difference in his mind between *knowing* that he will go to college and actually *making it happen.*

Much of your child's early thinking about college will be emotional. That's to be expected. After all, the context for young people is highly personalized. Teenagers are responding to a rush of enticing images, such as name recognition, big-time sports prominence, and seductive locations, not to mention love interests and the "herd mentality"—"all of my friends are going, so why not me!"

Lost in the shuffle for many young people are the more substantive matters such as the educational opportunities offered at different colleges, the track records of their graduates in various fields, the quality of life outside of class, and the question of who teaches the courses students take in the first year (faculty or teaching assistants). Your role is to help your child get past the superficial and emotional to the things that will truly have a bearing on his educational experience.

Start with a discussion about what he hopes to accomplish. What are his priorities? What are the three or four things that he hopes to achieve over the course of his college experience? How does he presume to accomplish them?

Early in his college search, my son, Kyle, spoke somewhat assuredly about his college plans. He knew that he wanted to go to a big school in the city. He didn't know where, exactly, but he had the "big school in the city" figured out. When I asked him why, he said that he wanted a place that was bigger than his high school, adding, "there is more going on in

Between the Lines

Hierarchy of Needs
As priorities emerge, it will be important to establish perspective. Despite the growing list of "must haves," not everything can be the top priority. Work with your student to establish a hierarchy of needs: is the item *essential* ("must have it"), *important* ("could live without it if necessary"), or *nice* ("nice to think about but not that important")? The hierarchy becomes a filter that will enable him to be more discriminating as he assesses different college options.

the city." Having heard this type of rhetoric before, I decided to probe a bit further.

"What is it that you hope to accomplish during your four years in college?" I asked. The question seemed to catch him off guard and he looked at me quizzically. "What do you mean?" he responded.

Now that I had his attention, I decided to push further. "What is really important to you as you look ahead to your college years? What are your top three priorities? On graduation day, what do you want to make sure you have accomplished?"

After a brief pause, he looked up thoughtfully and said, "I want to get a good education, I want to be able to study chemistry in a hands-on environment, and I want to be able to continue playing my trumpet in bands and orchestras."

All good answers! Kyle had sifted through the emotional baggage to identify matters critical to his education and was able to articulate a core set of priorities. Upon reflection, big schools and cities had taken a back seat to a good education (as he defined it) and the opportunity to pursue his passions. While he might still choose a big school in the city, he had been reminded that his options might also include smaller schools in non-urban settings.

You need to help your child discover and articulate his core priorities as well. In asking the question, though, you put the two of you at some risk of real discomfort. He may feel uncomfortable because he is afraid of saying something that will disappoint you or, worse yet, that he won't have anything to say at all! You may be asking him questions for which he doesn't have any good answers just yet.

The good news is that these questions should be rhetorical. He shouldn't have to come up with immediate answers. If he does, ask him "why" he has come to that conclusion. Your objective is not to get him to change his mind. Rather, you want him to challenge his assumptions. It is more important that you ask questions that will guide his thinking—that will open his mind to new points of discovery—rather than questions that will limit his thought process or make him feel trapped.

The answers that emerge—the priorities he is able to identify—should serve as important guideposts for him as he begins to evaluate his college options. As he shares information and impressions that he has been collecting about colleges, refer him back to his top priorities. Ask him: "How do the colleges you are considering relate to these priorities?" Deciding what criteria are important and then acting in a manner consistent with them is the essence of good decision making.

Moving Forward

As you work through the early stages of the college process, remember *it is not important for your child to find a college in the first days of the search*. Rather, he needs to get his feet under him and to be secure in the knowledge of who he is and confident that you are—and will be—with him at every step along the way. His self-assessment needs to be honest. He shouldn't be worried about having to please anyone but himself. And it is vital that he comes to grips with that which he *doesn't* know! This will be perhaps your greatest task. Once this is accomplished, the next step involves turning what he knows about himself in the direction of colleges and finding the one that fits him best.

Conversational Guide to Learning More About Priorities

If you want to help your child develop a better understanding of his priorities, try the following questions. They will enable him to think about the matter in terms with which he can relate based on his experience. As you might imagine, the "why" part of the question is the most important. There are no right or wrong answers, just good insights to be tucked away.

Q Who is your favorite teacher—and why?

A Is the answer framed in terms of the teacher's personality, the subject he teaches, the way he runs his class, or his passion for the subject? Your child's response will reveal a lot about the style of instruction to which he responds most comfortably.

Q What is your favorite class right now—and why?

A The curricular implications of this question probably are obvious. It gets fun when the answer is, "History and calculus." That's okay. Multiple interests are healthy and to be encouraged! They do, however, begin to provide clues as to where and how he finds some degree of intellectual engagement.

Q Do prefer your teacher to lecture or do you prefer to learn by doing? Do you like classes where you sit in the middle of a large group or do you like seminar-style courses—and why?

A Okay, there are really two questions here, but his responses will reveal the type of classroom environment in which he is most comfortable—small classes with lots of engagement or larger instructional arenas where he can remain relatively anonymous.

Q With what kinds of people do you want to spend the next four years—and why?

A Colleges have distinctive personalities. One of the keys to the personality of any campus is the people who are on it. The people—students and faculty—who comprise a university can make a huge difference in the "flavor" or personality of a campus. We all have preferences about the people we like to be around. Help your student become aware of his preferences. It can help him discriminate between one campus and another.

Chapter 4

Finding the Good College Fit

The Best College: Myth and Reality

Can you name the best college in the country? If your mind is racing through the names of four or five institutions that might vie for that title, ask yourself: "How do I know this to be true? Where is the evidence?" If you are honest with yourself, you will acknowledge that you really can't name the best school. Even if you were to make an attempt, you would be hard-pressed to defend your selection with anything more than hearsay.

In truth, there is no such thing as a "number one" or best college in absolute terms. It's a thing of fiction—the notion of the "best" college rests in our collective imagination. Such a place doesn't exist.

Because we need to attach worth to the things we have in life, though, we feel compelled to check the label. The best is something we believe we need to have. It holds value. In this case, it is the college that, more than any other, will set our students up for life—or so we believe.

While the concept of an absolute pecking order among colleges is merely an opinion, it sure does sell! Just check the magazine stands in the early fall. Publications touting college rankings are something akin to the sexy "swimsuit" issues for their respective publishers. To an audience starved for an orientation to the "best" in colleges, these publications seem to hold the answer.

Be cautious, however, about relying on such rankings to validate your child's college list. Most data are self-reported by institutions and there is very little of scientific value in what emerges. On the other hand, many of the ranking lists are accompanied by substantive articles and valuable insights about the process. Use them. But don't allow your student—or yourself—to be distracted by the rankings alone.

If you need comparative data, take a look at outcomes—how do students evaluate their experiences and how do they fare at graduation? The National Survey of Student Engagement (Indiana University Bloomington) annually examines levels of student satisfaction at participating colleges by comparing their expectations as first-year students with their sense of accomplishment at graduation. In addition, consult with faculty in graduate, doctoral, and professional degree programs for their assessments of the undergraduate programs from which their students originated. You might be surprised!

The reality of the best college is rooted in what is best for your child. Help her take stock of who she is and what she has to offer. Urge her to stay true to her priorities. In doing so, she will discover colleges that are best for her growth and development, that fit the criteria she has established for herself. The applicant pools at these schools define the "playing fields" on which she will compete. Helping your student find the *right* playing field—the colleges that represent the best college fit—will be vital to her success as she prepares to compete for admission at colleges that can say "no."

This is where the Pyramid of Selectivity can be instructive because it captures the competitive dynamic of every playing field. The same set of credentials will be viewed differently according to how hard it is to get in. The most highly selective institutions present the playing fields with the most intense competition. Less selective places provide playing fields that are more inclusive and more forgiving of less-than-perfect credentials. They embrace students as they are and help them to grow. Most students find happy college homes at such colleges, and the vast majority of the productive workforce in this country can trace its roots there as well.

If your student's credentials are superior and place her among the elite competitors, then she might have a fighting chance in an environment where the prospects for admission success are limited at best. But she still needs to be lucky. Otherwise, she would be wise to look for other playing fields, places where her credentials are better suited to the competition.

The good news is that there are quality options that extend beyond a cluster of elite colleges and universities to a spectacular array of diverse institutions. These options are found in colleges that are about as different as the students who wish to attend them. Somewhere among the 3,000-plus colleges and universities in the United States are places that provide academic venues for which your child is well suited. They are good "fits" for her.

The Best College "Fit" for Your Student

"Okay, " you say, "I'm persuaded that 'fit' is the key ingredient in a successful college choice. But what comprises a good 'fit'? How will I know when we have found the best college for my child?"

While a lot of factors contribute to a good "fit," I would like to offer the following criteria for the best college for your child. The best "fit" is the college that:

1. Offers a *program of study* that matches your student's interests and needs

2. Provides a *style of instruction* that is well suited to the way your student likes to learn

3. Provides a level of *academic rigor* to match your student's aptitude and preparation

4. Offers a *community* in which your student will feel at home

5. *Values your student* for what she does well

Each of the five elements counts. Students who overlook one or two of them in favor of others while choosing a college often find that they really are not as comfortable or as successful as they would like to be. Let's look at each in a little more detail.

Program of Study

Your student needs to make sure that her academic interests are well served by the curricula of the college in question. If she wants to pursue engineering, she needs to find an appropriate engineering program. Her interests won't be well served at a business school, just as the culinary artist won't find satisfaction at a *liberal arts* college, and the prospective lawyer probably won't find a teacher education program to her liking. In other words, if she already has some career direction, you need to help her find a place that will give her an opportunity to hone her skills.

This may be easier said than done, though, as most teenagers struggle mightily as they consider the future. The parent generation doesn't help by constantly peppering them with questions about their plans: "Where are you going to college?" and "Have you thought about what you want to study?" It begins to sound a lot like: "So, what are you going to do when you grow up?" I have heard kids make up answers just to get people off their backs!

In any case, it is probably unfair to put pressure on young people to have it all figured out

Between the Lines

To Be or Not to Be...

For parents who see great things for their children in the world, the inability of the young person to settle on a career direction can be incredibly vexing. The good news is that the indecisive student is normal. Most students who enter college in a given year don't have a clear sense as to what they want to study. It is estimated that approximately two thirds of all students in college change their majors at least once; half of them will do it two or three times.

before they even get started. They put enough pressure on themselves. Recall the path that you and many of your peers took to where you are today. Could you have predicted it? Could you have known when you were 17 that you would be in the career you have today? Just as your pathway to happiness and success may have taken on a different look from what you had imagined as you entered college, give your child the same opportunity to find and follow her path. She'll find her direction in good time. The best college fit may turn out to be one of the many places that offers her the opportunity to explore a range of options before making any firm career decisions.

Style of Instruction

The best college or university for your student will be the one that offers a style of instruction that is best suited to the way she likes to learn. You can be sure that there are as many styles of instruction as there are styles of learning! One might ask, then: How does your student like to learn? Does she learn best by "doing" or through memorizing? Does she like to write? Does she know how to do research or is she even interested in doing research? Does she like to be engaged intellectually—and be held accountable for her observations in classroom debate or does she prefer to absorb the material in relative anonymity? Each of these questions points to the fact that people learn differently. We all have different strengths, weaknesses, and intellectual comfort zones.

Imagine, for example, the scenario in which the student really wants the engagement of the small classroom but finds herself in a steady routine of classes that enroll hundreds of students. Would that environment give her the best opportunity to ask questions and pursue individualized learning tracks? Conversely, the student who is most comfortable in the larger learning environment might feel very out of place in the "fish bowl" of the small classroom. Our job as parents is to help students understand that differences such as these exist and to make discriminations between colleges based on them.

Academic Rigor

Just as styles of instruction vary across the board, the level of rigor in the classroom is quite different from one school to another. Finding a good fit in this regard is critical as your student seeks to put herself in the best position—on the right "playing field" academically—to achieve in college.

That said, be careful about encouraging your student to think about colleges that wouldn't be good matches for her. For example, it is easy to get caught up in the name game. People will say—and you will think—"if your child can get into XYZ college, she's got to go, she'll be set for life!" Maybe. She'll be set for life if she is prepared to deal with the pace and rigor of the classroom, if she is able to take advantage of the academic program to grow her talents. On the other hand, if it will take all that she has to merely keep up with the competition in the classroom, to prove that she belongs, then it will be harder for her to realize the growth and achievement that should come her way.

Conversely, quite a few young people of really good ability sell themselves short in choosing academic environments. Either they don't see much difference between what colleges have to offer or they don't care. The student who chooses a college that doesn't challenge her appropriately soon becomes bored. She might be having a good time, but if she is accustomed to meeting the "bar" at a level that cannot be experienced consistently at the college she has chosen, she'll soon be ready to leave.

If you are not sure about how to ascertain your child's ability *and* preparation relative to different colleges, it would be worth your while to touch base with her counselor and some of her teachers. They see her in action every day. They also have a pretty good handle on what different colleges will expect of their students and can be effective matchmakers if given the opportunity.

Community

Quite often, when students believe they've found the college of their dreams, they're hard-pressed to explain the attraction. Frequently, the explanation comes down to something like, "It's a gut feeling; it just *feels* right." *A gut feeling? It just feels right? Is this the best she can do?*

"Gut feelings" have a quality that is hard to define. Where do they come from? What do they mean? They can reflect a mood we are in—something temporary or fleeting—or they might be rooted in a deeply held passion. Regardless, there is certainly very little that is scientific or even logical about gut feelings. Nonetheless, the intuition that is revealed can be very insightful. Even though your student may have difficulty explaining what she means, there is a message in a "gut feeling."

The best college for your student, then, is one that feels right—the one that feels like home.

Observe closely as she becomes acquainted with different campus cultures. Does she seem to identify with individuals, groups, or activities? Are there people she would like to get to know better? Is there evidence of common values and shared interests? Is she content to respond to the superficial images, or does she seem interested in drilling down into the campus culture for a better understanding of how things really work? If she does the latter, it is good evidence that she is responding to a gut feeling.

The trick is to let her find her way in search of a new college home. Too much pressure to find or have answers can be intimidating. On the other hand, you need to be ready for those times when she will want to bounce ideas off of you. Listen carefully. In all likelihood, she is looking for validation rather than answers. She is testing the gut feeling on someone she trusts.

Values Your Student

Perhaps the most important element of a good fit is the relationship an institution has with its students. As your child gets to know colleges and universities, be sensitive to the difference between those that greet her politely and those that are eager to invest in a relationship with her. This is where it pays to be a tad cynical.

Most colleges will greet you well. After all, they are in the hospitality or, more specifically, the "approval business." They are predisposed to accommodate your student and your family. In order to attract students, they need to create a good feeling. As a result, they will treat your student well so she will feel good about her experience.

Some colleges will go the extra mile. They will make sure that she meets people in the academic program that interests her. They may extend special scholarships or internship opportunities. They will do what they can to demonstrate their willingness to invest in the talents she is bringing to the table. It is clear that they value her for what she does well and want her in their next freshman class.

In the final analysis, the process of admitting and financially supporting students is an expression of an institution's values. It is a college's opportunity to build a learning community that includes a myriad of talents and perspectives. When a college admits and chooses to support a student with financial aid (whether scholarships or other resources), it is a good signal that the student will be valued for what she does well.

Finally, if your student becomes frustrated by the admission process or by not being able to get answers to questions, it might be an indication as to how much she truly means to that institution. Places that value her will not let her "slip through the cracks."

Between the Lines

A Star or a Face in the Crowd?
Consider the saxophonist: the young woman who loves music, has enjoyed playing in the high school performing groups, and wants to continue performing in college. A competent and cheerful participant, her greatest distinction is having made first chair in the school band. As she looks at colleges, she finds a range of music programs in terms of the level of performance. With some, she might be given the opportunity to audition while others will embrace her as a future cornerstone of the brass section. At which college is she likely to be most happily engaged?

One More Criterion

In a perfect world, the cost of attending a college *would not* be a factor for you and your child. You could urge her to consider any college that appealed to her. She, in turn, could make a selection based on how well the college fit according to the criteria we just reviewed. Money wouldn't be an issue.

As you have come to know, we don't live in a perfect world. A college education does cost. It will rank among the most significant investments you make in your lifetime. As you approach the matter of how you will afford a college education, you may have begun to make value judgments of your own. For example, you may have an aversion to debt. The problem is that most colleges will expect students who receive financial aid to assume some responsibility, including debt, for their education. If educational debt is something that you have decided you don't want your child to deal with, then that decision will have a critical role in determining "fit."

Similarly, if you have independently determined a limit to the amount you will provide in support of your child's education, this decision will have an impact on determining fit. On the other hand, you might be perfectly willing to shoulder the full cost of tuition at one or two of the elite colleges but are reluctant to make the same payments to colleges of lesser prominence. In each of these cases, you are exercising a choice that will limit the range of options your child might consider. Or maybe you have no choice. Maybe your personal financial situation is such that you *can't* give her everything she might want.

In any case, you need to be candid with your student about the reality of your financial situation. Your ability or willingness to support the cost of her education can be a trump card in this process. Ideally, you are in a position where you can offer her the opportunity to explore a range of college options—to be funded by a combination of your own resources and financial aid. If this is not the case and issues of cost are likely to carry greater weight than any of the other "fit" factors, she needs to know this at the outset.

"Why Am I Here?"

We have talked about how emotionally driven young people can be, especially early in their college searches. When emotion speaks louder than reason and logic, they are bound to make decisions that put them in uncomfortable places and asking "Why am I here?"

So, what does that mean—"Why am I here?" It is the bewildered reaction of a first-year student in college who is suddenly uncertain that she belongs. She fell in love with a college for the wrong reasons. Her head and her heart were apparently confused about what defined a good college fit. Now, she feels stuck. Let's take a look at some of the *wrong* reasons to select a college.

The best college for your child is *not* likely to be your alma mater. If she grew up hearing stories about the "best four years of your life" and is now being encouraged to take a look at the place that got you to "where you are now," she may be finding herself in an increasingly awkward position. Should she go ahead and apply? And if she is admitted, isn't she supposed to enroll? Despite outward appearances, our kids want to please us. Promoting the school that means so much to you may put your child in the very uncomfortable position of having to choose against you in order to select the place that means a lot to her.

Your alma mater may have worked for you more than twenty years ago, but your student deserves the opportunity to find a place that works for her today. If, through the course of her own search, she finds the place that just happened to give you so many fond memories, then that would be great. But don't assume that she should start there. And don't assume it is still as it was twenty years ago!

The best college for her will not be the place that her significant other chooses! As young people get ready to graduate from high school, they become sentimental. They begin to think and then worry about the people and things they will miss by going off to college. This can be particularly traumatic for teenagers in love. You can probably recall from your own experience the friends who faced uncertain futures without the ones to whom they had sworn their love. Yet, with a grim determination that "love conquers all," they made their college plans—together! And off they went—together—only to find that love doesn't always conquer all.

Think about it. If your student were to follow her significant other to college—his college—just so they could be together for the next four years, the blissful happiness will likely give way—first to frustration as she realizes that she is not the only girl on that campus—because *he* has begun to attract a lot of attention—and then to the reality that she is no longer the most important person in his life as he has given his full attention to someone else! If your student chose that college because "he" was going to be there, too, now she can only watch and wonder—"why am I here?"

Finally, the best college will *not* be the one that produces the most impressive car decal! In our world, that is a metaphor for prestige. Much of your planning and conspiring over the last sixteen years has been done with this thought in mind: we *must get her into the best college*. The car decal will be evidence that she, or should I say *you*, has succeeded. I suspect that it is the secret desire of many parents to be able to put the decal on the car and drive slowly through the neighborhood so that everyone can see where "we" are going to college!

You need to be careful about this. If, indeed, the car decal is important to you, your child's eagerness and anxiety will feed off of your hopes and expectations. This puts her in the awkward position of having to reconcile her own sense of self-worth if she is unable to deliver. Even if she is able to make the grade and elects to enroll at the car decal college, she faces the potential for a huge disconnect. While she may have won the "prize," will she be heading off to a place that is truly good for her?

As you can see, finding a good fit will indeed place your child in the college that is best for her. In all likelihood, she will not arrive at this realization over night. And, frankly, it may take a while for you to place your trust in colleges that are not as well known but that might offer the best combination of educational experiences for her. Remember, though, that she is the one behind the wheel. You are in the passenger seat.

Keep her focused on her priorities. Help her to be disciplined about processing information through her Hierarchy of Needs and encourage her to conceptualize "fit" using the criteria that we have just discussed. As she becomes more practiced at this, the "ride" will become easier, and you will see her confidence grow as she approaches the point at which she will begin to compete for admission.

Chapter 5

The Agenda

Social Engineering

Colleges and universities are, in effect, planned communities that are picky about whom they will allow to join. By marketing themselves to parents and students, they can drive popularity in a manner that affords them greater selectivity. By becoming selective, they can literally pick and choose those students who advance *their* agendas, whatever they might be. The admission process allows these communities to choose their new members—those students who are seen as fitting best into the dynamic the college has defined for its community.

The question, then, is who on a college campus owns the "agenda"? What group of people has the greatest and most natural interest in informing if not shaping the selection process? Understanding where this ownership lies provides the context for making sense of the process itself. Who are the "social engineers"?

While many might aspire to this position, the faculty has historically filled the role of the gatekeeper. While faculty roles are not as direct or prominent today as they once were, their presence is still felt. In effect, the faculty owns the academic program. After all, the professors decide what will be taught, how it will be taught, and how their students will be evaluated for their efforts.

Indeed, the professors are the grand architects of the college experience and they provide the essential compass bearing for the admission committee as it begins its work. Without the faculty, a college campus would amount to little more than a playground—and an expensive one at that!

What Is the Agenda?

Given the opportunity, most faculty members would eagerly

Between the Lines

Chain of Command

So there's no confusion, the days of the faculty actually making admission decisions are long gone at most universities. The decision making is now accomplished by admission officers trained in what is often regarded as the art of the credential review. They, in turn, are ultimately accountable to senior administrators (presidents, vice presidents, provosts) who drive the agenda. At its core, though, any agenda will at least metaphorically reflect the influence of the academic program and the faculty.

define the qualities of the students who they believe would fit best in their classrooms. Whether their wishes are expressed formally through appointed involvement with an admission committee or discreetly at the water cooler or over lunch, the message is clear: We want more students who are:

- Bright
- Motivated
- High Achieving
- Diverse in Background
- Givers

Colleges Want Students Who Are Bright

It shouldn't surprise you that college professors want students who are **bright**. The professors have set the "bar" academically. They understand the rigor of the program and know what sort of talent and preparation will be required in order for students to find success. Their message to the admission office: "Bring us students who can work at this level of rigor."

Specifically, professors want students who can function well in their classrooms. If this sounds vaguely familiar, it should. Remember the third element of a good fit: The best fit is the college that "provides a level of academic rigor to match your student's aptitude and preparation." Finding this element of a good fit helps put your student on the academic playing field at selected colleges. It doesn't guarantee that he will get in, though.

Colleges Want Students Who Are Motivated

Professors *love* students who are **motivated**, who truly enjoy learning. These are the students who are curious, who ask questions, and who probe for broader understanding. They are willing to "push the envelope" intellectually. Motivated students are eager to do more than master the subject matter and are valued because they

Between the Lines

Measuring Motivation

To understand how motivation is assessed in the admission process, take a look at the "Teacher's Reference" forms that are part of most applications. Invariably, there is a request for the teacher to address the student's motivation, inquisitiveness, and academic leadership. For example:

- Is the student "enthusiastic about learning" or "excited by new ideas"?
- Is the student "able to ask insightful questions"?
- Is the student willing to "take educational risks" or "show initiative"?
- Does the student "contribute thoughtfully" to classroom discussions?

These questions are intended to identify the student who, however bright, goes beyond mastering the subject. They probe for insight into the student who is motivated to learn for learning's sake.

ask the "how" and "why" questions. They enrich the learning environment by helping to raise the level of discourse for those around them.

Motivation is difficult to measure because it is more a matter of attitude and determination than content or achievement. In some, it is reflected in a passion for learning or, more generally, a passion for excellence. We have all heard of the athlete who, despite having good but not great ability, proceeds to set records by simply outworking others. Academic motivation is much the same.

Many colleges attempt to measure a student's passion for learning by examining his exposure to curriculum over time. In particular, they look for breadth and depth. Breadth refers to five core courses: math, science, social science, English, and foreign language. Depth means four years—starting in ninth grade. In the final analysis, admission officers can gain some measure of a student's passion for learning by observing what he does academically *when he doesn't have to do anything.*

More than just desirable qualities, motivation and curiosity are good habits to be encouraged in your child. Do what you can to nurture curiosity in your child. As he approaches college, the ability

Between the Lines

Achievement

Achievement, not just participation, is a way of identifying the student who has ability, is motivated, and makes a determined and sustained effort to exceed expectations. The more selective the institution, the more likely that it will focus on how students are putting their talents to best use. Colleges near the top of the Pyramid will look beyond the candidates who meet expectations for those who consistently exceed them.

to take initiative, ask good questions, and think outside the box will be evident to those making selections in the admission process.

Colleges Want Students Who Are High Achieving

In the college admission process, **high achieving** often correlates with winning—with students who have proven themselves in the classroom. Bright and motivated, they have consistently put their talents to good use.

The trap that many people fall into is the assumption that good ability, native intelligence if you will, is all that it takes in order for students to find success. How often do you hear very capable students respond to queries into their academic progress with statements like: "I'm doing what I need to do" or "Don't worry, everything is under control" or "I know what I'm doing; everything's fine!"

Doing what is "good enough" has replaced "the best I can do" as the academic objective for this young person. "Good enough," however, is not likely to be competitive at a college that can afford to be very picky—a college that can look at every applicant under a microscope. If that is not important to your student, though, then there are no worries.

He will indeed have quality options among colleges that are not compelled to be quite so selective. He needs to remember, though, that in the face of competition, *potential is nice. Performance talks.*

Selective colleges want to see how well he applies the good stuff that he has between the ears. As an applicant to colleges that can say "no," the last thing your student can afford is to be regarded as an "underachiever," as one who has "it" but doesn't use it consistently. The classic expression of this type of student is the one who scores very well on the SAT but takes easy courses and/or has mediocre grades.

Colleges Want Students Who Are Diverse in Background

Including students of **diverse backgrounds** is particularly important to college and university faculty members as they seek to enrich the learning experience. They imagine each new class as the embodiment of a new community and are eager to find in it students who have diverse perspectives on the world, students who have seen life through different sets of lenses.

Between the Lines

Hide and Seek
Have you ever felt that your child is playing "hide and seek" with you? He might show flashes of brilliance one day but they are gone the next. As a parent, this drives you nuts! After all, his performance is supposed to be a reflection of the gene pool, and you are quite confident that there is more to the gene pool than he is choosing to reveal.

The good news is that he is likely to grow out of the "hide and seek" mode and blossom into a fine representative of the gene pool. It just might not be on a timetable that makes sense to you—or to the more selective colleges in which he is interested. And if you think that his prospects for a good life will be permanently damaged because he won't get into a *good* college, think again. Work with him to find colleges that "fit" him well—places that value him for what he *has achieved* as well as his potential to find greater success in the future—and he will be fine.

So, what comprises a diverse student body? What life experience or perspective will be of interest to a college or university? To be sure, his ethnic background may play a significant role in defining his life experience. So might his religious background or his social-economic background. The places in which he has lived—his geographic diversity—may play a definitive role in the shaping of his perspective. In all likelihood, some combination of factors or lenses has influenced his understanding of the world around him. In the admission process, it cannot be assumed that only one type of perspective will be valued.

It is important to note that the further up the Pyramid your child aspires, the less likely the *fact* of his diverse background will make the difference. Among the most selective colleges, a check in the ethnic minority box on the application ceases to be the hot button for admission. While less selective institutions may respond enthusiastically to such a notation, colleges and universities near the top of the Pyramid are not as impressed as they see many qualified students from diverse backgrounds.

By the way, students and parents often misinterpret the meaning of their status as members of a group that might reflect diversity. Specifically, a young person need not come from an ethnic minority background in order to have a cultural heritage that will be of interest to an admission committee. Two quick stories illustrate how the importance of one's background can be exaggerated or, in some cases, underestimated.

I once interviewed a student from Scandinavia who felt the fact he was born in Sweden was enough to make a difference—even though he had no real firsthand knowledge of his own culture. He had emigrated with his parents (both computer scientists) when he was 6 years old. He interpreted the value of "being Swedish" as simply being a member of a group with little (if any) representation on my campus. I tried to advise him that it wasn't "being Swedish" that counted; it was "the difference that your 'being Swedish' will make on my campus."

Conversely, I had occasion to meet with a young woman who had been placed on our Wait List. She was a fine candidate who had just gotten caught up in a highly competitive applicant group. Now, she was appealing her status. In the course of our conversation, I learned that her family had been exiled from their country when she was young. The longer we talked, the clearer it became that her culture and her family's place in that culture were very important to her. Yet, she had not shared this background information on her application because, in her words, she "wanted to be considered on my own merit rather than because of what had happened to my family."

Because of this noble intent, she had failed to acknowledge the impact of these circumstances in her personal development. When I asked if her family's odyssey and her cultural background had any bearing on the person she had become, she readily agreed that they had. Based on this revelation, she was invited to submit an essay that documented her story and was subsequently admitted.

THE UNDER-POPULATED ACADEMIC PROGRAM

Diversity can be important in another, more obscure, sense. Part of the agenda at many colleges is the need to populate all of the academic programs. When professors elect to teach courses, they do so for two reasons: they are passionate about the topic and they hold fervently to the belief that the topic should be studied widely—the seats in their classrooms should be filled!

The admission process, then, provides an opportunity to make sure that each program is populated with eager and interested students. This is never a problem in biology because there are lots of premed students to be satisfied. Similarly, the English, history, and political science departments rarely have enrollment concerns as there are plenty of prelaw students taking those classes.

Between the Lines

Making Diversity Count
The way a given college responds to diversity in a student's background will be determined by the degree to which the candidate separates himself from his peers. If his ethnicity or his geographic background or his religious background are integral to the person he has become, then he needs to make certain colleges know that. Simply checking a box may be all it takes at some schools. Other schools will want to see more compelling evidence that the student will share this perspective with others on campus.

One wonders, though, about the situations in departments like anthropology, classics, and religious studies where the faculty may outnumber the students majoring in the subject! In these instances the message to the admissions office is simple: "If you see a potential major for our program, grab him! We need more!"

It is worth noting, then, that if your child develops a *sincere* interest in an academic program that might be under populated on a college campus (versus finding an under-populated program and developing a sincere interest!), he may have an advantage in the admission process. The operative term here is *sincere*. If your student has demonstrably *invested* in learning more about the discipline in question, that evidence needs to be a part of his application.

Colleges Want Students Who Are Givers

The final category on the Agenda has to do with giving. College professors like students who raise the bar for other students—who make the interaction in the classroom, as well as the quality of life on campus, better by their participation. Bright, motivated, and high achieving, such students are also **givers**. They bring gifts—talents, interests, or perspectives—that enrich the experience of all within the campus community.

As a parent, you are quick to recognize your child's special gifts. You may also be quick to concede that, at this stage in his life, he is more often a "taker." After all, that's what teenagers do. This is especially true when it comes to things like money, food, clothing—and keys to the car! The notion of giving can be foreign and even threatening to young people. Quite often, when I ask students about their gifts, they squirm as if

Between the Lines

In Search of a Gift
I recently spoke with a young woman who was convinced that she didn't have any gifts. Visibly mortified, she asked, "What college would want me?" As we talked, it became clear that she was failing to recognize the things that she held dear in her life. I urged her to think about the thoughts, ideas, and activities that made her happy. "What do you do that makes you smile?" I then added, "Think of those things and do them more often. Do them until they become your passion."

to say, "What do you mean? I don't have any particular gifts." Even the question, "Tell me about yourself. What makes you different?" is often greeted with the classic deer-in-the-headlights response. Generally speaking, teenagers don't always feel that they are blessed with a gift. Moreover, they don't always have the ability to look within themselves to see their gifts—those qualities that set them apart from their peers.

The good news is that each young person is gifted. Relative to the student population of the colleges they want to consider, they possess talents, interests, or perspectives that *set them apart*. They are leaders, thinkers, and writers. They play basketball, the violin, and the stock market. They care about issues, give to others, and work to save the environment. And they have the opportunity while in high school to discover their gifts—to cultivate and nurture them so that when they apply to college, they can reveal them.

As a parent, you need to be sensitive to your child's potential to feel passionate about something in life. You can't force-feed passion. But you can give him time and encouragement as he discovers and cultivates those things that mean the most to him. Not only will the passion he discovers be healthy and definitive in his character development, it will help to define his space apart from his peers. It will become his gift. As he considers colleges, then, help him to find environments in which he will be valued for what he has to give.

The Agenda and Your Student

This, then, is what the "Agenda" might look like at most colleges. If you attend admission presentations or read about the selection process, the variables in the Agenda will get the greatest play. They will be revealed in discussions about courses, grades, essays, testing, interviews, and letters of recom-

Between the Lines

When Giving Makes the Difference
At some point in the admission process, someone on the admission committee will acknowledge the competitiveness of your student's academic credentials and then ask, "If we take him, what do we get?" In other words, what does he have to give? If he has enough academic prowess to get on the "playing field," then he needs to be able to compete by showing that he has something to give or contribute to the collegiate environment.

mendation. The rhetoric may vary, but the concepts will be the same.

As you come to understand the "Agenda"—especially within the context of the Pyramid of Selectivity—you begin to develop conceptual appreciation for the selection process. It is important to have this understanding well in advance of the application process so you can help your student *prepare* appropriately. (A constant lament of parents is that they are learning about the nuances of the application process when it is too late to help their students—that they should have been exposed to this information when their students were in middle school or just starting their high school experience.)

What It All Means

In assessing the academic credential (Bright, Motivated, High Achieving), colleges will focus on your student's transcript. They will look to see if he has used the available curriculum to his greatest advantage in developing his skills and broadening his perspectives. Has he moved to the next logical level of rigor in each year of high school? Has he applied himself consistently in meeting or exceeding the expectations of the classroom?

Admission committees will look for evidence of his passion for learning—a commitment to excel that is demonstrated by the choices he makes relative to his academic experience. Is he making good choices? Does he build on each experience? Will he sprint to the finish in his senior year?

They will factor in the evaluations of teachers and counselors to look for evidence of your student's initiative and sense of responsibility. They want to see that he has not only developed

Between the Lines

Where's the Passion?
If you have to sign your student up for music lessons or drag him out to participate in service projects, you're only wasting your time and making him miserable. Involvement in service is impressive when he persuades you to join the project. And the music lessons will be validated when he demonstrates achievement through his willful persistence and preparation.

effective learning habits, but also that he has adjusted well in the face of adversity.

Similarly, the extracurricular or "what do we get?" credential (Diversity, Giver) will get a lot of attention. The attractiveness of an All-State quarterback or an All-State Orchestra First Chair musician to selective colleges is undeniable. On the other hand, colleges are constantly on the lookout for young people whose gifts are still emerging. And sometimes they will latch onto the student with strong all-around involvements—not because they see a superstar in the making, but because they value the personal qualities required to manage multiple tasks and responsibilities. Or they might be attracted to the student with the strong niche credential.

The notion of the "gift" is intensely personal for many young people, and it easy for them to feel overwhelmed with a sense of inadequacy. You have an opportunity to coach your student through this reflective phase of his preparation. As you do, be sure to let him know that you value him for who he is and what he does well. Demonstrate that commitment by helping him find colleges that will, in turn, value him.

As you can see, the Agenda is rather simple in that many of the issues are common among institutions. The basic considerations of almost all colleges with regard to students are generally the same. It is complex, though, in that each college and university has its own particular needs and desires that determine who may or may not be admitted in a given year.

You have an opportunity and an obligation to help your student understand the simple reality that he does not get to choose where he will go to college. *He can choose where he will apply and, if all goes well, he can choose between admission offers.* The colleges and their "Agendas," however, control who gets those offers of admission. It is important, then, for you to be involved in your student's admission process as a stabilizing influence. Just remember, you can't, shouldn't, and *don't* control it. The colleges do that—according to their "Agendas."

A Parent's Guide to The Agenda

The following will help you guide your student toward the college admission process. Much of this information is covered with great emphasis in the student section of the book as well!

1. **Encourage your student to stay focused academically and to keep stretching himself.** When possible, it is a good idea for a student to follow an academic program that becomes progressively more rigorous. Colleges want to see that students move to the next logical level of rigor each year.

2. **Help your student assess his capacity to balance the various demands of high-level courses.** There is a growing tendency for students to load up on honors, advanced, or Advanced Placement courses in the junior and senior years in order to impress colleges. That strategy is not always healthy and can prove counter-productive if he over-reaches.

3. **As your student approaches the senior year, you will start to hear that "I don't need to take math next year because I have satisfied my graduation requirement in math,"** or "I already have four years of language (starting in eighth grade) so I don't need to take language next year." **Don't buy it**! These are rationalizations of choices that will undermine your student's competitiveness. Why? Because colleges that can say "no" to students want to see what their candidates do *when they don't have to do anything*!

4. **The most important year in high school is . . . .** How about this—the year your student is in! He needs to take care of business in the classroom now so next year can count for something. Help your student resist the temptation to put off really applying himself until "next year." Each year is foundational in his development. Moreover, selective colleges look at the courses and grades for each year, not just the junior and senior years.

5. **Speaking of important years, the great urban myth seems to be that the most important year is the junior year.** It is—until it is over. After the last exam of the junior year, the focus needs to shift to the senior year. Don't buy into the notion that colleges don't look at the senior year. *Most colleges will see grades from at least the first marking period*. The more selective the college, the more important the senior year will be as the determining credential.

6. **Balance between the academic and cocurricular is very important, especially as students aspire to more selective colleges.** Colleges want classes full of bright, motivated, high-achieving students who contribute from a range of talents, interests, and perspectives to the quality of life within a college community.

7. **Be careful not to program your student for college.** Let your student follow his own instincts in this regard. For example, colleges are interested in seeing where the students' passions have taken them and *not* that they have attended high-profile summer programs throughout high school. Too many young people are robbed of the joys of adolescence by well-meaning parents who schedule them into all of the "best" enrichment programs.

8. *IF* **your student is considering a summer program, it should be one that is truly enriching rather than one that "will look good on the application."** If it isn't truly enriching, save your money because that program is not likely to stand out as a competitive credential.

9. **A part-time job is a viable and important life experience.** If your student has the chance to engage in an activity that will help to define his life experience, including a part-time job, then that is a worthwhile activity—and colleges need to know about it.

10. **Resist the temptation to be a prescriptive parent—a parent who choreographs his student's every move in order to build a compelling college credential for him.** I can't tell you how often I hear parents tell me that they need to get their kids into sports or music or community service. When I ask why, I am told, "That's what colleges are looking for, isn't it?" The answer: "NO!" It's called résumé building and colleges are wise to that strategy.

Chapter 6

The Hidden Agenda

The Effect of a Changing Paradigm

Over the last 25 years, the high school to college transition has morphed from a student-centered venture into a corporate exercise that capitalizes at every turn on a student's desire to continue her education. Dramatic downward shifts in the college-age population from 1985 to 1995, declines in federal support for financial aid, and the introduction of college ranking guides conspired to change the way colleges and universities operate. Whereas they were once passively involved in the process of attracting new students, they are now highly strategic in their efforts to secure their enrollments.

The strongest catalyst in this alchemy is the college ranking phenomenon. Since their emergence in the early 1980s, rankings have turned the rather sedentary society of colleges and universities inside out. In ranking institutions on the basis of comparative data (albeit self-reported by the institution), guidebook editors presented higher education with a mandate that was as opportunistic as it was ominous: "Play with us and be judged. Don't play with us—and be judged harshly."

While institutions universally loathed the rankings at the outset, they felt compelled to play along in order to avoid being left out. Before long, college officials were being drawn into a vicious and endless cycle of having to measure up on matters ranging from facilities development to student outcomes to factors reflecting the comparative strength of the admission process. No longer content to enroll classes of the size and quality to which they were accustomed, institutions found themselves playing the "fame game" by manipulating various elements of the selection process in order to gain a statistical advantage in the competition for placement in a mythical pecking order.

This brings us to the "Hidden Agenda" in the admission process. As they seek to protect or improve upon their places in the pecking order, colleges are prone to act in ways that fall outside the reason and logic that previously defined their processes. Consequently, it is difficult to predict outcomes—and surprises are more frequent. The Hidden Agenda, as I am defining it, includes many of the little-known caveats—the exceptions to the rule or deviations from the commonly held assumptions that have crept into the process. They reflect the various financial, political, and public relations pressures that places of higher learning don't wish to discuss with—much less reveal to—prospective students and their parents. This type of disclosure is difficult for colleges and universities because they are driven by ideology. That's why they like to talk with students about matters that can be defined and defended within the neatly packaged logic of the "Agenda." Sworn to educate and create opportunities for intellectual advancement, theirs is the rhetoric of an unspoken morality and determination to do the "right thing."

Unwrapping the Hidden Agenda

Driven by the need to compete for positioning in the world of ranked colleges, admission officers will often discreetly invoke criteria for decision making that are inconsistent with the rhetoric they deliver to students and parents. For example, when they discuss the selection process, most of the focus rests on the strength of the academic record and the ability of the candidate to make a compelling presentation with regard to what she has to offer. While all of this sounds good and promising, there is often more to the story.

Lost in the shuffle are factors that can actually tip the balance—*after* the student's credentials are considered. They are:

- Demonstrated Interest
- Ability to Pay
- Standardized Tests
- Special Interest Admission

As your student prepares to compete, it is essential that she understand *all* the variables that might influence her outcomes. Fair or not, they could have a real bearing on the outcome. The greater her awareness of these matters, the easier it will be for her to adjust her expectations going into the competition.

Demonstrated Interest

The concepts of "*selectivity*" or the admit ratio—the ratio of applicants to students selected—and "*yield*," the percentage of selected students who enroll, have become important markers in the fame game. The greater the selectivity—the wider the margin between applicants and acceptances—the stronger the evidence that a college can choose whomever it wants from a wide array of candidates. And the higher the yield, the greater the perception of desirability.

The two statistical relationships actually work hand in hand as colleges build enrollments. The more a college is able to control its yield on offers, the more easily it can influence selectivity. Invariably, the critical review of thousands of candidates—really good candidates—leads to questions about the student's level of demonstrated interest. "What confidence do we have that this candidate is truly interested in us—that she will enroll if accepted?"

The best indication to an institution that a student is interested and will enroll if accepted is the student's participation in the school's Early Decision or Early Action program. High-yield applicants with competitive credentials are like "money in the bank" for colleges as they build their enrollments.

It is no wonder, then, that many places encourage early applications of one type or another. (You will read in Chapter 13 why, despite disclaimers to the contrary, institutions are incited to grow the percentage of high-yield matriculants.)

COVERT OPERATIONS!

At some point in the Regular Decision process, the following question will likely be raised about your student's application: "If we admit her, what is the likelihood she will come?" She might be a very strong candidate—maybe the best from her high school or even her city or region. Nonetheless, admission officers at the college in question may not be inclined to offer her a place simply because she is good. They want to know where their school "fits" in her thinking.

This may not seem fair—and it isn't—but where would you

Between the Lines

Campus Visits
The fact that a student has visited its campus is the best indicator, short of an Early Decision application, that a student has high-yield potential for a college. As you visit college campuses with your student make sure that she documents her visit in the admission office!

place your bet if you were a college admission director—on the student who has clearly developed a relationship with your college or the one whose application has appeared out of thin air? Your student's success in the selective admission process may well depend on her ability to eliminate questions about her level of interest.

If Early Decision is not in the cards for your student, it is incumbent on her to make sure she gets on and stays on the radar screens of the schools she likes. It starts when she first expresses an interest in a college. The college will be happy to send her everything she needs. It will also create a data file with her name on it.

This is the beginning of what will sound like a covert operation by the college. Every subsequent contact she has with the college will result in a new entry in the data file. The file grows. When she applies, the admission office will collect all of this data in summary form and place a notation in her file. Some colleges will show, in single digit codes, all of her contacts on a mailing label. Others will create a numeric value or index that represents the sum of the contacts. A snapshot for the person who reads her file, the code or the index can tell the story of her level of engagement with the college prior to applying. An admission officer can look at the code list and know in an instant the number of contacts your student has had with the college. A similar label reveals the *nature* of your student's experience on that college campus. Did she visit, take a tour, participate in an information session, attend a class, meet with a professor, or stay overnight?

As you can see, a short string of contacts or a modest "interest index" can undo the strength of everything else in the application. The result: the student is placed on the wait list with the proviso that "If she's interested, she'll let us know and we can take her later."

"THE CARD"

The number and type of contacts with a college give a good indication of level of interest and likelihood of enrollment if admitted. It would behoove your student, then, to take advantage of opportunities to demonstrate interest—she must make sure she gets credit for the things she does to learn more about a college. This requires just a simple investment of time. Whenever your student is able to meet with a representative in school, at a college fair, or on a college campus, she needs to make sure she gets credit for being there by filling out an inquiry card. The card travels back to the admission office where someone will make a new entry in her data file that says she participated in that activity. That's how the file grows.

Between the Lines

Money...and the Good Fit
Remember, the admission process is an expression of institutional values. The best college for your student will *value* her for what she does well. It will make sure that she is admitted and supported according to her needs.

Generally speaking, kids loath cards! They get in the way of other things they would rather be doing, and they force the young person to be accountable for a certain level of information about herself. That in itself can be a hassle. Filling out the card, though, eliminates the question about her level of interest and forces the admission committee to return its focus to the good stuff—the academic record and the question of *"what do we get?"*

Ability to Pay

When we think about education and our children, we are easily distracted by issues of cost and funding. It is an unpleasant but necessary part of the process. We are not prepared, however, for the prospect that our ability to pay may have a bearing on our student's selection into the class. Like it or not, money *does* matter.

Admission committees need to make certain the classes they enroll are able to (collectively) generate the revenue that will pay the bills.

Charged with attracting the brightest and best, they also use the financial aid resources at their disposal to strategically leverage the enrollment of these students. This is when things get interesting because, invariably, there are more deserving students than dollars to go around. Admission officers want to give themselves the best chance to enroll their high-profile candidates but must be mindful of budgetary limitations.

As the process of matching dollars with targeted students progresses, the candidates with the highest quotients in areas defined by the "Agenda" will be given need-based financial aid. Students without need who fall into this talent category may be the recipients of merit scholarships in amounts that are calculated to influence their college choice. (We'll get into this in greater detail in Chapter 12.) Merit-based aid is troubling to some because it is often awarded at the expense of needy students who may not get financial aid awards—or may not be admitted at all. Regardless, those making the offers are being very deliberate to extend their funds to the students they value most.

Similarly, critical judgments must be made at the end of the selection process when the financial aid office is given an opportunity to run the roster of students on the tentative admit list through its yield models. Let's suppose these yield projections indicate that proceeding with the financial aid offers on the table will take the college over its financial aid budget by a million or so dollars. The enrollment managers are now faced with a dilemma: risk going over budget in financial aid—and deal with the attendant budget shortfall in the coming year—or correct the situation before it becomes a problem. They need to make a business decision. Before long, the order comes back to the admission office. Fix it!

Since the admission letters haven't been mailed, "fixing it" is relatively easy. The admission committee will review the roster of students slated to be admitted and find 50 to 60 students who are on the competitive "bubble" *and* who have substantial financial need—who will require support in excess of $25,000 per year in order to enroll. The question will be asked in each case: "Is this someone in whom we want to make a four-year, $100,000+ investment if it means putting our bottom line at risk and compromising our academic program next year?" When the answer is "no," the applicant is quietly moved to the wait list for possible consideration later in the process.

At the same time, the committee will revisit students on the *other* bubble—those initially ticketed to the wait list—in search of 50 to 60 students who don't need financial aid. These students will be moved up and offered admission. When the juggling is finished, it would be impossible to tell that anything happened unless you were in the room with the decision makers. The students who have been moved up and those who have been moved down are virtually indistinguishable—except for their financial needs.

NEED-BLIND ADMISSION?

Perhaps you are familiar with the concept of "need-blind" admission. It is a time-honored notion that colleges should, or in the minds of many *must*, consider students for admission without regard to their family's financial circumstances. In other words, the admission folks should look at the academic record, not the bank record. It's a great and noble concept that most colleges strive to achieve. Unfortunately, the concept is much easier to describe than it is to achieve. It's fiction. When you think about it, the term itself—NEED BLIND—is absolute.

Between the Lines

The Bubble

In just about any competition, there are the stars and those who want to be stars. The stars are the sure things, the people who always get the lead roles. The "wanna-be's" may be good. They may even be stars on the rise, but in this competition they are relegated to back-up status. They are on the "bubble." In the competition for admission, the candidates on the bubble are always vulnerable. Logic suggests that the farther up the Pyramid of Selectivity a student might aspire, the greater the likelihood that she will find herself on a bubble and in jeopardy of coming up short in the competition should the admission committee need to justify her offer of acceptance against the bottom line.

It leaves no room for equivocation. An institution that claims to be truly need blind must be so in every circumstance of the selection process with every student. That's a pretty tall order. Consider the following exceptions:

- The admission of a student with modest or weak credentials whose family is or could be a major donor to the institution

- The awarding of any type of scholarship based on talent or merit even if those awards fall "out of the realm" of the normal admission process

- The decision to discreetly change the admission status of candidates due to their financial aid requirements

- The administration of different price structures to students based on the state of residency

The statement of need-blind admission should not be regarded as a matter of moral imperative. This is not about good guys and bad guys. It's a matter of colleges and universities taking care of business. You can be sure that any institution with financial aid to offer will make sure that it goes to the students it values most—the students with the highest quotients in areas identified within the "Agenda."

From the outside, this maneuvering can seem to be arbitrary and unfair. When you look at it from the institution's point of view, however, these are rational decisions and not at all arbitrary. The admission committee members

Between the Lines

ROI

Imagine that you are holding the credentials of a candidate whose family has expressed interest in building a new library for your school. She is good enough to be admitted but barely. You might consider the ROI (return on investment). Without her, you don't have a shot at the money for the library. If you admit her and get her into the right courses with the right professors, she just might make it—and your school gets the library. What would you do? If you admit her or others like her, are you still need blind? No. You have just made a business decision that makes you "resource aware."

may not like to see financial considerations enter the picture, but they will act in the best interests of the institution. If the committee cannot justify the expense associated with admitting and enrolling your student, it will simply move her to the wait list with the notation that she might look good later if there is any money left.

Standardized Tests

That standardized tests are included in the Hidden Agenda might surprise you. After all, tests have been around forever. Nobody seems to like them, but they are a necessary evil—or are they?

The underlying premise of the SAT® is that it provides colleges with a metric that enables them to predict whether a student will be able to perform academically in the first year. That's it. Neither the SAT nor its counterpart, the ACT®, is an intelligence test. While high scores may correlate with high intelligence, they do not measure it.

With that in mind, let's assess the competitive admission environment and the role standardized tests play in the decision making. I would begin by observing that a very high percentage of students (perhaps as high as 90 percent) self-select onto playing fields (i.e., applicant competitions) at colleges where they should be able to compete academically. In addition, validity studies have consistently shown that the best predictor of a student's success in college is the strength of her record in high school. The presence of standardized tests adds only marginally to a college's ability to predict success.

This combination of factors would suggest that, for most students applying to most colleges, standardized tests are no longer relevant for the purpose for which they were intended. They hold very little diagnostic value. Despite assurances from colleges that score results aren't that important, test scores are still required by many of them. A reasonable person might ask why.

The profit motive of test-makers notwithstanding, the answer is found in the inherent need of colleges to produce an easily recognized measure of their relative strength. Just as selectivity and yield provide evidence of popularity and accessibility, standardized test results have become a widely used "indicator" of the talent level of the student population. Higher scores seem to connote higher ability and better students. As a result, many colleges continue to require standardized tests, not as a measure of admissibility but as competitive credentials. The bigger the numbers, the better one's chances of admission.

Don't be surprised if, one day, you are within earshot of a conversation your student is having with an admission representative and the topic comes up. After talking casually about things your student likes to do, the rep might turn the focus to things academic. They'll talk about courses and grades. Then comes the ominous lead-in: "So, tell me about your test results." That's when it hits your student—sudden amnesia! "I can't remember exactly" she'll stammer. "I'm not sure if I got my results yet." Sensing the awkwardness of the moment, the admission rep will jump to the rescue, "That's okay. The tests aren't that important for us anyway."

If this response seems hard to believe, you can check it out. After all, you don't want your student acting on bad information. Colleges that are true to their rhetoric will make the submission of tests optional—and over 700 fall into that category. They can be found at all levels of selectivity on the Pyramid. In effect, these colleges are saying to young people that they can make sound decisions based on the strength of the information that is provided on the application. They are saying that they will *value* candidates for what they do well. (You can find a list of the colleges that have made score submission optional at www.FairTest.org.)

Special Interest Admission

It happens every spring. Shortly after admission decision letters are received, whispers of amazement and, at times, outrage spread through the neighborhood. They sound something like this: "Can you believe that Choosy U. turned down Allen but took Harry? Everybody knows that Allen is a much better student!" An injustice was passed down. Certainly, somebody made a mistake!

Such assessments are rooted in the notion that the outcomes will be fair and logical. By now, you should know that such assumptions are groundless at universities that can make fine distinctions between strong candidates. You know that selective colleges will do whatever they want with a group of qualified candidates. Why? Because they *can*. They are not accountable to anyone for the decisions they make. The farther up the Pyramid your student aspires, the more likely the process will seem arbitrary and capricious.

Between the Lines

"Can the Student Do the Work?"
A basic concern of any admission committee is: "Can this student do the work in our environment? Does she have the necessary ability and preparation to achieve passing grades?" (The bottom- line question of "Can the student do the work?" is the underlying premise of the NCAA's Proposition 48 threshold for extending scholarships to Division I athletic recruits.) If a student provides evidence that she *can* "do the work" then the question turns to "What do we get if we admit her?"

In any applicant pool, the students run the gamut academically from those who are projected to make the Dean's List to those who "just might make it" to graduation. If a college is convinced that it will get something substantial (talent, perspective, etc.) in return, it might elect to admit students who, given the chance, just might make it. If your student is admitted under such circumstances, it does not mean that she is entering an environment that represents the best "fit" for her. You'll have to help her separate the *glow* of the opportunity from the *glare* of the reality.

In choosing from the academically able, colleges will refer to their own list of needs and priorities in fleshing out their programs and perspectives. It is not uncommon for the needs to shift from year to year. One year, they might need poets, field hockey goalies, and cellists. The next year they might need writers, left-handed baseball pitchers, and bas-soonists.

Whatever the year, colleges are looking for students who, by virtue of their backgrounds, interests, or talents, stand apart from the rest in some way. When such applicants pass through the admission process, they are warmly embraced, even though their academic credentials may be relatively modest. If they are admitted, it is not because they possess academic brilliance. Rather, it is because they possess points of distinction in other areas—and they are *good enough* academically.

The Reality

The whole point of this chapter is to illustrate that admission outcomes are often driven by factors that are sometimes beyond your control. This revelation may leave you feeling numb and helpless. On the other hand, it could help to frame your student's college prospects in terms that are more manageable for her from the outset.

Surprises are an inevitable part of the selection process. There is no conspiracy here. We tend to forget—perhaps we want to forget—that there is a business side to colleges and universities. If they performed badly as businesses, they would close. It should not come as a surprise, then, that financial health and competitiveness among their peers will prompt colleges to engage in practices and behaviors that are reflected in the "Hidden Agenda."

The more your student stretches *against* the realistic range of her credentials in compiling her list of colleges, the more vulnerable she becomes to the potential heartbreak of the Hidden Agenda. A clear understanding of her competitiveness—and how it relates to the Pyramid—will put her in situations where she is more likely to be valued as a candidate rather than as just an applicant to be counted.

Navigating the Hidden Agenda: Ten Tips for Parents

1. **In assessing colleges, focus on outcomes rather than rankings.** What percentage of entering students will graduate from the university? What percentage is gainfully employed or in graduate programs a year after graduation? How have graduating students fared as applicants to professional or Ph.D. programs? Ask for the data.

2. **Remember that rankings featured in guidebooks are merely someone else's opinion.** They are the "sex that sells." Buy them for what they are—but be sure to read the articles as they often contain valuable insight.

3. **Resist the temptation to buy into Early Decision as a strategy.** I have heard more than one parent volunteer, "we are looking for an ED school." In doing so, they remove the focus from doing what's right for the student and place it squarely on the institution and "getting in." The better approach is to support a college search that is based on elements of a good fit. If/when a clear first choice emerges, then—and only then—consider the ED application.

4. **Resist the temptation to pool your resources in order to make your family look rich to enhance your student's chances of admission**—thinking that you will be "poor enough" in subsequent years to qualify for financial aid. Colleges base their financial aid budgets for returning students on the needs they have demonstrated upon entry. Your student won't find much sympathy in the financial aid office if she shows up pleading poverty in the second year after having gained admission as a "full pay" candidate.

5. **The Internet can be a valuable point of access to your student as she demonstrates interest in a college, especially if time and distance are prohibitive factors** with regard to a campus visit. Urge your student to identify the admission representative who is responsible for recruiting in your area. Then, in brief but substantive messages, she should introduce herself. In doing so, she should be prepared to ask a question that would require a response. For example, this is a good opportunity for your student to get an opinion about critical course selections for the senior year.

6. **If possible, have your student take both the SAT and the ACT.** Why? Colleges like to have options. If a college is otherwise predisposed toward your student but suddenly gets cold feet at the sight of her relatively modest SAT results, it may well decide to admit her on the strength of the ACT result. Besides, nearly every college in the country now considers the ACT in lieu of the SAT.

7. **Some colleges may play down the importance of demonstrating interest (filling out the card).** Don't buy it! Your student should continue to do the things she would normally do to get to know the college better.

8. **Students in the application process are prone to shortcuts.** An example of such a shortcut is the Common Application®. Three hundred colleges and universities belong to the Common Application® group and, as such, agree to accept the Common Application® as their own. The advantage to the student is that she can complete the application one time and send copies to multiple colleges. The potential downside to the Common Application® is that, while member institutions promise not to discriminate against students who use it, they may become cynical about the student's level of interest if she has not visited and has not been terribly engaged prior to applying. The solution: she should demonstrate interest and put to rest concerns that she is taking a random shot in the dark with this application.

9. **If your student is considering an Early Decision application at a first-choice university,** but you have concerns about managing the cost of her attending the institution, a little research in advance of the application might provide needed answers. Contact the financial aid office at the university in question and ask for a meeting at which you can present your financial situation and ask for an early read of your "expected family contribution (EFC)." Armed with this information, you will be able to advise your student regarding the feasibility of an ED application.

10. **Special interest admission can work in your student's favor *if* she has applied to colleges that will value her for what she does well.** This is where it pays to research colleges carefully to understand what *their* needs might be. Then, she needs to position herself so that the college in question will feel compelled to admit her.

Chapter 7

Recruitment 101

Before officially starting the college search, be reminded that the exercise will not be purely one-sided. Just as you and your student are gearing up to learn about colleges, colleges are preparing to launch an all-out marketing offensive designed to generate student interest, increase selectivity, and improve yield (i.e., the Hidden Agenda). The resulting engagement will be like surfing in the ocean. If you are able to catch the wave and maintain your balance, you can ride it to shore. If you aren't ready for it, though, the wave will crash over you leaving you churning in the surf.

The same is true of the college process. If you and your student are ready, you can catch a good "ride" all the way through the application process. Let's take a look, then, at what you can expect from colleges and how you can productively tap into the energy and resources that the colleges bring to bear as they recruit students.

The Admission Funnel

The enrollment process at each college is based on the principle of "yield." Colleges identify and target a very large number of students with recruitment messages in order to *yield* a group of prospects that will *yield* an applicant pool of a size that will enable them to accept the right number of students that will eventually *yield* an entering class.

In effect, colleges are playing a numbers game. At each step of the process, the numbers diminish—as students choose other options or are not chosen by the college—until the class is achieved. The sequencing of the numbers from greater to smaller produces the image of a funnel. In order to get a class of X number of students, a college will reverse the yield progression to forecast the number of students required at each stage of the process.

The Admission Funnel

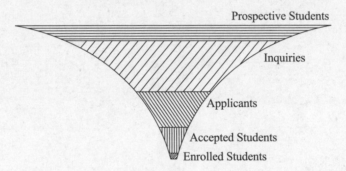

Prospective Students

Inquiries

Applicants

Accepted Students

Enrolled Students

As you can imagine, colleges want to keep the brim of the funnel as wide as possible. The more students who express an interest, the greater are the prospects for increases in applications. Like modern day "Pied Pipers," institutions invest heavily in marketing and recruitment outreach efforts that enable them to establish an active following among prospective students.

Your Student, the Free Agent

Think of it this way. Your student begins the college process as a free agent—an eligible but uncommitted college prospect. Institutions everywhere will court his brains and talent, not to mention his loyalty and affection. Much of the mail he receives will have the "you have been preapproved" ring to it. It will include free offers ("guides to the interview process" or "frequently asked financial aid questions" or even application fee waivers) in return for his interest.

Colleges and universities—even small enrollment schools—mail search letters or "feelers" to nearly 100,000 students each year. Any student who meets an institution's minimal admission criteria (score results, self-reported GPA), has compatible academic interests, and lives within specified geographic areas will be targeted with personalized letters and colorful brochures. If he possesses a GPA and a PSAT result, someone will want him. Owners of particularly high scores will begin receiving "love letters" from dozens of "top ranked" universities.

As flattering as it may be to receive so much mail, your student must understand that these mailings are essentially feelers. He should expect e-mail and/or snail mail from literally hundreds of col-

Between the Lines

A Healthy Dose of Cynicism
As colleges recruit your student's interest and application, beware of empty promises. The literature can sound promising and the recruiters—especially athletic recruiters—can seem highly encouraging. A healthy dose of cynicism is warranted. What may seem like promises of "happily ever after" are attempts to get you and your student to buy-in at the next level of interest. Wherever you perceive a "disconnect," look for evidence to support the rhetoric. Without it, you are left with nothing but . . . rhetoric.

leges, all of which are "trolling for nibbles." Their initial "bait" will be colorful, flashy, and full of promise. In order to receive more substantive information—the really good stuff—he will need to complete and return a reply card.

The recruitment continues as college representatives visit high schools, attend college fairs and college nights, and host information receptions to generate interest. They conduct open houses, provide tours and, in many cases, offer interviews in an attempt to build relationships with students. And it won't stop there as they pour hundreds of thousands of dollars into creating and producing interactive Web sites, chat rooms, e-mail blasts, and iPod messages designed to woo your student.

It pays to be a bit cynical about all of this. On the one hand, there is an ego rush that comes with being recruited by College X. "Wow! Can you believe College X wrote me a personalized letter? They must really want me!" Then reality hits. They are sending the same letter to thousands of other young people. It is part of a marketing scheme calculated to generate interest. That said, if a college seems to interest your student, it costs nothing to receive additional information. Encourage him to read the material carefully and then decide.

The greater reality is that colleges want more applicants in order to afford themselves a measure of selectivity later in the process. It's a volume business. The more students who respond and eventually apply, the more flexibility—and selectivity—afforded the institution in choosing its class. The sender wants your student's business, his application.

The Disconnect

Don't be mistaken, though. This is not a plan by colleges to increase access. While the brim of the funnel may grow wider each year, the narrow neck that determines the number that get in remains the same. In many cases, it becomes tighter as institutions become more selective. Consequently, you will find a disconnect between the rhetoric (what colleges proclaim publicly) and reality.

The rhetoric is warm and promising, almost altruistic. Colleges want your student to apply and they want you to feel good about making the investment. In fact, they want lots of students to apply.

As colleges roll out their marketing efforts, be sensitive to the often subtle differences between reality and rhetoric. For example:

Rhetoric	Reality
SATs aren't that important.	They are—colleges love high scores!
Don't worry about cost. We have aid.	They don't have enough aid for everyone.
We have great internships!	Very few students get them.
You would be a good candidate for us.	They might reject you—others are better.
We've got a place on our roster for you.	But you have to try out first!
You get used to the snow.	Yeah, right!

You can probably add to this list without much difficulty. The point, however, is not to bash colleges. Rather, it is to alert you to their motives and make you and your student sensitive to the fact that things are not always as they seem. Colleges have a lot at stake in promoting themselves. The more students they can get into the funnel as applicants, the stronger their admission profile.

Chapter 8

Putting It All Together

Gaining Traction

So far, we have taken a look at the college process from the perspective of ownership and agendas. You know who is going to college and you now have a better idea about how to talk with your student regarding what lies ahead. Moreover, as she prepares to enter the competition for admission, you will be able to guide her decision making so she is able to put herself in the best position possible to achieve success.

While getting off to a *good* start in the college planning process is instrumental to achieving happy endings, an *early* start can also make a big difference. Starting "early" does not mean, however, that your student needs to have it all figured out by the end of the freshman year. She doesn't need to have a short list of colleges ready by the sophomore year. And you certainly don't want to start prescribing activities for her so she has a "better chance of getting in." Starting early simply means that the two of you gain exposure to the bigger picture sooner rather than later.

The insight gained can be a strong guide and powerful motivator as she makes her way through high school.

On the other hand, teenagers are unpredictable. What seemed like a given ("I want to study premed at an urban university near the ocean.") in October of the junior year is reduced to entertaining trivia by October of the senior year as interests and directions change daily. Regardless of when this process starts to gain momentum, it is vital that you remain flexible and find patience with what will be an uneven and, at times, emotional series of events.

Between the Lines

Take the Initiative
Urge your student to take the initiative in researching colleges. A simple yet direct letter or e-mail to a college requesting information will put her on the mailing list. When she is able, she should attend college information sessions at her high school where she can also request additional information. College nights/fairs provide similar access to dozens of institutions— all under one roof!

The College Search: A Three-Phase Process

The best time to actually start the college search process—to really dive in and start shopping for colleges—is in the middle of the junior year of high school. It's okay to begin collecting information prior to that, but be prepared for a fairly light treatment by colleges. Your student will begin to experience the really substantive interactions with college personnel after the high school class that precedes hers has been "put to bed."

Starting in the junior year allows your student to collect information while there is still time to process it systematically. No pressure. No deadlines. No commitments. The more time that is allowed for processing and decision making, the better. As you'll discover quickly, your student will not be at a loss for source material! In order to help her maintain focus and direction, you might try conceptualizing college planning in three sequential phases: data collection, analysis, and decision making.

Data Collection

For each new institution that appears on your student's radar screen, she needs to *collect data* and impressions from a range of sources. While she can expect to be inundated with unsolicited mail from colleges around the country, much of that information is designed to grab her attention. She needs to be disciplined in her approach to this information. If she pauses to read through a flyer she has received, ask her what has caught her attention. Is she responding emotionally or has the college's message resonated with her own set of priorities? Urge her to check the place out on the Internet or in a comprehensive reference guide. If her research turns up something substantive, then she should request more information and add the school to her list.

College catalogs, videos, and Web sites are also great resources. Campus visits as well as conversations with current students and

Between the Lines

Give It Time

If you or your student prefer a "go, see, and buy" approach to college shopping, this process of data collecting may seem tedious. Being targeted and tactical is fine if your student knows unequivocally what she wants. It is rare, though, that "shopping" for a good college match can be accomplished at that level of efficiency. In the long run, a patient, strategic approach will serve her best.

recent graduates provide valuable perspective. She will also find that an investment in a college guidebook—preferably one that is an objectively reliable data source—is money well spent.

Generating original research is the best solution to finding a college that represents the best fit for your student. She is more likely to internalize such information if *she* is at the point of discovery. A well-organized and systematic search gives her ownership of the critical data as they are uncovered. The risk is that she will be inconsistent—that she won't always be inclined to collect, organize, and distill information about colleges. This is where you can be helpful.

As she begins to think about colleges, urge your student to develop a spreadsheet onto which she can chart critical information *for each place that interests her*. Call it the Essential Data Checklist (EDC). Each revelation about a college or university should serve as a prompt to update her EDC.

Essential Data Checklist (EDC)

1. **Application fee/deadline** She needs to be respectful of deadlines in all cases.

2. **Interview** Is it offered and where? She shouldn't miss it if it is offered.

3. **Required tests** What is required? Note where test submission is optional.

4. **Location (city/state)** How does a school's location fit with her priorities?

5. **Population center (urban, suburban, rural)** She needs to assess the type of community and neighborhood environment in which the college is located.

6. **Distance from home (travel time)** Some students want to get away; others want to stay close. Note the time and cost associated with travel as well as miles to be traveled.

7. **Travel costs** Estimate roundtrip expenses. What it will cost for her to make the trip several times a year if not several times a semester?

8. **Size** Styles of instruction vary dramatically with size of institution.

9. **Type of support (Public, Private)** An important insight with regard to institutional mission and support.

10. **Structure (College, University)** Institutions vary in their organization and complexity. Note the impact of different structures on styles of instruction.

11. **Student/professor ratio** This ratio reveals a lot about the access your student can expect to faculty and various individualized learning opportunities.

12. **Program** Your student needs to note the availability and relative strength of the academic programs in which she is interested.

13. **Ratio of undergraduate operating budget to undergraduate student** This ratio speaks to an institution's ability to support the undergraduate educational experience. It is powerful information if you can get it and use it comparatively.

14. **Cost** Sooner or later, you will need to deal with issues of cost and affordability.

15. **Availability of financial assistance** Find out what your student might expect in terms of need- and merit-based assistance.

Urge your student to customize her list to reflect special needs and interests, particularly as they relate to the priorities she established earlier. For example, access to major transportation outlets, availability of support for learning differences, access to kosher kitchens, and opportunities to play in the band or write for the newspaper might be factors worth noting.

Armed with the EDC, your student is ready to organize data objectively and strategically. In the interest of her sanity—and yours—it will pay to invest in a small file cabinet (file the materials in an organized fashion) and a spreadsheet program (to keep track of the key data).

While the data collection process will be most intense at the outset of the college process, it is an exercise that will serve you and your student through the final decision making. Patterns will become clear, enabling her to make critical distinctions between colleges. She will quickly learn that not all colleges and universities are alike. In fact, they can be very different. The objective: find those that have the right educational package for her.

Analysis

In the *analysis* phase, your student needs to *gain perspective* on the idea: "what would it be like to be a student at College X?" Have her roll it around in her head for weeks

Between the Lines

Crossing Over
Your student's relationship with colleges will change as she makes her way through each phase of the process. At the outset, she will regard herself—and be regarded—as a "prospective student." She is very much on the outside of an institution tentatively peering in to see if it is a place she would like to enter. She's "just looking." As she begins to arrive at a short list of colleges, she needs to be more accountable for information. Even though she may be well ahead of deadlines, she must be sensitive to requirements for testing, auditions, essays, and any other elements of the application process that will otherwise sneak up on her.

or, if possible, months to see how it feels. She should talk with recent alumni and get opinions from teachers. She needs to move beyond the data to impressions she can draw from her own experience.

As your student begins to sort through the college possibilities, her objective should be to come up with a "short list" of highly compatible colleges to which she will eventually apply. These are the colleges at which she can see herself performing—and living—comfortably. They are the best "fits" for her. At the outset, though, the distinctions won't be so clear. Finding clarity will require sorting through a much longer list as she samples a range of options!

Allowing the list to grow is actually a good exercise. The broader your student's exposure to colleges, the greater is the chance that her ultimate decision making will be thoughtful and knowledge based. Make sure she is exposed to colleges of all sizes and types. Let her see the difference between large, complex universities and liberal arts colleges, between urban campuses and those situated in the countryside, between residential campuses and commuter campuses. Challenge her assumptions and, in the process, broaden her understanding of the possibilities.

Attacking a long list of colleges can be daunting, though. At times, it will seem like an exercise gone out of control. That's why the EDC is important. By keeping the data organized and using her list of priorities as a guide, she should be able to control the pace and the direction of the college search as she begins to examine the possibilities.

The analysis or critical review stage of this exercise should take place over the eight-month period from April of your student's junior year through November of her senior year. As she becomes more involved in this activity—especially through original research—her interests will become more defined and the range of options will begin to narrow.

CALCULATING THE ODDS

An important element of the analysis phase for your student is determining whether she is likely to be on the "playing field" at the schools that emerge on her short list. While it is impossible to predict admission outcomes, she can increase her comfort level (yours too!) by gauging where her credentials stand in the competition. At which colleges does she have a reasonable chance of competing for admission?

In order to make this assessment you need to know her best SAT scores (or highest ACT result) as well as her rank in class or grade point average (if her school does not rank). Next, compare her results with the admission profiles for each of the respective colleges. Look at the score ranges for the middle 50 percent of their enrolled students. This is where the real competition takes place. To get a reasonable approximation of your student's chances, plot her results on each continuum.

The same is true of her grade point average. The best combination would be for both her scores *and* her GPA to be in the top 25 percent of those reported. Even then, however, there can be no guarantees at colleges and universities near the top of the Pyramid.

The following chart offers a rough approximation of your student's chances for getting into a college based on its selectivity and where her credentials fall on its profile. For the purposes of this discussion, assume that both her scores and her GPA fall at the same point on the admission profile.

	Where Student's Credentials Fall on the Profile			
	Selectivity	Top 25	Middle 50	Bottom 25
	1/8	1:4	1:8	1:16
College	1/4	1:2	1:4	1:8
Admits	1/2	3:4	1:2	1:4
	6/8	9:10	6:8	1:2

Note that, at the top of the Pyramid—among the most highly selective colleges—there really are no guarantees or even "probable" admits. Even the strongest candidates must compete against long odds to gain admission. And being in the ballpark at the places on the Pyramid that are somewhat less selective (admitting 1 out of 2) is not a guarantee that your student will get in. It does mean that she has a fairly even chance of admission.

A COMPETITIVE TWIST

It is common for universities to apply different standards to their various degree programs due to the varying levels of demand for them. For example, the competition to get into the engineering program may be much more intense than the competition for the nursing program. The College of Arts and Sciences might operate under yet another set of expectations.

As your student explores the various degree programs that exist within universities, make sure she understands the admission profile for each specific program that interests her. The standards will not only be different from program to program within an institution, but the required application elements may be different as well.

Decision Making

Finally, she must *decide* where to apply. How does College X *fit* according to the priorities she has established? Compared to others that "fit," how well does College X match her needs and interests? What is its value to her?

This is the affirming phase of your student's relationship with a college. It embodies her decision to move forward—to express an interest, to visit, to apply and, if accepted, to enroll. As your student's priorities crystallize, the spreadsheet she created will prove its worth in giving her comparative data that will be useful in her final decision making. By focusing on critical needs regarding outcomes and matters that will define her satisfaction with the college experience, she will be able to eliminate many colleges, including some that had been very attractive at first blush.

It is as she makes decisions about where to apply and where to enroll that you need to be most vigilant. Challenge assumptions and make sure that your student has been true to her priorities in pursuing a good fit. Despite her best intentions, she may still be holding fast to ideas or perspectives that are not valid relative to her own set of priorities. Allowing emotions to drive her decision making can prove costly in terms of tuition dollars spent and delays toward graduation. Barely half of the young people who begin at four-year colleges actually graduate from those original colleges. More often than not, the failed starts are the result of ill-fitting college choices.

Separate Fact from Fiction Tip-Sheet

As your student processes the information she receives from colleges, be careful to separate fact from fiction. It is a rare college that will volunteer its weaknesses or shortcomings to students it would like to recruit. If you begin with a healthy dose of cynicism, you'll be off to a good start. Observe the following to make sure you and your student know what she is getting *after* she takes off the wrapping.

1. **Check the numbers.** You are bound to hear about small classes and impressive student to faculty ratios as you learn about schools. Make sure you know what these numbers mean. Ratios and averages are only useful in comparing schools if the methodologies for reporting them are the same across institutions.

   A good question to ask is: "What percentage of the classes includes 20 or fewer students?" If you are concerned about the student to faculty ratio, ask if teaching assistants or non-teaching administrators with academic credentials are included in the faculty count. Or, better yet, find out the percentage of undergraduate classes taught by tenured (professors formally granted the right to hold their positions until retirement) faculty. You get the picture. Make sure you understand the numbers you are given.

2. **Who gets the perks?** Every college and university wants to give the impression that its students have access to enhanced learning opportunities. Internships, independent study, research with faculty, and study abroad are examples of such activities. The good news is that such opportunities usually do exist. The question to ask is: for whom? Find out what is required in order to participate. What percent of graduates has taken advantage of such opportunities? Ask

to see lists of completed projects. If a perk sounds good in a college's presentation, look for evidence that it can become a reality for your student.

3. **Understand course availability.** In the recruitment process, colleges will tell your student about the amazing range of academic experiences for undergraduates. They may even offer a thick catalog as evidence of a broad curriculum. In order to determine how well she will be served by this curriculum, she needs to dig further. What will happen if she changes her mind about a major? How easily can she move from one program or college to another? Will she lose ground in her progress toward graduation? And what about access to interesting courses outside of her major—how available are they?

4. **Who graduates—and when?** The choice of a four-year college should represent a four-year investment of time, energy, and talent that results in a bachelor's degree. At some institutions, though, it is not possible for a student to complete a full program of undergraduate study in four years due to inaccessibility of required courses. Your student needs to factor this into her decision making. The financial consequences will be obvious in terms of tuition expectations. Be sure to consider the cost of her lost income opportunity as well.

    There are no guarantees that your student's progress toward graduation will happen according to script and you should be aware of the probabilities. Look for evidence that colleges will actively support her progress toward graduation. Who will notice if she has difficulty or needs assistance? What is the availability of summer school? What are the graduation rates for students in four years? Five years?

5. **Outcomes** What happens when your student graduates from college? Her experience and her degree should be instrumental in introducing her to opportunities for jobs as well as graduate school placements. You will hear lots of promising rhetoric. Make sure it is grounded in reality. Also make sure your student asks the career counselors about their placement activities. How do they help prepare soon-to-be graduates for the job market? Do they facilitate internships or provide alumni mentoring programs for their students? What support is there for applicants to medical or law school? And what are the results?

Get the Best Data

Career counselors at each college should be able to produce information about job placements by major for a five-year period. Look for patterns of quality and consistency. Consult independent studies that show baccalaureate origins of Ph.D. recipients, medical school placements, and business executives. Most of that information is available through the institutional research offices of the colleges your student is considering. Other sources of information are advanced degree programs and their graduates. Your student can find out from graduate schools which of the undergraduate programs are "hot" in her discipline. And she should talk to the professionals. If law is a career possibility, she should talk with lawyers in your community about their educational experiences. What worked for them and where?

College Planning Timeline	
The following planning timeline highlights key dates and decision-making periods for the college-bound student. A similar timeline is included in the reading for your student as well. That version features a more directive commentary. You will want to keep this timeline, along with key dates established by your student's high school, handy throughout the college planning process.	
9th Grade	
All Year	Reinforce good habits in the classroom. Help set goals for personal and academic achievement.
Fall	Encourage your student to "test the water" and become part of the action in places where her interests or talents might lead her. She can try out for the team, audition for the play, join a club, or volunteer in the community.
Winter	When it is time to choose courses for 10th grade, encourage your student to remain focused on moving to the next level of challenge.
Summer	Your student should look for constructive opportunities to find enrichment in her areas of interest (sports, performing arts camps, travel).

10th Grade	
All Year	Reinforce positive and productive academic efforts. Your student needs to stay focused. It's okay to get good grades!
Fall	Encourage your student to do the little things that keep her engaged and allow her to grow in the areas that interest her. Urge her to consider taking the PLAN in October (in advance of the ACT). She might also take the PSAT (just for practice).
Winter	In planning courses for 11th grade, your student should look for ways to move to the next logical level of rigor.
Spring	Year end examinations are offered for accelerated courses (AP, pre-IB) your student may have taken as a sophomore. The results will validate her classroom performance as well as the strength of her school's program.
Summer	Your student should continue to pursue enrichment opportunities. Part-time work and community service are respectable pursuits. Take advantage of family vacations and business trips to visit college campuses.

Help your student develop a system for organizing the admission materials she will receive/collect from colleges.

Fill in your personal calendar with registration deadlines and test dates for the PSAT, SAT, ACT, AP, and SAT Subject Tests that will take place during the junior year. Test dates vary from year to year, but you can find them at www.collegeboard.com and www.act.org. |

11th Grade	
All Year	It is time for your student to bear down academically. Expectations continue to grow and the pressure to perform will be greater than ever.
Fall	Begin a conversation with your student about what she wants to get out of college. Don't worry about the specifics (what, when, where) just yet. And don't feel that she must be absolutely certain about what she wants to study. That will follow. At this point, simply get the conversation started.
	Your student should take the PSAT/NMSQT in October. Results will arrive at her school in December.
	Encourage your student to attend college information sessions with visiting admission officers at her school as well as any school meetings for juniors that deal with selecting and applying to college. Keep an eye on opportunities to attend college nights and college fairs as well.
	If your student is going to pursue test prep, now is the time to explore her options and get registered somewhere.
Winter	Help your student map out a plan to take the ACT, SAT, and SAT Subject Tests that extends through her senior year. Help her take stock of her priorities for college. Why does she want to go? Begin working with her on a list of possibilities.
	Urge your student to choose a senior year course load that continues to stretch her. Forget the notion that the junior year is most important—it's a myth! If she wants to compete for admission to selective colleges, she needs to make her senior year count!

Spring	Plan college visits during your spring break. Many colleges offer Open Houses for juniors. Participate where you can. Go to the parent workshops while your student is doing the things scheduled for students.
	Your student should take the SAT or ACT as well as any appropriate AP tests.
	Along with your student, attend a college fair in your area.
	As your family plans summer activities (jobs, camps, youth conferences, etc.), be sure to include college visits.
Summer	Continue college visits. Your student should interview wherever possible. She should also register for fall SAT/ACT examinations and investigate community-sponsored scholarship opportunities. She should find a part-time job and/or continue enrichment activities related to her passions.
	Late in the summer, after the college visits, help your student narrow her list of colleges. She should start her senior year with a "short list" of six to eight colleges, including one or two in each category of selectivity (Reach, Match, Probable).
	Along with your student, become familiar with the application requirements for each college and talk through the essays she needs to submit. By late summer, she should have developed strong outlines if not rough drafts of her critical essays.

12th Grade	
Fall	Prepare yourself for a busy year. The college application process will seem like another course or two on top of everything else for your student. She should continue doing the things she loves, assume leadership roles where appropriate, and stay on top of her grades!
	By the end of September your student should meet with the teachers who will write letters of recommendation for her, notify her counselor of the colleges to which she may be applying, AND complete good drafts of her essays.
	Encourage your student to prepare supporting material (portfolios, tapes, CDs) that speaks to her special talents. She should continue to attend college information sessions.
	If your student has a favorite college (where she might apply Early Decision), she should plan an overnight visit there AND at another of her favorite colleges. She should compare her impressions of each before completing any ED forms.
	Your student should take the SAT/ACT at least once between September and December. She should also plan to take the SAT Subject Tests necessary to satisfy the requirements of the colleges where she is applying.
	Your student should inform her counselor of her final college list and provide a list of application due dates. You need a copy of this list as well since you will be writing the checks for application fees. She needs to release test scores to colleges if she is applying ED/EA by October 15.
	File the College Scholarship Service (CSS) PROFILE, if appropriate. The PROFILE is typically required by private institutions to determine your family's eligibility for assistance.

Winter	By early December, your student should have finished applications that are due between December 31 and February 15. If she applied ED and was admitted, she must withdraw all of her outstanding applications. She should take the ACT/SAT /SAT Subject Tests, if appropriate, and complete and submit applications with later due dates.
	File the Free Application for Federal Student Aid (FAFSA) as soon after January 1 as possible. The FAFSA will determine your eligibility for government assistance.
	From early February through mid-March, your student should consider returning to some of her favorite colleges to stay overnight and attend classes.
Spring	Final admission decisions will arrive between late March and early April for colleges that do not have rolling admission. Financial aid awards will typically follow after a week or so.
	Take advantage of opportunities to attend receptions/programs for accepted students. Ask lots of questions! Help prepare your student to declare her commitment by May 1.

Chapter 9

Road Trip!

Buckle Up!

As the college process warms up, you will likely find yourself sharing lots of quality time on the road with your soon-to-be college student. Given your work schedule and his school commitments, such opportunities have probably been few of late. Get ready. Once you are buckled in and heading down the interstate, you'll either find things to talk about or be graced with long periods of silence!

Why is this necessary, you might ask? After all, your time is valuable and "couldn't these college visits wait until we find out where he gets in?" You *could* wait, but that would be counterproductive for a couple of reasons. One, the campus visit is critical to your student's ability to validate his selection process. Two, most colleges regard the campus visit as the *best indicator of yield*—that a student is likely to enroll.

As a result, the college visit will rapidly emerge as the most important element in your student's college planning process. Everything else—the talking, the searching, and the planning—is based on theory.

Your student researches his options and develops a list of schools based on what he thinks he knows about himself and the respective colleges. The moment he steps on a college campus, he puts the theory to the test. How will the people, the place, and the culture match up with your student's interests? How will it fit? Will it resemble the pictures? How will he like it? So, get ready. If the college selection process is to go to the next level—if your student is going to test the theory behind his initial thinking—he needs to hit the road.

The Strategy of Visiting

Two frequently asked questions about college visits are "how many places should we visit?" and "when should we visit?" The

Between the Lines

"Drive-bys" Not Allowed!
Whenever in proximity to a college campus, take advantage of the opportunity to see what is there. Make sure he gets out of the car at least long enough to find the admission office—there is no such thing as a "drive-by" college visit! He needs to fill out a registration form, collect whatever literature he needs, and, if time will allow, take a tour. Even if the college is not on his radar screen, he benefits from the visit as it broadens his perspective with regard to what's out there.

answers are tied to the logic presented in the opening paragraphs of this chapter. Frankly, *the best time to visit is when you can*—whenever your schedules will allow. Just make sure your student has an opportunity to visit the colleges on his short list before the application deadline. Beyond that, there is no limit to the number of colleges you and your student might visit.

Ideally (time, distance, and funds allowing!), your student will complete three rounds of visits to colleges that make it to his "short list." The sequence begins with the "Look/See" or exploratory visits and is followed by those that are more investigative in nature. Finally, he will want to make one more visit prior to making his final enrollment decision. Each round of visits will include fewer campuses and serve a different purpose in his decision-making process.

Look/See

This is the initial "survey" or exploratory visit. Your student should take a tour and, if possible, attend an information session. If the college is far from your home and an interview is offered, he should take it—even though he is still learning about the school. The purpose of this visit is to determine if he wants to keep the college on his list. He should visit as many colleges as possible and resist the temptation to make emotional commitments right away.

The best time to make this initial visit is during the junior year or the summer prior to the start of the senior year. The real benefit to visiting prior to the junior year would be in giving him additional exposure. Don't push a lot of other activity unless he is genuinely interested.

Between the Lines

Fill Out the Card!
Whenever your student visits a college campus, he needs to get credit for being there. Make sure he signs in at the admission office. He needs to fill out the card even if it is the second or third time he has visited. In fact, if he is on a campus after hours and the admission office is closed, he should go to an information desk where someone can at least pass along the message that he was on the campus. *He should never leave a campus without making a record of his visit.*

Investigate

When your student has determined his short list of colleges, work with him to begin planning a second round of visits. The point of these visits is to learn about the place from the insider's perspective. In order to become immersed in campus life, he should visit when the college is in session. He needs to become a student on that campus for 24 hours—to breathe the air, meet the people, and taste the food.

This is his opportunity to thoroughly assess his theories of "fit." The more he internalizes the culture of the place—especially those elements of campus life that are important to him (athletics, music, theater, volunteerism, etc.)—the easier it will be for him to make critical distinctions later in the process.

Fast Forward: Time to Buy

Imagine that your student has been accepted to several colleges and now it is "time to buy." Assuming he used his priorities and the five points of a good fit as a compass thus far, he will need to rely on his gut feeling in making a final decision. He should seize any opportunity to visit again, including programs for accepted students. He needs to try the experience on one more time—to imagine himself in the classroom, the residence hall, and the dining hall before making a commitment to enroll.

What's in a College Visit?

Once your student knows which campuses he would like to visit, sit down with a calendar to plot out a travel strategy. Depending on the complexity of his agenda, he needs to plan well in advance. If he is planning an ambitious itinerary that covers more than three schools

Between the Lines

Don't Hesitate to Ask the $$ Questions
If your student finds that a college is becoming his favorite, ask the financial aid folks if they will provide an "early read" of your financial family contribution. Using the previous year's financial data, they can give you a close estimate of your anticipated expenses.

or more than two days of travel or hopes to accomplish a lot on each campus, he should begin to contact the schools at least six weeks in advance of the designated travel time. In doing so, he improves his chances of getting appointments on the dates and at the times he would prefer.

As you and your student prepare to visit colleges, keep in mind the various options that you might find at your disposal while on each campus. At most colleges, the admission office will be happy to help your student assemble a campus visit itinerary to suit his interests and needs. If any of the following opportunities are not presented automatically during a visit, it is worth inquiring about them.

Campus Tour

The tour is usually an hour-long presentation of the campus by a current student. Wear comfortable walking shoes and be prepared for the hike. Listen carefully as tour guides don't always project well and, with large tour groups, they are not always attentive to those at the rear of the procession. When possible, encourage your student to stay close to the front of the tour so he can take advantage of conversational opportunities with the guide.

Special Facilities Tour

Some colleges offer tours that feature in-depth presentations of program areas. This is particularly true of the sciences and the arts. If your student has interests in these areas of study, he would benefit from the added exposure that such a tour would give him.

Personal Interview

Many colleges offer interviews for rising seniors. The interview is usually conducted by a member of the admission staff, although an increasing number of colleges now offer interviews conducted by upperclass students or interns. Regardless, if an interview is offered, your student should take it. Can it help? Absolutely! Students are often reticent about submitting to a personal interview. The prospect of having to carry on a conversation with a stranger behind closed doors for more than 5 minutes sends chills through most teenagers. If they would just relax and give themselves a chance, though, they would do just fine. Besides, making a good impression can be important later during the credential review as the admission committee struggles to make fine distinctions between strong candidates. I once found myself in an interview with a young man by the name of Christopher who presented solid but not spectacular academic credentials. He was good enough to be on the "playing field," but he needed a hook in order to compete for a spot in the class. I was immediately impressed by the satchel of inventions he had brought along. Christopher proved to be an enthusiastic and engaging conversationalist and I enjoyed listening to the explanations behind his creations.

Before long, the conversation shifted to his recent activities in school. I learned of his passion for musical theater and that his school had just completed a production of *South Pacific* with Christopher in the role of the Frenchman, Emile Dubec. No sooner had I expressed my fondness for the show when he offered to sing. He stood up and launched into a rendition of *"Some Enchanted Evening"* that was worthy of Dubec himself!

Whether or not Christopher was calculating in his approach, it worked. He was later admitted and went on to become the cornerstone of several musical performing groups on our campus. Your student doesn't need to sing in his interview. He just needs to be prepared to share himself with the interviewer. The fact of an interview may not always get a student in, but the lack of an interview has kept many deserving students out.

Information Session

Often offered in lieu of personal interviews, these sessions offer little opportunity for personal interaction with staff but do allow ample time for questions about college life. Your student should be prepared with one or two questions to ask in one-to-one conversation afterward. Among other things, this extended conversation presents an opportunity for your student to secure the presenter's business card for later follow-up.

Between the Lines

A Campus Too Far

No one expects a student from a great distance to visit if time and finances do not allow it. What a college would like to see in that case is a determined effort *by the student* to find out about the college through the various means available to him. An e-mail to the admission representative working your area that explains the circumstances and opens a dialogue about his interest can be very helpful.

Attend a Class

During the investigative or decision-making visits, it is vital that your student immerse himself in campus life. When possible, he should attend a class or two in areas of his interest. You can attend, too, although a different class might be a good idea. Regardless, it is important that the professor be given the courtesy of advance notice of your presence. Remind your student to introduce himself after the class has been dismissed.

Meet a Professor

In many instances, your student will be able to arrange brief meetings with professors in their offices. This is a particularly valuable opportunity late in the process as it will give your student a flavor of the academic expectations—and opportunities.

Stay Overnight

Before making a final decision about a college, it is very important that your student plan an overnight visit. This will give him an opportunity to talk with the "natives" and immerse himself in the culture of the place.

Eat in the Dining Hall

Your student might as well check out the food. It won't be home cooking, but will it be tolerable?

Hang Out

At some point in his visit, your student should find a comfortable place in a public area (i.e., snack bar, reading room) where he can simply observe people to determine how he might fit in. He should be sensitive to the way people regard him (welcoming and friendly versus cool and disinterested).

Attend Open Houses

The open house is a great opportunity for you and your student to become acquainted with a college.

Between the Lines

Dig Deeper

If your student is interested in a special program of study or learning opportunity (research, internship, etc.), he should ask professors and students to talk about their respective experiences and get evidence of undergraduate involvement. Similarly, if he has an interest in the performing arts, he should speak with professors in those areas to assess the opportunities he might have once enrolled.

While it may seem like a mob scene, colleges usually orchestrate such programs well to give families a basic orientation to the academic and cocurricular opportunities on their campuses. If you attend an open house with your student, make a conscious decision to split up. The two or three of you can cover more ground that way—and your student will begin to find his own voice as he meets people on his own.

Student Athletes

Students with special talents are likely to be treated to a round of recruitment apart from that which is offered to the general public. This is particularly true of student athletes. While you might expect that scholarship athletic (NCAA Division I) programs provide special on-campus recruitment programs, the degree to which nonscholarship programs engage in similar activities may surprise you.

Tips to Remember

The chapter dealing with campus visits on the flip side of this book goes into much more detail about the process. The reason is simple: You are the coach in this "game," not the player. The following tips will guide you as you coach your student through the college visitation process.

Between the Lines

Review the Rules

When your student accepts an opportunity to stay overnight on a college campus, he is suddenly on his own in "someone else's house." Some colleges will expect that both of you sign acknowledgments that he will be responsible for his actions. An overwhelming majority of overnight visits come off without incident. Regardless, he will be known by his actions. You may want to review with him the need for accountability on both his part and that of his hosts. He may bristle at the need to have such a discussion, but it is better to be safe than sorry. Colleges have been known to revoke offers of admission and scholarship due to bad behavior on an overnight visit.

1. **This is your student's process.** While you might work together to develop a travel plan, he should make the arrangements. It is best to schedule visits at least six weeks in advance.

2. **Make the visit count.** Make sure he never leaves a college campus without filling out a registration form that will give him credit for being there!

3. **If the opportunity to meet with an admission officer is available, encourage your student to take it.** The corresponding chapter for your student will provide greater detail and instruction about preparing for the interview.

4. **Remember that this is the twenty-first century.** *No one* dresses in coat and tie for campus visits anymore. The equivalent of business casual will work.

5. **If your student is struggling with the process, do your best to insert appropriate empathy and humor.** Your unconditional support in this very public forum is vital to his confidence and, ultimately, his ability to relax and benefit from the visit experience.

6. **Remind your student to follow up.** A simple "thank-you" e-mail to the admission office is always appropriate and does not take long. If

an admission officer has met with you individually, a thank you note is appropriate (and it goes into his file).

7. **Remember that the issue is not whether *you* were impressed with the residence hall** or the exercise center or the class you attended or the architecture. Be wary of expressing your own opinions too eagerly. When your student wants them, he will let you know.

8. **When getting into the car at the end of the visit, resist the urge** to ask your son, "Well, what do you think?" In truth, he probably doesn't know what he thinks. He is still new to the experience and needs time to process the events of the day.

9. **Encourage your student to make notes about his impressions of the college.** Wait to *compare* notes even though you probably noticed something he may have missed. That can come later. For now, you are helping him gather facts and impressions.

10. **Most of all, *Do Not Embarrass Your Student!*** A little encouragement and a lot of staying in the background on your part can go a long way toward establishing a relaxed and confident approach by your student.

As you work with your student in planning itineraries, remember your role. You have to know when you can push the envelope and when to wait for another day. Yours is an important yet simple job when it comes to visiting college campuses. You provide the cash, a car, and a map. Mix in healthy doses of good humor and encouragement—and you'll be all set.

Chapter 10

Testing

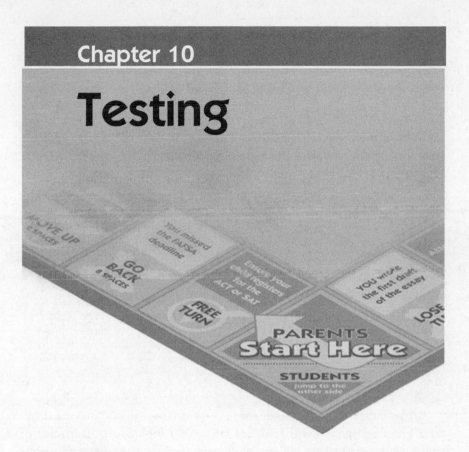

"The Tattoo"

Few topics bring more trepidation to the hearts of teenagers than standardized testing. The prospect of having to sit 3-plus hours for a college entrance exam leaves many in a cold sweat. And can you blame them in light of what seems to ride on the outcome? One Saturday morning test can determine your student's admission to college, eligibility for scholarships, and an entrée into a world of future employment.

And let's not forget the impact the scores will have on her self-esteem. Long before an admission committee views them as part of her application for admission, the test results will have unalterably changed the way others regard her—not to mention the way she feels about herself. Before the test, she's simply "Susan, the cool kid who does well at school." After the test, she will be "Susan, the kid with the 1930" (new three-part SAT scoring scale). The newly revealed score will figuratively leap off the page and onto her forehead like a big tattoo for everyone to see!

The results will also affect the way your student views her college options. If the number that smiles up at her as she opens the envelope bearing the results is "big," she may suddenly see herself as having options at the top of the Pyramid. On the other hand, she may be devastated if her results fall out of the competitive range for the schools she had in her sights. In either case, you need to be prepared to offer appropriate counsel. The student with the "big" score may need a reminder that big scores without big grades can be a problem and that, even with the combination of big scores and big grades, she will be competing with thousands of others like her if she applies to the most selective colleges.

Between the Lines

Beware of Score Laundering
Score reports published by colleges in their new student profiles must be viewed with a "jaundiced eye" as the reported numbers are subject to "laundering." Information for students enrolled under special circumstances is often purged in order to inflate the result that is passed on to the public. The *complete* data set for an enrolled class would probably produce mean scores and ranges that are lower than those that are reported.

An indicator that your student is on the competitive "playing field" at a given college is that her scores fall within the middle 50 percent of those reported for that college. Will such scores ensure her admission? No. They will, however, position her so that other personal strengths and attributes can give her the competitive edge—where she can be valued for what she does well. If her scores are in the bottom 25 percent at a particular college, then she is looking at the definition of a true long shot.

And if your student's scores don't match expectations, you must be quick to point out that it is *just a test*—not a reflection of her character and achievements. The results are only a beginning point in her search for a good college fit. Help her build on the many good qualities she has to offer. Don't allow her to wallow in the notion that she is a failure. She deserves much better than that.

Tests, Tests, and More Tests . . .

Two major testing organizations sit at the center of the college-entrance testing world. They are the ACT (founded in 1959 as the American

College Testing Program: www.ACT.org) and the College Board (founded in 1900 as the College Entrance Examination Board: www.CollegeBoard.com). The ACT is a widely used measure of achievement across subject areas while the SAT is a reasoning test designed to determine the likelihood that a student can do the work in her first year of college.

If you live an area where the ACT is more popular, your student likely will take the PLAN in the fall of the 10th grade and follow with the ACT in 11th and/or 12th grades. If you are in an area where the SAT (administered by the College Board) is more popular, your student will take the PSAT in

Between the Lines

Registration Is the Student's Job! Your student's testing record will become her property so this is a good time to establish ownership. Let *her* go online to complete the registration forms. You'll need to provide the credit card and the reminders for some reason, teenagers don't attach the same importance to deadlines! If she misses a deadline, she may be forced to take the test at a site that is not within easy range of your home.

the fall of the 11th grade and the SAT Reasoning Test later in 11th grade and/or 12th grade.

Despite the differences in origin and intent, colleges use the two tests almost interchangeably. A few will accept only one test. It is extremely important that you review your student's research on this topic to make sure she is planning to take the tests that will be required of her. A look at a college's Web site under the "Admission" or "Prospective Student" tabs or pages will reveal which tests are required and which tests are accepted. If possible, your student should plan to sit for the ACT and the SAT at least once. The following is a summary of the tests to which your student will be exposed in the coming months of college planning and preparation.

Preliminary SAT (PSAT/NMSQT®)

Nearly 2¼ hours in length, the PSAT consists of two 25-minute Critical Reading and two 25-minute Math sections and a 30-minute Writing Skills section (fill in the ovals but no writing). The three sections of the PSAT are scored on a scale of 20 to 80 (add a zero and the score translates into a projected SAT score). The PSAT is offered in October of the junior year at your student's high school. Consult your guidance counselor for the procedures your school uses.

The junior year PSAT results double as the National Merit Scholarship Qualifying Test (NMSQT) that is used to select candidates for the National Merit Scholarship and National Achievement Scholarship program. Each state has a different qualifying threshold based on test results. More information about this program is found in the PSAT information flyers given to all juniors (as well as any sophomores who want them) in advance of the testing. The information is also available online at www.CollegeBoard.com. *Only the PSAT taken in the junior year counts as the NMSQT.*

Tips for the PSAT

- In interpreting the PSAT results, the "actual score" (the 59 or 63) is less important than the "range" that is reported several lines below it. The results are really snapshots of where the test-taker is on a likely *range* of scores. For example, it is helpful to know that a student who scored 62 on the Critical Reading section is likely to score between 570 and 670 when taking the SAT.

- The PSAT is designed to be taken in October of a student's junior year. Taking the test in 10th grade gives the student early exposure to the test and experience with the testing environment. There are, however, no reliable predictive measures to estimate a student's 11th grade PSAT score or later SAT scores based on 10th grade scores.

- Your student can familiarize herself with the test through free information and sample tests from the College Board provided by the school each fall.

- In the final analysis, the best preparation includes a good night's sleep, breakfast before the exam, and a stress-free, on-time arrival at the test site.

SAT® Reasoning Test™

The SAT is 3¾ hours long. Administered seven times each year, it consists of nine sections: three Critical Reading sections, three Math sections and two Writing sections (one of which is a writing sample). One section is unscored: the results from this section are used to validate future questions (there is no way of knowing which section this is in advance of the test). Scores range from 200-800 in each area. Students take the SAT at a test center (usually a high school) of their choosing. Not all high schools administer the test. Your student can register by mail (using the form provided in the SAT Registration Booklet), by phone, or online at www.CollegeBoard.com (recommended).

Tips for the SAT

- How many times should a student take the SAT? There is no simple answer, but most college counselors and test prep services agree that students should:

  Take the SAT twice: in spring of the junior year (March or May) and in the fall of the senior year. If needed, take it again in December or January of the senior year.

  Not take the SAT more than three times. Generally, twice is sufficient. Studies indicate that there is usually no advantage to keep retaking the test.

- When viewing your student's SAT scores, remember to look at the projected score range reported in the box immediately to the right of the test score. The range indicates the approximate high and low scores she might have made on that test date.

- There is considerable speculation as to how colleges use the writing component of the "new" SAT in reviewing applicants (will they put less emphasis on the personal statement, use it to authenticate personal essays, etc.). While each college will respond differently, my opening premises still hold: test results are largely irrelevant for diagnostic purposes and the writing results will be another set of competitive credentials.

- Some students have taken the SAT for entrance into an enrichment program in 6th, 7th, or 8th grades. These scores are rarely indicative of how a student will perform on the test in 11th or 12th grade.

SAT Subject Tests

SAT Subject Tests are 1-hour tests that measure knowledge and skill in particular subject areas. Students may take up to three tests on the same test date but may not take the SAT and SAT Subject Tests on the same date. Nineteen (19) Subject Tests are offered six times a year.

Tips for the SAT Subject Tests

- Most colleges and universities do *not* require SAT Subject Tests. Those that do tend to fall into two groups:
  —Institutions that require Math 1C or 2C exams for placement purposes
  —Institutions that ask for one, two, or three Subject Tests. These schools tend to be either highly selective (looking for additional points of distinction) or very technical (looking for specific levels of competence) in their orientation. The latter usually specify the exam results they want students to submit whereas the former give the student total discretion with regard to the exams they take.

- Some colleges accept the ACT in lieu of SAT Subject Tests. Your student needs to know what tests *each* of her colleges requires or accepts. There is only one way to know this: Check with the college. *Don't* let her make the mistake of assuming that because Choosy U requires one set of tests that Persnickity College wants the same tests. Your student may have a rude surprise.

ACT

The ACT is a four-part test that measures general education development and the ability to complete college-level work in four subject areas: English, mathematics, reading proficiency, and science reasoning. Scores range from 1 to 36. The Writing Test, which may be optional for some colleges, measures a student's skill in planning and writing a short essay.

Tips for the ACT

- The ACT has traditionally served students in the Midwest. In recent years, colleges and universities that had only accepted SAT results have begun to accept ACT results as well, and some accept the ACT in lieu of *both* SAT Reasoning and SAT Subject Tests. Moreover, ACT test sites are now more accessible to students across the country.

- Since colleges like to have a measure of flexibility in considering students for admission, it is a good idea for your student to include at least one administration of the ACT in her portfolio of testing. A college that is otherwise predisposed to her application but finds her SAT results to be modest may find the ACT results more appealing.

Advanced Placement® (AP®) Tests

Many high schools feature a roster of Advanced Placement courses for students who are high achievers in various disciplines. The courses are taught from a nationally standardized syllabus. At the conclusion of a course (May), students have the option of sitting for a comprehensive exam. Scores range from 5 to 0, with 5 being the highest. While colleges often award credit for scores of 3 to 5, credit policies vary widely across institutions. Students are responsible for understanding institutional policies to ensure credit is attributed to their records.

Tips for the AP Tests

- *Theoretically*, AP test scores are not used in admission decisions. That's like saying that if you are in a car dealership you will only look at one model as you make your decision. In fact, some colleges will expect your student to report AP scores from tests taken prior to the senior year as part of the application.

- The question of whether students should sit for AP exams for courses taken in the senior year has sparked a great deal of debate. I recommend that students take the exams. Even though the results may not affect their own applications for admission, their participation in the testing is part of their legacy in validating the strength of the AP program at their high schools.

International Baccalaureate (IB) Program

The IB program is a two-year, college-preparatory curriculum offered in some high schools for high-achieving students in their junior and senior years. The curriculum features courses taught at both the "higher" level and the "subsidiary" level. Students preparing for the full IB Diploma will take six IB courses per year, three of which must be at the higher level.

At the end of the second year, the students must take examinations for each of the six courses. The exams are graded on a scale of 1 to 7 with 7 being the highest. In addition, students must complete 150 hours of service over two years, take a broadly based capstone course called Theory of Knowledge (TOK), and complete the Extended Essay during the second year. Students who score between 5 and 7 on the exams are often extended college credit for that work; those who complete the diploma requirements are frequently given a full year of college credit depending on their aggregate scores.

Tips for the IB

- It is not uncommon for U.S. high schools to offer students the option of taking courses from both AP and IB curricula. While the courses are similar in rigor, the IB typically is more reflective and writing intensive.

- The IB program's popularity is growing fast both in the United States and overseas, as is the respect for the programs among colleges and universities. Selective colleges see quite a few applications from IB candidates and are well aware of the strength of the program.

TOEFL®

The Test of English as a Foreign Language is designed for international students whose first language is not English and who have not been in English-speaking schools for more than a few years. It is meant to help colleges assess whether the student's English skills are adequate to understand college-level texts. Generally, if a student is not a U.S. citizen and is from a non-English speaking country—even if she has a "Green Card"—colleges will ask for a TOEFL. It is important to understand the requirements of the colleges to which your student is applying.

Tips for TOEFL

- More than 5,000 colleges and universities in 90 countries accept TOEFL scores.

- Your student's test scores will be considered together with other information she supplies to the institution to determine if she has the appropriate credentials to be admitted to a regular or modified program of study. Each institution that uses TOEFL scores sets its own minimum level of acceptable performance.

"My Student Doesn't Seem to Be a Good Test Taker"

There's no denying it. Some students struggle with tests. Whether it is a classroom test, a semester final, state-mandated testing, or a college entrance test, they suffer sleepless nights in fearful anticipation of the next test. Such students seem bright enough. They do well on projects and papers, but when they take tests, it all falls apart.

If this sounds like your student, dig beneath the surface to find out what is going on. While there is no universal antidote for this phenomenon, there are some things to keep in mind that might help:

- Find out how well she *really* does outside of the tests. Talk with her teachers. Is she really doing as well as you think (or as well as she reports) in the classroom *except* for tests? Are tests really the problem? It could be that the level of rigor associated with the course content or the way she applies herself to the content are the more critical issues.

- If tests really are the problem, investigate how she prepares for them. Perhaps some work with a study skills coach or tutor might be the answer. Enabling her to address the problem in a general context may be less stressful than ramping up the stakes for the SAT or ACT.

- There really is such a thing as "test anxiety." Could that be the problem? If so, you might explore strategies your student can learn and practice to help alleviate the problem.

- Has your student seriously tried to engage the tests? The problem may have more to do with the value she attaches to the test. If she just isn't into it, she is not likely to produce results commensurate with expectations.

- It may be that your student has a learning barrier of some sort that makes taking tests a problem for her. Over the last ten years we've learned a great deal about how brain functions relate to performance. If testing is a continuous problem and not just a "localized" issue centering on the college-level standardized tests, then you might look into educational testing to see if there is a real barrier to success on tests and, if so, how to deal with it effectively.

Keep Testing in Perspective

Two things are certain about college entrance tests: one, they are not terribly relevant within the context for which they were established—they don't add measurably to a college's ability to predict a student's success —and, two, they should not be confused (as they often are) with intelligence tests.

The degree to which self-selection lies at the root of the application process means that most students applying to most colleges have already predetermined their qualifications. Given the chance, they can do the work at some level. They may not be superstars, but they are at least qualified. The decision by a college to admit them will then rest on their desirability as applicants. When everything is equal, higher scores tend to be more attractive.

It is also clear that standardized tests do not measure intelligence. Yes, smart kids get high scores. Smart kids also get modest scores. If a student improves her score on the SAT by 200 points, does that mean she has become 200 points "smarter?" Or, if a student's results go down by 50 points, does that mean that she has suddenly become stupid? The answer in each case is "no."

Test results are more likely a reflection of a student's exposure to different thought processes and problem-solving opportunities than a reflection of native ability. Success on the test can also be attributed to the student's ability to remain relaxed and calm under pressure. Moreover, there is good evidence that, with certain amounts of coaching, students can improve their scores.

Regardless of how they are used—as a diagnostic or a competitive credential—they are a fact of the college admission process. Unless your student makes a conscious decision to consider only those institutions that will allow her to apply without submitting test results (see www.fairtest. org for the list), she will need to face this fact.

Test Preparation Instruction

If you and your student believe that current test results do not represent her well (results from the PSAT in 11th grade and the ACT's PLAN in 10th grade are fairly reliable indicators of what a student's first set of SAT or ACT scores will be), consider test preparation.

Between the Lines

Score Improvement

Even though the tests are coachable, there is no guarantee that test prep will produce measurable results for your student. If you are considering a test prep program, make sure he is prepared to make it work. He must invest in the course the same way he approaches his course work at school. If he doesn't, he will be wasting his time and your money.

Test preparation comes in many forms from books to online courses and from very expensive classes to private tutoring. Decide what the goal is, then examine your options. Perhaps all that is needed is a few sessions with an experienced test tutor to help your student learn how to take the test (there is nothing like the SAT in a high school curriculum). If there is a problem in a content area (math or grammar) or a skill area (writing or solving trigonometric functions), then a customized class or online course might be the right answer.

The point is to take stock of what your student really needs. "Better scores" is the obvious but incorrect answer. Rather, she needs an orientation to the test and the content that will enable her to score higher. By understanding the structure and content of the test, your student can develop strategies that will help her focus on questions that she has a better chance of answering well and, then, help her deduce the correct response among several that are designed to trick her.

As you contemplate test prep options, take into consideration the impact that investing in test prep will have on the rest of your student's life. At what point does she reach overload and go "tilt?" Is the possible score improvement worth it? One of the best forms of test prep is reading—and reading can probably fit into her schedule comfortably. The evidence is universal that students who read often do better on the tests than students who don't—even in the quantitative (or "math") sections.

Tips for Considering Test Prep Options

As you review test prep options for your student, look for evidence that the provider/instructor will provide:

- Feedback on incorrect answers (where are the problems and how can they be fixed)

- Customized instruction—this is not a "one size fits all" business

- Practice tests at the beginning and at the end of the course

Between the Lines

Test Optional: Practicing What They Preach

Colleges that do not require test scores are practicing what they preach when they say "tests aren't that important." The most liberating day of my professional experience was when my institution declared itself to be test optional. We could focus on kids not scores.

- Results from previous students that show improvement from one "live" or actual test administration to another. Many claims to score improvement are actually based on comparisons of an initial live test with a subsequent practice test.

- Ongoing support throughout the course, not just at the beginning and the end.

- Strategically, it makes sense for her to prepare for the testing. Reading, working with a tutor, and even taking a test prep course can make a difference. Be careful, though, that preparing for the test does not become an obsession. If she reaches the point where testing and preparing for the tests have taken over her life, you need to call a time-out. The likely returns are not worth the sacrifices.

- Even if she were to improve her scores by 200 points, there is still no guarantee *they* will get her in. Remember the elements of a good fit. It is better to find colleges that fit the scores—that value her for the scores she has produced as well as what she has done in life—than it is to try to create scores that will fit the college's expectations. She has one shot at being a kid. Don't let her lose it to test paranoia.

Final Thoughts About Testing

Successful SAT- and ACT-takers share many of the following attributes:

- They are readers. They internalize good language mechanics, have an expanded vocabulary, and know how to get through a passage and understand its main points.

- They do not allow stress to affect the way they process information.

- They are effective problem solvers.

- They have the stamina to take a 4-hour test with only two 5-minute breaks.

- They are reasonably good, if not excellent, students who are experienced writers and have had math through at least algebra II.

Students with documented learning disabilities may be eligible to take college entrance tests in extended-time environments. They will need to submit written documentation (from a licensed psychologist) of their learning differences to the respective testing organizations (check their Web sites for more details) well in advance of the registration for the tests.

Chapter 11

Engaged Parenting

MOVE UP
SPACES

GO
BACK
8 SPACES

You missed the FAFSA deadline"

Realize your class register for the ACT or SAT

FREE
TURN

YOU wrote the first draft of the essay

PARENTS
Start Here

STUDENTS
Jump to the other side

LOSE
TI

Transitions

The end of the high school junior year signals the beginning of several important transitions for young people. Just as they begin to emerge as kingpins in their own school environments, they come face-to-face with the prospect of graduation and the inevitability that they will soon move on to the next chapters of their lives.

Eager as they might seem to move forward, many students find themselves looking back somewhat wistfully as the all-important college admission process comes into sharper focus. The time for getting ready has passed them by—the accomplishments of the previous three years are a matter of record and will soon appear as competitive credentials on their applications. "Will it be enough?" they wonder.

This is a time of transition for you, the parent, as well. The period of preparation that seemingly spanned a young lifetime is coming to a rapid end. Years ago, you shaped the agenda while doing your best to provide opportunity and encouragement. As your student has grown and matured, though, he has gradually taken a stronger voice in determining that agenda. Now, both the agenda and the opportunity rest with him as he begins to compete for admission to college.

Questions remain as you shift uneasily into the passenger seat. "Does he have what he needs?" you ask. "Is there more that I might have done to prepare him for this? How can I help him move forward? What can I do to make sure he finds success?" To gain perspective on your understanding of the process and your student's readiness to enter the competition, consider the following.

- Do you understand the "big picture" about college admission—the Agenda and the Hidden Agenda? Does your student understand it?

- Have you separated your wants and needs from those of your student?

- Do you understand the Pyramid of Selectivity and how to interpret it for someone with your student's academic, extracurricular, and social profile?

- Do you have a sense that your student understands the implications of selectivity and the realities of the Pyramid?

- Have you begun conversations with your student about what he wants—and needs? Are the two of you on the same page with regard to what constitutes a good college "fit?"

- Have you articulated any concerns you may have about the process to your student?

- Does your student understand that he owns this process? Does he understand what he needs to do in order to get from where he is to where he wants to be?

- Does your student have a general calendar of events in mind for the admission process?

Strategic Nagging

Staying on top of your student's involvement in the college planning process without actually doing the work for him will require that you employ the fine art of *strategic* nagging—not just any nagging, but strategic nagging.

It is easy to be a nag—to give in to our anxieties as parents and our own sense of what *ought to be* going on in the college process. We know our kids well enough to know the difference between when they are striving and when they are coasting. We recognize the difference in effort between a commitment to doing "the best that I can" and doing that which is "good enough." It is because we know these things that we become *their* living consciences! We nag.

Be careful. Experience tells us that nagging usually results either in defiance or compliance. When nagging induces defiance, everybody loses and the objective is effectively abandoned. If nagging results in compliance, there is a good chance that you have retaken ownership and are dictating the action. You may see immediate, tangible results, but the long-term consequences may not be so positive.

Between the Lines

Invoke the College-Free Zone
Do you find tensions rising around the college process? A friend has suggested that every house needs a "college-free zone." It is a place where the family gathers with the promise that college may *not* become a major topic of conversation. The idea is simple, really. Instead of that place becoming one where you and your student confront each other about college, it is the place in the house where the two of you can be together without that dreaded topic coming up—it's off limits!

Strategic nagging, though . . . that is very different. Strategic nagging is the delicate craft of communicating your need to know about where your student is in the process so that you both can operate from the same page. It is not assertive or intrusive. It is a calm statement of fact ("You need to let me know when your application fees are due so I can write the checks.") that demonstrates to your student mutual benefit in his response.

Above all, strategic nagging involves an implicit knowledge of the process that enables you to provide timely prompts for your student (not on the cell phone on the way to work!) to take the next step. You become supportive, not directive. Reminders certainly are a part of strategic nagging; ultimatums are not. If you find yourself issuing ultimatums, something has gone wrong. Your child is either stymied or overly anxious and needs help, not orders.

Other College Planning Resources

As you consider the competition that lies ahead for your student, think of yourself as a coach. Make sure you understand the game and begin to think about others who can assist you in coaching him through the competitive admission process. You won't have to look far to find people and resources that will prove invaluable in the college admission process.

The High School Counselor or College Adviser

Theoretically, your student's high school counselor or college adviser is in the best position to lend assistance with college planning *due to his knowledge of the game*. Not only does he manage the process of paperwork and deadlines at your child's school, he is the primary point of contact with the colleges. Among other things, he is expected to provide a thorough overview of your student's high school experience when he submits his applications. Your student *should* know this person well!

Between the Lines

Telling the Story

When a young person is on top of his "game," there is a rhythm to his performance. Periodically, things happen in life—injury, illness, family problems, changing schools, or the loss of someone close—that can cause him to lose focus and fall out of rhythm academically. When this happens—when his program or performance deviates from what is normal for him—he has a story to tell. In addition to addressing the story personally in his application, he must make certain that the people who write on his behalf *know* him and his story. The counselor or college adviser is responsible for giving colleges the "big picture" orientation to your student's performance. It is incumbent on him to make certain that his story is known to this person.

Unfortunately, counseling situations vary greatly across the country. While college counseling is a dedicated responsibility at some schools, it is an afterthought at others. The pressures of having to deal with scheduling, discipline, testing, and students with special needs are so great at the latter that the college counseling function gets what is left over. In between, college counseling takes on all different shapes and forms. Unless your student is enrolled in a school with the resources to staff the college counseling function adequately, the counselor may or may not know who your child is.

Regardless of the scenario that confronts your student, he must accept responsibility for making it work. Armed with the information your student shares, his counselor can be an effective advocate for him *in a voice other than his own*. That said, even the most engaged counselors don't know everything there is to know about each student. Unless he is taking the time to become known to his counselor or is otherwise on the counselor's "radar screen," he is leaving a lot to chance.

Urge your student to get to know his counselor. Kids are often reluctant to take initiative as it seems "un-cool" or they don't know what to say when they are face to face with an administrator. Do what you can to ease the stress and take the edge off the anticipation. For example, talk through some conversation starters (i.e., "I'd like to know more about colleges but don't know where to start."). Suggest that he prepare a résumé of his activities and achievements that can serve as a talking point in the conversation.

However you do it, help your student understand how he will benefit from the conversation—that the counselor can only provide assistance from a base of knowledge. The more the counselor knows about your student the better—not only in orienting him to the college process, but eventually in presenting his case to the admission committee. And if your student has difficulty gaining access to or making the connection with the assigned counselor, explore with him the potential to switch to another counselor—or, at least, find someone else at the school in whom he can confide about the college planning process.

And what about you? Should you meet with the counselor? Absolutely! If the counselor requests a meeting or makes one available, by all means take it! Even though this (the college process) may be your student's adventure, you have every right—and need—to know what's going on. You might as well make sure you are all on the same page!

Five Tips for Staying Engaged with Your Student's College Counselor/Adviser

1. **Attend an open house at school where you can introduce yourself and make sure you have access to important program information and process deadlines.**

2. **Read newsletters that are sent home.** If you think that you may have missed something, call the office.

3. **Don't assume that you are getting the full story about college orientation activities from your student.** Be wary of "It's not that important" or "Nobody goes" or "It's just for parents"—when clearly it's not!

4. **Attend college fairs and orientation activities *with* your student. It's best that you both hear the same messages!**

5. **Offer to provide a brief written summary of your hopes and expectations with regard to your student's educational future.**

You will discover a number of benefits in meeting with the counselor. One, you should receive a thorough orientation to your student's school record. Up to this point, you have seen report cards (if you're lucky). Now, you will see the entire transcript—*just as a college will see it*. Be sure to ask questions so that you understand everything that is being presented to you.

Two, with the school record in hand—and your student in attendance—you can begin to think aloud about the appropriateness of various college options. Take advantage of the opportunity to ask questions about financial aid and scholarships. At the very least, the counselor should be able to orient you and your student to resources at the school that will help him discover and explore his options. Finally, make sure you are clear about what your student must do to have transcripts and test scores sent to the colleges to which he is applying. Having this information safely tucked away will save you potential aggravation as application deadlines draw near.

Teachers

In team sports, position coaches are the specialists. They work with the players to develop their areas of special interest or expertise. The same is true of the teachers who work with students to broaden their awareness and sharpen their skills academically. The good ones are very passionate about their work and eager to instill the same passion in their students.

They are also well positioned to mentor, advise, and *coach* young people—and to champion their performances.

As a result, teachers—especially those who are respected, the true champions—can be instrumental in the college process. Having seen their students in action on a daily basis, they know what these young people can do. Moreover, teachers are usually thrilled to talk with students about college programs and career possibilities. It is not surprising that dreams and ambitions are born in the classroom—and that teachers are frequently cited as the inspiration behind the achievements of many young people.

Your student's teachers also know his strengths and weaknesses. They know when he is realistic in his academic choices and when he is not. Take advantage of opportunities to get feedback from these teachers about your student's performance. Learn what you can about the teachers' academic backgrounds—and encourage your student to do the same. This may lead him to discoveries that could become pivotal in his thinking about college and his future.

Between the Lines

The Parent-Teacher Alliance

Take advantage of opportunities to get to know your student's teachers. As your student gets older, there will be a tendency toward forgetfulness and nondisclosure when it comes to reporting the events of a day at school. Don't assume that "no news is good news." It just may be that evidence of poor performance is getting "lost" along the way.

I discovered this with my son. Despite an affinity for chemistry and glowing reviews from his teacher regarding his mastery of the subject matter, his grade revealed a far different outcome. A subsequent three-way conversation revealed that his grade would have been much higher had he handed in his homework! As you get to know your student's teachers you will realize quickly the mutual benefit to open and frequent communication. You are important allies to each other in the advancement of your student's education.

Four Tips for Staying Engaged with Your Student's Teachers

1. **When possible, attend parent-teacher conferences** *and* **ask questions!**

2. **Exchange e-mail addresses and/or phone numbers.** Ask the teacher to contact you if he has concerns about your student's performance.

3. **If your student's school does not provide regular detailed feedback regarding his progress,** schedule at least one meeting with the teacher that includes your student. It is a good idea to make sure everyone is "on the same page."

4. **Ask the teacher what he knows of your student's future ambitions and how these ambitions square with current competencies.**

The Independent Educational Consultant

If time and resources allow, you might consider engaging an *Independent Educational Consultant* to work with your student in the college planning process. Independent Educational Consultants are individuals outside of the school itself who provide a range of college planning services for a fee. While some carry credentials as former admission professionals or college counselors, many come into this environment from careers as teachers or simply parents who have sent children to college. Make sure you know what you are getting before making the investment! A good consultant will:

- Provide reliable guidance about colleges and the search process itself

- Know where to go to find answers to questions that may arise

- Work in concert with your student's school counselor or college adviser

- Regularly visit colleges to keep "college knowledge" up to date

- Help students evaluate specific colleges and their admission chances at those colleges

- Work with your student throughout the admission process, including reviewing essays

- Often provide other, customized services to help your student with the college planning and application process

Before engaging an Educational Consultant, ask yourself why you want the help. Is the college counseling available through your student's school deficient? Does your student have specific needs to be addressed? Or do you simply want the peace of mind of having access to an expert who can interpret the process for you as you move forward?

Many consultants are expert about particular areas such as learning differences, family relocations, or financial assistance. Get referrals and ask for references. You and your student should always meet with a consultant before "signing on." Then consider cost and credentials. You should not have to pay the equivalent of private school tuition to retain the services of a good consultant! Educational consultants who are members of the National Association for College Admission Counseling or the Independent Educational Consultants Association (IECA) have met minimum standards of experience and peer review. The Higher Education Consultants Association (HECA) is another membership organization. Consultants who hold the Certified Educational Planner (CEP) credential have met the highest peer review standards in their field.

Between the Lines

Beware of the Guarantee!
If you are considering a consultant, always remember that consultants do not get students into college. While their experience and knowledge of colleges and people on the admission staffs make them valuable sources of information and guidance, the admission decision still rests in the hands of the respective college's admission staff. In the end, it is the student who must compete.

The IECA offers a valuable pamphlet that will help you understand what a consultant can do for you and your student and how to identify the right one for you. (www.IECAonline.com)

Five Tips for Considering Educational Consultants

1. **Make sure your student agrees that such an arrangement is a good idea.** You don't want him to "stonewall" the consultations because he doesn't want to be there!

2. **Meet with the consultant in person in advance of contracting for her services.** Make sure there is a good fit between her style and character—and your family.

3. **Get references.** With whom has this consultant worked before and how is her work regarded by previous clients? Remember, "getting kids in" is *not* the measure of a good consultant. You want to learn about honesty, reliability, accessibility, accuracy, and consistency relative to the consultant's relationship with past clients.

4. Ask to see a prospectus that includes a summary of professional development activity over the last two years and an outline of services to be rendered.

5. Make sure the consultant supports the process *but does not* assume the responsibilities that typically fall to the applicant in completing the application.

College Guidebooks

As you learn about colleges and the admission process, it is important to find a reference guide you can trust. You will find three types in most bookstores: descriptive, subjective, and comparative (ratings).

Descriptive guidebooks present comprehensive data regarding an institution's academic programs and admission process. Some are merely books of lists; others are extensive compilations of program information. The biggest difference between guidebooks in this group is the manner in which the information is organized.

Based on survey results of current or recently graduated students, editors of subjective guidebooks attempt to offer the "inside scoop." The resulting narratives tend to be sensational if not controversial. Make sure the authors provide data to validate their assertions. It is worth noting that a college is rarely as good, bad, or distinctive as it is made to appear in guidebooks.

Preying on our seemingly insatiable desire to rate consumer items—to identify the "best"—comparative ranking guides attempt to do just that to colleges and universities. Popular magazines have taken turns at producing such ratings. Not surprisingly, the results are never the same! It is difficult to quantify differences in the manner attempted by these guides.

There are no absolutes in higher education. Rather, there are a myriad of quality options. Perhaps the best solution with regard to guidebooks is to utilize one of each type. As your student becomes acclimated to college possibilities, he should move toward a stronger reliance on his own research and good instincts regarding "fit." There are no reliable shortcuts in the college search process.

If you must compare institutions, look at outcomes. What better way to measure a college than to look at how its students believe it has helped them grow personally and academically? The National Survey of Student Engagement (NSSE) provides an assessment of outcomes for participating institutions (http://nsse.iub.edu/news/index.cfm).

Web Sites

Web sites offer a creative and interactive alternative to the guidebooks. The range of possibilities is wide and varied and includes sites produced by guidebooks, lending institutions, news media, test prep organizations, consultants, and authors. You will even find excellent information on the Web sites of the colleges themselves. The best sites will not only answer your questions but also expose you to more questions and answers than you could have imagined. They will take you and your student from start to finish in the college planning process. Savvy surfers can access and complete most of their applications through these online connections.

Between the Lines

Headline Grabbers

Be careful about relying on comparative rankings. They tend to be headline grabbers that presume there is an absolute order among colleges and universities. If your student becomes distracted by the rankings, he will take his eyes off the real substance of the colleges he is considering.

Some sites, both independent and college-sponsored, will guide your student through a self-assessment that may reveal more about his aptitude for certain types of career tracks—and then give him links to colleges that offer compatible programs. Most provide an orientation to the admission process (what counts? where? and how much?). Other Web sites reveal strategies for test taking and essay writing.

Many colleges now offer access to chat rooms *for students.* (It's not a good idea to tap into such spaces unless you see a specific invitation for parents.) Don't be surprised if your student has already availed himself of the possibilities. At designated times, he will be able to join a free-form discussion of campus life with students, both current and prospective. While this can be a valuable opportunity to get the "scoop" on a college, urge him to process the information carefully. One or two voices can dominate the conversation. As a result the perspective he gains could be limited if not very one-sided.

As you utilize Web sites and guidebooks, make sure the impressions and data you are gathering are consistent across all sources. Test your impressions with those of your student, his teachers, and other parents. If you discover discrepancies, know that you need to dig a little deeper in search of the truth.

Frequently Asked Questions from Engaged Parents

Worried? Nagging? Anxious? All are terms that might describe your frame of mind in the college planning process at this time. You are not alone! The following FAQs form a common refrain from parents as they work with their children in preparing to compete for admission.

Q How can I tell which is the best summer program for my student?

A The quick answer: the program to which he is drawn naturally. The value of summer programs (enrichment programs on college campuses, leadership workshops, volunteer programs overseas, etc.) *as college credentials* is vastly overrated. The choice of summer activity should hold intrinsic value to him—it should speak to his true passions. Whatever he does, your son should spend his summer—especially the summer between the junior and senior years—doing things that are an organic extension of his interests, abilities, needs, and desires—and *not* activities that are planned to impress college admission officers.

Q Is it better for my student to take courses where he knows he can do well or should he take courses that might be harder and risk getting lower grades?

A With few exceptions, it is better to err on the side of rigor. From a developmental perspective, it is good for young people to keep stretching their intellectual capacities while building their skill sets. Moreover, advancing rigor speaks volumes with regard to a student's ability to handle new challenges at higher levels of instruction in college. That is why the more selective colleges expect students to take high school courses at the higher level. They can't proceed with confidence in your student's ability to take on challenges in the college classroom if he has shied away from them in high school. By the way, don't be too quick to concede that lower grades will necessarily follow if he takes harder courses. Quite often, the biggest difference between the "A" and a lower grade is not what he has between the ears, but how he puts it to use.

Q My son has taken four years of language starting in 8th grade. He is a math/science whiz and wants to pursue premed in college. Does he need to take language in his senior year or can he double up on his science classes?

A It depends on where he aspires on the Pyramid. If he wants to compete for admission to colleges that are admitting fewer than half of their applicants, he needs to keep his program broad. At less selective colleges, this selection will not be so problematic. On the other hand, if he is trading quality for quality—a high-level language for a high-level science—then the switch that you propose may be acceptable. If your son has identified one or two colleges to which he might apply, he should contact them for their advice. In making the judgment calls within the context of their competitive environments, they become the experts.

Q Do colleges look for students who are good at a lot of things or really good at one thing?

A Contrary to popular belief, there is no formula for success here. Resume building, however strategic, is pretty transparent—and not highly regarded in the admission process. It is most important that the student follow his passion(s). Colleges want to see consistency and substance as well as evidence of personal growth through involvements. Relative to the other applicants at colleges to which he will apply, he will have to possess at least one "gift" that will set him apart. *Colleges that value him for what he does well will embrace him as an applicant.*

Q How important is community service in the selection process?

A Community service has become a hot button in the selection process at many colleges as they value students who give selflessly to others and/or the environment. They also value singers, actors, athletes, and writers. If community service is your student's "thing," then it will generate its own energy in the selection process. If it's not, don't force the issue.

Q My student goes to a huge high school. How can he find someone who will know him well enough to write a good letter of recommendation?

A This is a good question regardless of the size of the high school. Too often students fail to invest time in making sure that the people who write on their behalf *know them*. If your student is concerned that his teachers or counselor don't know him that well, then he should introduce himself and make sure they get to know him, his goals and ambitions, the experiences he has had, and the factors that have influenced his performance. If he can't seem to get the attention of a particular teacher or counselor, then he might try another or ask for assistance from the principal or headmaster.

Q How important is it that my student knows what he wants to study before applying to college? Will the fact that he is undecided affect his chances of getting in?

A This is a myth of the college planning process—that students need to know what they want to do with their lives before choosing a college. If your student is clear about what he wants to do, that is one thing. Then finding a good college fit means finding a place that will accommodate his academic and career interests. On the other hand, if he is uncertain about his future, then he is better off choosing from colleges that will allow, if not encourage, him to explore. Remember, to be undecided at age 17 is to be normal. Most college students change their minds about majors at least once. There is no sense in pushing him to a conclusion that may be temporary at best.

Q I have heard that some students are taking the SAT as early as 7th and 8th grades. When is a good time for my student to start taking the exam?

A The best time for your student to gain exposure to the SAT is in 11th grade. In fact, that is an underlying premise of the PSAT. It is intended to be an introduction to the SAT. For the most part, younger students who are taking the SAT are doing so in order to qualify for enrichment programs.

Q I have a student whose grades are just above average. Does he have any chance of getting into a four- year college?

A He sure does! You will recall from our discussion of the Pyramid of Selectivity that there are hundreds of excellent colleges and universities all over the country. Most of them accept a fairly high percentage of their applicants. That means that they can be more forgiving in the admission process. It also means that they are likely to have academic programs that are geared to students who may need more remediation as they transition into the college classroom. Your student should look for a "good fit"—a place that will take him as he is and invest in his success.

Q We can't seem to get our student to work up to his potential. He knows that college is right around the corner but doesn't seem to care. He's a good kid, but he just isn't stepping up. What can you recommend?

A Patience. In all likelihood, there are underlying issues that are affecting his emergence as a student. One of them might be maturity. It could be that he just isn't ready to take the next big step. In situations like this, you have to be careful not to impose your expectations on him. Too often, we assume that the high school to college transition will proceed like clockwork. You may simply need to step back and let him proceed on a different schedule.

You must also face the possibility that he *is* ready to move on. It's just that the destination and direction may not be what you had in mind. If that is case, then the problem is yours, not his. One of the hardest things that we, as parents, must face in life is the realization that the dream that we have worked to create and support for our children may not be possible—or even shared. We must allow for the likelihood that there is a different reality for each child. In embracing that reality—whatever it might be—we validate it as well as the young person who lives it.

Chapter 12

Managing College Costs

It Costs How Much?!

The early stages of college planning with your student should be a lot of fun. Mixed in with the excited feelings of anticipation, though, are the sharp reminders that this college education isn't going to be cheap. In the "not-so-fine" print, you discover that four years of a college education can cost anywhere from $30,000 to $180,000—or more! "How in the world am I going to afford this?" you ask yourself. You always knew that college would cost, but price tags of this magnitude are a shock to your system.

Indeed, the prospect of having to manage college costs has the potential to haunt you throughout the college planning process. It doesn't have to be that way, though. Rather than being indiscriminately affected by the cost variable, you can manage it to your student's benefit. Your ability to get your arms around the related issues of affordability *and* to help your student project herself into colleges and universities that are good "fits" for her—*places that will value her for what she does well*—will be critical to the happy endings you envision.

Know What You Are Buying

As you look at colleges with your student, you will hear the dueling perspectives that "you get what you pay for" and "they're all the same." The truth is somewhere in between. While there is good evidence that the college a student attends will have a bearing on the first job/income opportunity, there is equally good evidence that, once on the job, one's performance—and not pedigree—dictates the prospects for long-term success. This is all the more reason to be attentive to your student's priorities as you weigh the cost variable.

In considering these options, you and your student *will* have to reconcile the price tag for a college against the perceived value of the educational experience to be gained. If you are of the mindset that it really doesn't matter—that your student can get the same education at institutions of any price—then you might find her gravitating toward lower cost options. On the other hand, if you are persuaded that there is a material difference, that there is value to be found in a more "fully loaded" experience, then you might be willing to pay more for the education offered at an institution with a higher price tag.

Making the Price Tag Work

Most parents who want desperately to give their children the gift of a college education simply don't have the means to extend the opportunity carte blanche. The will may be there, but the cash isn't. Regardless of their income and asset situations, most parents find a gap between the price tag and their ability to meet it. If you are in this number, the next section is written to give you insight into what financial aid is all about.

If you haven't already, you are about to encounter three types of financial aid: need-based, merit-based, and want-based. *Need-based* aid is the support your student receives when she can demonstrate that your family does not have the means to cover a college's costs. Colleges and universities often extend *merit-based* assistance in the form of scholarships to students whom they value regardless of the family's ability to pay. *Want-based* aid, however, is the number you carry around in your head. It is the consideration you *want* the institution to give your student: "If they would only give her a $5,000 scholarship, that would make it easier on our cash flow and she could enroll." Sadly, this type of aid doesn't exist. Let's take a look at the two aid opportunities that might be useful to you.

Need-Based Financial Aid

Most colleges offer financial assistance based on a student's demonstrated need. Unlike your demonstrated "want," demonstrated need is the difference between the cost of attending an institution (tuition, room, board, travel expenses, books, academic supplies) and the resources your family has at its disposal to cover the cost. Need-based financial aid is the funding awarded to the student to help cover that differential.

Between the Lines

The Cost of Attendance—All of It!
The actual cost of attendance is not always the price tag you see. Many schools will list their tuitions only or lead you to believe that the tuition *is* the cost of attendance. Unless your student plans to commute, though, you need to factor in room and board as well. Depending on the school, that combination can range from $4,000-$8,000 per year. And don't forget books—about $1,200 per year—and lab and other obscure program fees.

In order for your student to qualify for need-based aid, you will need to reveal your family's income and assets to determine your *expected family contribution* (EFC). For the purposes of this discussion, "family" is defined as both biological parents *and* the student. Financial information will be required of each, including the student for whom savings and projected summer earnings will be considered. If, in the case of divorce or death, the custodial parent has remarried, the stepparent may be expected to contribute a portion of her/his assets as well—more on that to come.

Formula for Determining Expected Family Contribution
    Family Income/Assets
    – Cost of Living Allowance

    Expected Family Contribution (EFC)

Financial "need" is determined simply by comparing your EFC with the cost of attendance at a given university. Be prepared to see your need cover a range that is as wide as the variance in pricing at the schools on your student's list. At one end of the spectrum, an EFC that is greater than the cost of attending means you have no "need" for assistance. This can be particularly troublesome when your own estimate doesn't agree! On the other hand, if your EFC is less than the cost of attendance—there is evidence your family cannot cover the cost of attendance—then you have demonstrated "need." The greater the differential, the greater the need.

Here's the twist. The methodology for determining the EFC and, potentially, the "need" varies from school to school. The notion that a student's EFC should be determined the same way at each university to which she applies disappeared when institutions began responding aggressively to opportunities to attract top talent. Now, schools actively exercise the prerogative to apply their own standards in defining and determining "need." It is no longer a certainty, for example, that two admitted students at the same institution with identical family financial circumstances will receive identical financial aid awards or that two institutions of the same cost will treat your student in the same manner.

Colleges and universities typically subscribe to one of two methodologies for determining need. They are reflected in the *Free Application for Federal Student Aid (FAFSA)* and the *College Scholarship Service PROFILE*. You need to find out which financial aid applications are required by the schools to which your student is applying and make sure the necessary forms are submitted by the posted deadlines. It is possible that some institutions will require their own forms as well.

The FAFSA embodies the *Federal Need Analysis Methodology*, a formula used to determine your student's eligibility for grants, loans, and work study (campus jobs) funded by the Federal government. "Federal Methodology" is the formula of choice for state-supported universities as well as quite a few private institutions in determining the EFC for their applicants. The FAFSA does not require as much information about your family finances as does the PROFILE and is likely to project a lower EFC for your student (and greater eligibility for need-based financial aid).

On the other hand, the CSS *PROFILE* was established to give institutions a more comprehensive look at a range of financial factors in determining a family's EFC. Afforded this extra measure of scrutiny, a good number of private colleges and universities employ this "institutional methodology" as the basis for determining how they will distribute their institutional "funds." Many will, in fact, require both the FAFSA (to determine eligibility for Federal assistance) *and* the PROFILE in order to complete the need analysis for their applicants.

There are at least two major differences between the PROFILE and the FAFSA:

1. The questions on the PRO-FILE probe much more deeply into family finances, often uncovering assets that are overlooked by the FAFSA.

2. Institutions using the PRO-FILE can elect to customize a portion of questions to gather information specific to their own need assessments. While 80 percent of the PROFILE includes standard questions, the remaining 20 percent may be institution-specific questions. In any case, the PRO-FILE gives institutions a much broader look at your family finances that invariably leads to a *higher* EFC for your student.

Between the Lines

Same Information, Different Outcomes

If your student is considering private institutions, you will discover quickly that the FAFSA and the PROFILE offer similar, yet divergent, assessments of your family's financial picture as the latter typically requests more information and greater detail. Depending on the methodology used by the institution, "family income and assets" may or may not include the equity you have in your home, or consider the finances of the non-custodial parent or the stepparent. Similarly, the "cost of living allowances" may or may not credit you for having other concurrent educational expenses. The result can be a difference of $5,000–$7,000 in the EFC determinations *for the same family.*

When you have completed the necessary forms—you can do this online—the information is processed independently during the same time period that most colleges are reviewing their applications for admission. The FAFSA review is usually completed first and your student will receive a Student Aid Report (SAR) within about six weeks asking for confirmation of the information that has been submitted. The PROFILE may take longer to process as it may include various supplemental forms if you are divorced or separated or own your own farm or business.

If you have submitted your forms on time, the basic need analysis is usually complete by the first week of March and the EFC reports have reached the university's financial aid office. If all goes well in the admission process, the selection committee will release a tentative roster of students to be admitted to the financial aid office *that includes your student's name.* It is at this point that institutions make critical value judgments about the students in whom they want to invest their financial aid dollars. The outcome of these deliberations will go a long way to determining whether there will be happiness in your house when the decision letters arrive.

Meeting Need

At this stage of the game, the financial aid officers take stock of the resources they have at their disposal:

- Institutional need-based scholarships and grants
- Institutional merit-based scholarships
- State grants and loans
- Federal grants and loans
- Federally subsidized Work Study funding (FWS)
- Institutionally subsidized work award funding

Between the Lines

When Things Aren't as They Seem

For most students, the EFC and financial need are derived from either the FAFSA or the PROFILE. An extended illness, the loss of a job, or a family move may put an undue hardship on a family that is not fully captured by the aid applications. In such instances, you should document these circumstances directly to the school's financial aid officer as that person is permitted discretion or "professional judgment" in arriving at a final determination of need.

The largest pool of funding available to most colleges and universities is that which is used to address *need-based scholarships and grants*. This is free money. It doesn't have to be repaid. In fact, it isn't really even money—at least not in the sense that you can see it, touch it, and bank it!

Despite what the label—scholarship or grant—might suggest, colleges are *not* giving out money or hard cash. The award is really a discount—a coupon for $5,000 or $10,000 or whatever amount has been determined necessary to cover the cost of attendance—your student receives because she has demonstrated need. These awards are usually renewable as long as your student remains in good academic standing.

By contrast, *merit-based scholarships* are directed at a college's top applicants regardless of their "need" in order to lure them away from other schools. Such scholarships might recognize valued talents and achievements in areas ranging from academic prowess to leadership and community service and from music and theater to NCAA Division I athletics. These scholarships are typically tied to some performance criterion and can be revoked if the student fails to meet expectations. Not all institutions offer merit scholarships.

Most *states* will award grants and loans to students who plan to enroll at an in-state institution and who demonstrate need. Access to these awards may require that your student submit additional application forms around the first of the year when she is applying to college. While colleges cannot literally award these grants and loans directly to the student, they are aware of the student's eligibility for such awards and, when possible, will include references to this *eligibility* in the financial aid awards they send to students.

Federal funding may be available in the form of grants, loans, and work study. The Pell Grant, the Federal Supplemental

Between the Lines

Scholarships About Which Nobody Knows

It is not uncommon for colleges and universities to provide scholarships that are relatively obscure. These awards are designated for the redheaded, left-handed cellist or the student from a designated county who wants to pursue nursing as a career. As endowed scholarships, they are easily overlooked and, as a result, not awarded on a regular basis.

Educational Opportunity Grant (FSEOG), the Federal Perkins Loan, and the subsidized Federal Stafford Loan are all need-based (FAFSA) funds. Your student's eligibility for these funds is determined apart from her relationship with a given college, though, and she is not obligated to accept any of the grants or loans for which she is eligible. The funding she does accept is portable and will be released to the college at which your student enrolls in her name *after she has begun classes*. Then, and only then, will your student be able to apply these funds to college costs.

The amounts of the Pell Grant and the FSEOG will vary according to the cost of attendance at the schools to which your student is accepted but usually range up to $4,000. Like institutional grants and scholarships, these funds displace the need for dollars from your pocket to meet college costs. The maximum Federal Stafford Loan eligibility for students is $2,625 for the first year, $3,500 for the second year, and $5,500 for the third and fourth years.

Most students, regardless of need, can qualify for Federal Stafford Loans. While the loans are low interest and repayment can be deferred until after your student has completed her education, the interest on need-based loans is subsidized by the Federal government as long she is a full-time student. Students whose Federal Stafford Loans are not subsidized will find that the interest on the loans begins accruing immediately. Payment of that interest can be deferred as well. Your student may elect to accept all, part, or none of these amounts.

In meeting demonstrated need, colleges expect that students will assume some measure of responsibility for helping themselves. This expectation of "self-help" is implicit in the awarding of the loans just mentioned—low-interest, deferred payment funding opportunities for which the student is responsible. In addition, some institutions will extend their own loan programs to students in amounts that exceed the eligibility determined by the FAFSA.

Similarly, students may be given the opportunity to work part-time (10-15 hours per week for about $1,500 per academic year) on their campuses in order to earn additional money to cover incidental expenses. The majority of these opportunities are underwritten by the Federal government (*Federal Work Study*). Many colleges also budget monies of their own to cover situations where students may want to work even though they are not eligible for need-based assistance. The degree to which students accept self-help opportunities will have a bearing on their family's cash flow as they otherwise make plans to cover the EFC.

Other Scholarships

Scholarship assistance is available from many sources apart from the colleges and universities. Local service organizations, scholarship foundations, employers and individuals/groups with ties to your student's high school make awards annually. Among the most prestigious are the awards made by the National Merit Scholarship Foundation in recognition of academic achievement and standardized test (PSAT) results.

Some of these awards will find their way to your student. She might be nominated or recommended for consideration by teachers, counselors, or community leaders. Other awards are more elusive because they are either relatively unknown or they are highly competitive. In these cases, your student needs to do her homework if she hopes to find money for college.

If your student wins such an award, she will need to report it to the college where she enrolls. What happens next varies from college to college. Colleges will:

1. Apply the entire amount of the outside scholarship against the amount of self-help (loan and job) that would normally appear in her financial aid award, or

2. Apply the entire amount of the outside scholarship against the amount of need-based grants that would normally appear in her financial aid award, or

3. Split the amount of the outside scholarship so that one part replaces a portion of self-help and the other replaces a portion of need-based grants.

Between the Lines

Parents Can Borrow, Too!
Parent Loans for Undergraduate Study (PLUS) are available to parents of dependent students who don't feel as well off as the need analysis might suggest! These variable rate loans are available, regardless of need, in amounts equal to the cost of their student's annual education. PLUS can become a parent's best friend in meeting the expected family contribution and working through the cash flow crunch of the college years.

As she explores scholarships awarded outside of those offered by colleges, your student needs to be sensitive to this dynamic. Too often students win substantial scholarships in the community only to find that the institutions at which they will enroll plan to substitute the outside award for money that would have been part of the need-based grant. That being the case, she would be wise to survey colleges early in the process to determine their policies regarding the administration of outside awards.

The College Dollar

As you can see, colleges possess an arsenal of options as they prepare to make financial aid awards to students they will be admitting. The options fall into two categories: gift aid and self-help. While the gift aid (grant/scholarship) is self-explanatory—it's free money—the self-help is comprised of the loans for which the student is eligible and the opportunity to work on campus. Generally speaking, the amount of gift aid that is available to entering students is a function of an institution's endowment. The larger the endowment, the more money that is available to underwrite the discount.

In theory, the dynamic variables in the awarding process are the EFC and the gift aid. As your expected family contribution changes, up or down, it is offset by corresponding adjustments to the amount of the grant or scholarship. For example, a low EFC will result in a larger portion of gift aid.

College Price Tags

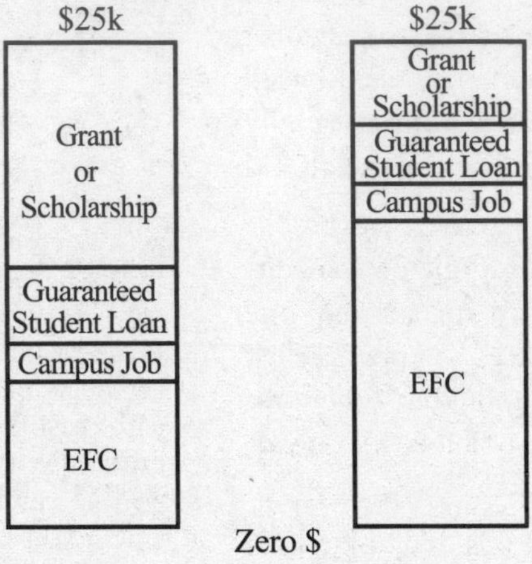

$25k		$25k
Grant or Scholarship		Grant or Scholarship
		Guaranteed Student Loan
		Campus Job
Guaranteed Student Loan		
Campus Job		
		EFC
EFC		

Zero $

The graphic, above, illustrates how this can be the case at colleges that list the same or comparable prices but use different formulas to arrive at your EFC. Note that the self-help values tend not to change, although there can be exceptions as you will see in the next section.

Now, imagine that the expected family contribution (EFC) is constant at institutions that carry different price tags. As you can see, the same EFC that comes well short of meeting the costs at one school may cover most if not all of the costs at another.

Same EFC, Different Cost of Attendance

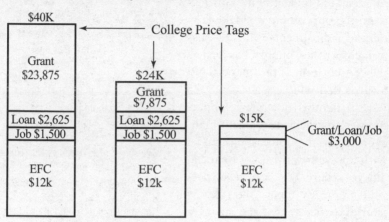

Enrollment Management: Who Gets What?

Let's fast forward to the moment of truth in the enrollment planning process—the time, usually late in the application review process, when the admission officers become enrollment managers and begin to assess the "big picture" of enrollment to determine how they can utilize their financial aid resources to leverage the best class possible. This is the point at which they ask the questions: "Who do we value most?" and "What will it take to get this student to enroll?"

This seemingly obscure activity is really the defining moment for colleges as they determine the students in whom they will make their investments. By referring to the yield statistics on offers of admission in previous years, enrollment managers can predict the likelihood that students will enroll according to the value ratings that have been assigned them by the admission committee as well as their respective financial needs. This is the time when the final "tweaking" of the class takes place.

To visualize this exercise, imagine a matrix that shows the relationship between the value ratings assigned to applicants and their respective financial needs. Each cell of the matrix includes the numbers of applicants and students to be admitted as well as the projected enrollment based on the previous year's yield rates. The matrix enables admission officers—now wearing the hat of enrollment managers—to gauge the likelihood that their tentative offers of admission and financial aid will be accommodated by the financial aid budget. It also affords them the opportunity to make last-minute adjustments in the class (remember the "bubble") as well as the composition of the financial aid awards that will be sent.

A number of strategic opportunities emerge as enrollment managers scan the forecasting model with an eye toward using financial aid to secure the best class possible. For example, they know from experience that the stronger ("High Value") students who don't need financial aid are potentially the lowest yielding students be-

Between the Lines

Value Ratings
"Value ratings" is a term used here to loosely define the value an admission committee attaches to each candidate. Factors that determine value are found in answers to the questions: "What do we get?" and "What is the likelihood that she will enroll?" While ratings at some institutions are highly quantified, they can take on a very subjective look as qualities that are valued by an institution can change by the season.

cause they will have lots of college options—many of which carry with them offers of scholarships. In order to compete for these students, enrollment managers may consider offering scholarships of their own. In looking at the matrix to find funding flexibility, they will find large numbers of students who are on the bubble ("Low Value"), many of whom needs large amounts of financial aid.

If aided with standard awards, the students on the bubble are likely to show up in large numbers as the school in question represents a highly attractive option that will cost them very little. While enrollment managers may well let some of these financial aid awards stand, they may also decide that some of the gift aid that is targeted at students on the bubble might yield stronger students if directed at "High Value" students in the form of merit scholarships. As a result, they will either reconfigure the financial aid award for the student on the bubble to include less gift aid and more self-help—or they will simply decide not to admit the student.

Similar strategies will be played out across the matrix as colleges seek to use their resources to affect enrollment outcomes. High Value students with low to moderate financial need might find that the self-help (loan and work study) in their financial aid awards is replaced with scholarships while Low Value students in the same financial situation might find that all of their need is being met with self-help.

As we noted in the discussion of the "Hidden Agenda," the decisions about whom to admit and aid are business decisions. When colleges and universities admit students, they will exercise discretion within the values that guide their decision-making to admit or not admit. And among the admitted students with financial need, they will strategically determine how much (or how little) financial aid will be required in order to gain an enrollment. This practice is known as preferential packaging.

Each matrix at each school reflects a different set of institutional values—values that can change or be applied inconsistently, values that are rooted in qualities from the academic to the eccentric. The Pyramid provides the perspective of selectivity. The same applicant qualities that might not gain much attention at one school may be highly valued at another. This is why, if your ability to fund a college education is a critical concern, you really need to work with your student to find the right playing fields—the places where she will be valued for what she does well.

Reflections on the Financial Aid Game

The *strategic deployment of financial aid*—yes, that's the term used by many enrollment managers—to enroll a class is really a fitting end game for colleges and universities that must treat their affairs in a business-like fashion. The ability to balance the budget is just as important as the ability to get the class. The ability to corral a larger share of high profile talent is just as important as the ability to enroll "good" kids.

And this is just the beginning. The decision making at each institution is so heavily nuanced with pressures to perform and compete that the procedures employed to determine need and award aid will leave you scratching your head. For example, many institutions will use the FAFSA and the PROFILE interchangeably depending on their needs. If they want to be able to justify a larger financial aid award based on demonstrated need, they will use the FAFSA to determine the need. Conversely, the desire to issue a smaller need-based award may invoke a reference to the PROFILE in determining need. Or an institution might simply admit one student and proceed to ignore his demonstrated need while admitting another student of similar credential and giving him an athletic scholarship. You have got to ask yourself, "Who is being valued and why?"

These tactics are a part of the process that is largely invisible—and that's probably a good thing. No parent likes to see his/her student treated as an object of lesser value. This is often the reality, though, in the "smoky" backrooms where the real decisions—the business decisions—are made. Like it or not, institutions are not completely altruistic as they manage their enrollments.

College price tags can be likened to the prices charged by airlines for tickets. If you are on an airplane with 100 people, it is likely that each of you has paid a different price for your seats: 100 passengers, 100 prices. The same is true of a college education. Your job is to make sure that when it comes time to pay, you and your student are convinced that, among the "good fit" options, she is getting a "seat" that is worth the price you are paying.

Ten Tips for Parents in Managing College Costs

1. **If you think you need assistance, ask for it.** Yes, colleges are likely to discriminate at some point. They will wait, however, until they see evidence of the demonstrated need that they can weigh against the merit of the application.

2. **Be prepared to appear wealthier on paper than you might feel.** Many parents have become accustomed to lifestyles that include discretionary purchases (extra appliances, summer homes, boats, vacations, etc.) that constrict their cash flow. As you apply for financial aid, you will be reminded these are choices you have made—choices that hold a cash value that you could redirect toward college expenses

3. **Adhere to deadlines.** This is not the time to be coy about your intentions or your needs. Waiting until after your student is admitted to complete the financial aid process can have disastrous implications if your student truly needs financial assistance. The money in the financial aid "pot" begins to diminish with the first offer that is made. If you wait to apply for financial aid until your student has a letter of acceptance in hand, the money will be gone.

4. **If your student is considering Early Decision and you are concerned about being able to afford the costs of the college in question,** plan to visit with the financial aid office at that college in August or September of the senior year. Take your most recent pay stubs as well as your tax returns. Most financial aid officers will take the time to work with you in establishing an "early estimate" or preliminary read for EFC.

5. **Saving for college can cut both ways.** Unfortunately, college costs have grown at such a rate that saving "a little at a time" leaves you with an empty feeling when the bill arrives. If saving is a part of your strategy, whether through a 529 program, a set-aside account at your bank, or under the mattress, you'll need to squirrel away large amounts in order to meet college costs. If you live on a modest income, then it is better to do what you can financially to take care of your family. Saving a little at a time will put you in the *Catch 22* situation of having too little money to cover costs but enough that your eligibility for financial aid is reduced.

6. **Don't pool your resources to create the illusion of affluence when your student is applying for admission.** Families that try to appear rich in order to get their kids into favored colleges on the assumption that those colleges will respond to their impoverished state in subsequent years are making a big mistake. Colleges plan financial aid budgets for years 2 through 4 of your student's experience based on the expectations in the first year.

7. **Understand what is going on when institutions promise to meet the full financial needs (no loan expectations) of families below certain income levels.** These institutions are not promising *to admit and give aid* to all students who have high need. Rather, they are promising to extend *to all who are admitted* aid packages that are free of loan expectations.

8. **Read the fine print about "renewability."** Students must reapply for *need-based* assistance every year. Some merit scholarships are awarded for one year only. For those that are renewable, recipients are often required to attain minimal GPAs. Make sure you find out about the potential of a scholarship to grow in subsequent years to match increasing costs.

9. **Tell the whole story.** If your family financial situation is confusing due to unusual circumstances that can't easily be explained on financial aid forms, most schools will welcome additional information in the form of a letter with documentation. Such letters should be sent to the financial aid officer at the college in question and NOT the financial aid servicing center.

10. **Don't assume that all colleges and universities are alike.** Such assumptions lead to the conclusion that "where a student goes to college doesn't matter" and the further conclusion that "we might as well send her someplace that won't cost us that much." Each school is indeed different and the differences your student might identify in seeking a good fit should be factored into any affordability discussion. And, as you have that discussion, make sure you distinguish between what you *can't* do to support her and what you *won't* do.

When It's Too Good to be True . . .

As your student becomes fully immersed in the college planning process, be wary of "free" financial planning workshops that promise to deliver scholarships and cut college costs. If any of this sounds too good to be true, it usually is. I say this with the caveat that there are scores of well-trained certified financial planners who will indeed provide sound, comprehensive advice regarding the way you manage your assets in anticipation of educational expenses. They can usually count on you finding them, though.

Remember, "free" usually has a price tag. If you register to take advantage of a free opportunity, be prepared to hear heart-warming testimonials and a pitch for fee-related services. And know that the people offering these services are simply giving you information already in the public domain. If you have specific concerns about meeting college costs, you are better off contacting the financial aid directors at the schools to which your student is applying. They will be able to give you good direction at no cost. They might not always tell you what you want to hear, but they should be able to help you find solutions to your financing dilemmas. If you aren't satisfied with the service you receive, you might rethink your commitment to that institution.

If you are uncertain about the credibility of the information you are receiving as it relates to financial planning and/or scholarships, visit the following Web site: www.finaid.org/scholarships/scams.phtml.

Chapter 13

Time to Apply

Assembly Required!

So far, you have navigated the early, reflective stages of the college search and selection process with your student. Now, the calendar says it is time for him to get serious about his college applications. Unfortunately, your student can't push a button that will immediately produce the contents of an application. Assembly is required.

If your student is like most, he will see the deadline as the target date for getting things done. And "getting things done" means exactly that—working from start to finish to beat the deadline! In the other half of the book, I stress the need to work from a plan *well in advance of deadlines*. This is where you can put strategic nagging to good use! He must stay on task at this stage of the game.

On the other hand, resist the temptation to do the work for your student or have it done for him. I have heard parents explain that they didn't see any harm in completing the applications *themselves* because their students were "too busy." Besides, "you could never read his writing." One parent even told me that he had his administrative assistant prepare the materials—not a good idea!

If the parental tendency to take over and get it done "right" is beginning to overwhelm you, stop now! Do you really want to head down that slippery slope? Completing your student's application for him under any pretense sends a bad message regarding accountability. It removes him from an exercise that is integral to the admission process and denies him ownership of his application. Think about it. Will you complete his college registration forms? Will you write and edit his papers in college? I hope not.

Make sure your student does *his own work*. His applications for admission are akin to personal statements. He is making the case

Between the Lines

Maintain a Working Checklist
Work with your student to develop a spreadsheet or checklist that references the requirements, as well as the steps needed to meet the requirements, for each of the colleges on his short list. It is vital that he be intimately familiar with the guidelines and deadlines for the submission of application materials as established by his school. Post the spreadsheet on your refrigerator or family activity board (or next to the bathroom mirror). Make sure he checks each item as it is completed. He should never "not know" what needs to be done.

for himself in his own words—"Here I am. Take me." *He* needs to make the sell. You can review everything with him to make sure it is presentable, but he needs to be responsible for presenting the content in his own voice.

The application your student completes for many colleges could include more than ten pages of courses, grades, test results, activities, honors, and awards. It is his past, his present, and his future all wrapped into one. While much of it is in his words, he will also include letters of recommendation from those who have observed him in the classroom—and in life—that validate and provide context for his performance.

The challenge—and the opportunity—for students is to use each element of the application to make a compelling statement to the admission committee. The application represents the sum of his experiences over the last four years as he competes for admission. What does it say about what he can do? What he has accomplished? Who he is? And what he can become? As was noted in the discussion of the Agenda, he needs to be able to answer the question, "What do we get if we admit him?" The further up the Pyramid he aspires, the more compelling the statement needs to be.

The Application as an Empty Canvas

The blank application, then, is like his empty canvas—his opportunity to paint a picture that reveals each element of his being. Wow! That's pretty heavy, but shouldn't it be? It's his life in a nutshell. That's why students have trouble with the application and, more specifically, the personal statement. So much is at stake and they feel inadequate to the task.

You can help your student reflect on the opportunity that stands before him—to make a statement with his application that tells his story and reveals his gifts. He needs to reflect on who he is, what he has to offer, and how these things will resonate with the college to which he is applying. For guidance, he might reexamine the early stages of the college planning process. What can be learned from his priorities for college or the perspective that emerged as he examined elements of a good college "fit?" Keep the following in mind as he prepares his applications:

- Many students have stories to tell that provide real insight into who they have become. Some are stories of hardship while others reveal extraordinary, "mountain-top" types of life experiences. The application is your student's opportunity to tell his story.

- He should consider the "lens" through which he has seen life. His cultural heritage, his relationships, his values, and his spirituality each give definition to the person he is becoming.

- If nothing else, his application needs to reveal his passion for learning and living, for trying new things, for taking risks, and for making a difference.

- He *should not* try to make himself into the image of someone who is attractive to colleges. Rather, he needs to be himself. Colleges that value him for who he is will respond accordingly.

Parents and the Personal Statement

One of the most stressful tasks that will confront your student in his young life is the personal statement or college essay. It has the potential to absolutely stop him in his tracks mentally and emotionally—to paralyze his thought process at a time when he needs to be more lucid and reflective than ever. The essays are so daunting that students will complete everything else in the application quickly and efficiently only to sit and stare at the essay requirement for weeks or months waiting for some kind of inspiration.

Your role in this project is four-fold. One, *show empathy.* After all, if you've been there, you know that writing an essay like this isn't easy. You also know that he will survive. Two, *resist the temptation to take over.* Do not write a draft for him. Do not pay someone to write or edit a draft for him. Think about the lessons of own-

Between the Lines

The Personal Statement
Addressing the personal statement or college essay will be one of the more difficult tasks to confront your student in his young life. It requires him to be creative and introspective. He must demonstrate that he has mastered the technical aspects of writing while at the same time revealing a part of himself that may not be apparent anywhere else in his application.

ership and ethics you are teaching him. This exercise is about more than getting into college, it is helping him learn to rely on his own talents as he makes his way in life.

Three, *get him to think—and to talk about his thoughts.* Challenge him to own his thoughts. Make him accountable. I once had a professor who challenged me to try to disprove everything he said. If I could "disprove" him, he claimed, I would discover a new truth. If I couldn't disprove him, then I would validate an old truth. Regardless, I would have a better understanding of the truth.

Challenge your student to understand the truth about himself. The question "why" is a powerful point of inquiry. It elicits self-examination. It brings him into touch with who he is—the person that stands apart from the rest of the applicants. If you ask him why something is important and he answers with "I don't know," then he's got a problem. "I don't know" doesn't work very well on a college application! The more comfortable he becomes as a critical thinker—the owner of a thought process that reveals the connection between himself and the world around and within him—the more comfortable he will be as the author of a college essay.

Finally, at some point you should have an opportunity to go over your student's essay with him. I say "should" because some kids are pretty crafty about keeping their parents out of the loop. (My eldest daughter waited until I was out of the country to write *and submit* her essays!) When that opportunity presents itself, restrain yourself. No pencils or pens. Don't throw any hip-checks at the PC or workstation followed by: "Move over, honey. I know how to fix that for you!"

Your job is to read and react. Read the essay and provide feedback. When I was a student, my parents would routinely review my papers. My mother, the English major, loved to talk me through extensive edits. My dad, the veterinarian, would read the paper, hand it back, and simply say, "You're

Between the Lines

Let Your Student Find the Answer
One of the problems with 'hands on' or corrective editing can be that the person doing the editing is often the first to find the best solution to challenging word selections. When this happens, the student is faced with a dilemma to accept the proposed language or try to find something even better. To the conscientious student, the latter is the only option. Your well-intended advice, however, has just made that task frustrating, if not impossible. Do what you can to lead your student through a reflective thought process that will enable him to find—and own—the best solution.

not going to hand it in *that* way, are you?" He knew that *I knew* what needed to be done to make the paper better. The technical orientation that I gleaned from my mother notwithstanding, that was all that needed to be said.

Consider an approach that is somewhere in between. Show an interest in your student's essays. Read them and *be prepared to talk about them*. Ask questions that get him to think and talk about the ideas that he is trying to convey. Get him to defend his thought process, but give him room to find his own solutions. And, if you need to, remind him that he can always start over!

The Application

The application form itself captures important information about the candidate, his family background, and his academic achievements and extracurricular activities. Your student will encounter application options ranging from the hard copy version that a college sends him in the mail to an online version provided by the same college. In addition, 300 colleges and universities are members of the Common Application® group. The "Common App" is an application form that each member institution has agreed to use as its own even though it may produce and distribute an application bearing its own mark. A student can complete the Common App and submit copies of the original to any number of the member institutions.

Some colleges use a two-part application process. The first part is essentially a form that collects your student's biographic information. Students may be encouraged to submit Part I of an application, with the application fee, well in advance of the application deadline. Admission officers will use this information to begin building the student's applicant file.

Five Tips for Completing the Application

As your student prepares and compiles his application materials, urge him to:

1. **Establish folders for each college into which he can file important forms and documents.**

2. **Include a list of submission deadlines in each folder.**

3. **Complete a draft of the application in pencil.** Type or print the final copy in pen.

4. **Present everything legibly.** When admission officers have to struggle to read or interpret information, they lose interest.

5. **Make copies of every document that is to be submitted.** Date each copy.

Information Produced by High Schools

While the procedures for submitting the applications to colleges will vary from one high school to another, the basics are similar across the board. In general, guidance counselors or college advisers will produce:

- Academic transcripts showing courses and grades and, in some cases, test results

- Documentation that describes the scope and rigor of the school's academic program

- Basic demographic information about the school population

- Letters of recommendation

Some guidance counselors will expect the student to submit his applications to colleges directly with the provision that the counselor will follow-up with transcripts and letters of recommendation. Others will coordinate the collection and preparation of the application materials at the school and then submit bundled packages to the colleges. Generating the application, though, is the student's responsibility.

The Official High School Transcript

A record of courses and grades, this form will show the history of your student's performance since the beginning of 9th grade. Some transcripts will show a single grade for

Between the Lines

"Will They Know?"

A common concern among students and parents is "will they (admission officers) know" about the rigor of the academic program at our school? The short answer is: "Yes!" For every high school, there is a slightly different interpretation of courses and grades. Admission officers go to great lengths to understand the nuances of the academic programs at high schools around the world.

each course each year. Others may show grades for each marking period *and* exam grades for each course. Transcripts may also show credits earned for each completed course as well as the results from testing (state assessment, Advanced Placement, college entrance exams). In all cases, the responsibility for preparing the official transcript rests with the school personnel.

You should check with your student's college counselor regarding the school's practice with regard to reporting standardized tests results. If your student has elected to apply without standardized tests (to colleges that have made them optional), *he will want to make sure the scores are not inadvertently posted on the transcript.*

School Profile

The School Profile is designed to give colleges a comprehensive snapshot of the learning environment so admission committees can make critical, contextual assessments of students. Each profile is different with regard to what it reports, as the courses, levels of rigor, grading systems, and student outcomes vary greatly across schools.

School Report/Counselor Evaluation

In addition to submitting an official transcript, the college adviser will provide a narrative assessment of your student's high school experience.

The confidential Counselor Evaluation speaks to the "big picture" with regard to your student's performance by providing insight into your student's growth and maturation as a student and as a citizen within the school. The accompanying school report provides a brief statistical summary of your student's academic record.

Mid-Year Report

Contrary to popular belief, many colleges will consider classroom performance well into the senior year. The Mid-Year Report form enables high schools to do just that: report grades at the mid-point of the senior year. This form is submitted to the admission committees by the college adviser.

Teacher Recommendations

Most colleges require at least one letter of recommendation from a teacher who can comment on both your student's proficiency and potential as a student. Your student should provide the letter-writer with a preaddressed, stamped envelope.

Supplemental Form

Colleges that subscribe to the Common Application® or generic online applications may require your student to submit an additional form that includes information that may not have been collected. This information could include a statement of interest in merit scholarship opportunities, a declaration of Early Decision or Early Action intent, or a review of audition dates and procedures. Colleges that use a Supplemental Form usually do not regard an application as complete until that form has been received.

Application Options: How and When to Apply

Each institution is different in the way it receives applications. Some begin receiving and making decisions on applications early in the senior year and continue until their enrollment goals are achieved. A few will even encourage applications during the summer prior to senior year. Others will collect applications through a deadline period after which they can evaluate each candidate within the context of the overall competition. The following are examples of application processes your student may encounter as he applies to different colleges and universities.

"Rolling Admission"

Thumbs Up: The student receives prompt feedback regarding admission and, if admitted, is able to secure enrollment with necessary financial assistance.

Thumbs Down: The process gets bogged down when additional information (i.e., grades, scores, financial aid data) is required. Merit scholarships are not always awarded within the context of the original application evaluation time period.

Works Best for . . . the student who has a clear sense of where he wants to go to college within a narrowly defined set of parameters (cost, location, academic program) and/or wants to secure a viable option early in the overall application process.

Rolling Admission is utilized by colleges that do not expect to see many applications beyond the number they will need to admit. Designed to accept and give financial aid to qualified applicants on a rolling basis until their respective classes are full, Rolling Admission processes are fairly open. Depending on the student's circumstances, this could be right up until the first day of classes. The opportunities diminish, though, with each student who is admitted and each financial aid award that is made. It is easier to gain admission and financial aid through such programs by applying early in the senior year. If your student is considering colleges with Rolling Admission *and* needs financial aid, he would be wise to begin the process sooner than later. Applicants typically learn of their admission and financial aid status within a month of applying.

Many colleges that operate Rolling Admission programs offer on-site credential reviews. Such reviews can take place during campus visits, at open house programs, and in conjunction with presentations made in local high schools. Based on a favorable review, a student might be offered admission contingent on submitting a completed application to that college.

"Deadline Admission"

Thumbs Up: Student is able to compete for admission and financial aid/scholarship at multiple colleges at the same time.

Thumbs Down: The candidate review processes are long and often arbitrary with very little communication from the college until the decisions are made. The deadlines for scholarship competition may fall ahead of regular deadlines for admission at some schools.

Works Best for . . . the student who wants to be able to weigh multiple college options (and the affordability of each) before deciding where to enroll.

Deadline Admission institutions anticipate large numbers of applicants and impose deadlines for candidates who are seeking regular (non-binding) offers of admission. This allows them to see all the applicants before determining who will be admitted and aided. Students who apply by the deadline are notified of their admission status at the end of the credential review period. This can range from the beginning of March to the beginning of April depending on the size and competitiveness of the applicant pool. Students admitted through the regular decision process have until May 1 (the Candidate's Reply Date) to declare their enrollment intentions.

"Early Decision"

Thumbs Up: Student is able to wrap up the college process early in the senior year. Acceptance rates are higher for ED at most schools.

Thumbs Down: Students who use ED strategically are often not thinking logically and are prone to inappropriate selections. In addition, ED may not be a good idea for students who need to shop for the most affordable option.

Works best for . . . the student who is absolutely certain of his first choice college and has resolved any concerns regarding affordability.

Early Decision (ED) is a subset of the Deadline Admission process through which a student and a college exchange promises of commitment. By making an Early Decision application, the candidate promises to enroll if the college in question commits to offering him a place in the class.

While most Early Decision deadlines fall in advance of those for Regular Decision, many colleges and universities have gone to a tiered Early Decision program with multiple deadlines and decision-making periods. For example, Round One of ED at College "X" might have an application deadline of November 15 and a target for notification of December 15. College "X" may also extend a second ED opportunity (Round Two) for students to make ED commitments with a deadline of January 1 and target for notification of February 1. Students who may not be ready to commit on the Round One calendar, or who are rebounding from bad news with an initial ED application at another school, may consider ED at College "X" through its Round Two program.

At some colleges, you may discover that the distinction between ED deadlines and regular deadlines is a bit blurry. It may even seem that the ED door remains ajar in what amounts to a rolling deadline. That is intentional. As you will see when we discuss the "Doors of Enrollment" in the next chapter, colleges are very strategic in their use of different enrollment options. The more students who commit through ED, the fewer students a college needs to admit through Regular Decision. As a result, the yield goes up and the college appears to be more selective.

It is important to note that your student may not apply ED to more than one college *at a time*. He may submit any number of regular applications at the same time he is an ED candidate, but he does so with the understanding that he will withdraw those applications as soon as he is accepted at his ED school. Colleges take seriously the mutual commitment that defines their relationship with every ED candidate. If your student applies ED, he is saying "if you take me, I *will* enroll."

Most colleges will require an ED candidate to sign a statement acknowledging that commitment. Moreover, you and your student's college adviser or guidance counselor will need to sign similar acknowledgments. In doing so, you acknowledge the rules that govern the ED program and the guidance counselor agrees not to send transcripts to other colleges if your student is admitted ED.

"Early Action"

Thumbs Up: Gives the applicant an early indication of his admissions status at his first-choice school without compelling him to enroll without seeing his other options.

Thumbs Down: While growing, the list of institutions that offer EA is still relatively short. Applying as an EA candidate does not enhance the prospect of getting in.

Works best for... the highly competitive candidate whose admission focus rests on a few of the most selective colleges and who wants the security of knowing that he has been admitted to at least one of them.

Early Action (EA) is a nonbinding, early notification opportunity extended by a growing number of selective institutions. As is the case with Early Decision, students who respond to the EA deadline (in advance of the regular application deadline) are notified early of their admission status. Unlike ED, however, accepted EA applicants are not obligated to enroll if accepted. They may wait until the Candidates Reply Date (May 1) to declare their intentions and may, in fact, choose another college. A variation on this theme is "single choice or restrictive EA." Institutions that offer "single choice" Early Action insist that an EA applicant designate only one college as his EA choice.

Five Tips for Determining the Best Way and Time to Apply

In preparing college applications, your student should:

1. Err on the side of applying sooner than later. Give the people who are processing the information more time to get it organized and entered.

2. Choose to apply without regard to a college's decision-making process (Deadline or Rolling). Whether a college offers Deadline Admission or Rolling Admission is incidental to the fact that it is a good fit for your student.

3. Use the form and process that enables him to best illustrate his talents and interests.

4. Be sensitive to separate deadlines that relate to scholarship eligibility.

5. Consult www.nacacnet.org with any questions that might come up with regard to ethics of the admission process. NACAC (National Association for College Admission Counseling), a membership organization that includes most secondary and postsecondary institutions in the country, has articulated a comprehensive *Statement of Principles of Good Practice* to which members must subscribe.

Frequently Asked Questions from Parents About The Application

Q *My son attends a very competitive high school. Will colleges know that he is getting B's at this school when he could be going to another school and getting A's?*

A The academic programs at high schools across the country and around the world are so heavily nuanced that it is nearly impossible to take information such as a grade point average at face value. Colleges are very attentive to context when they review applications. Before they attempt to assess your son's courses and grades, they will make sure they understand the academic environment in which he is competing. How rigorous is the course load? How competitive are the students? How well do students from your son's school perform on end-of-year assessments (AP, IB exams)? This is where the School Profile and letters of recommendation help the admission committee triangulate on the rigor of his program.

Q *My daughter is trying to figure out which teachers to ask for letters of recommendation. Her favorite was her 9th grade English teacher. Should she ask him for a recommendation or someone who has taught her more recently?*

A First, she should choose a teacher who is familiar with her most recent work. That said, the teacher most likely to provide credible insight into your daughter's growth and achievement as a student will be the one who challenged her the most—who forced her out of her comfort zone and into new patterns of discovery. Such a teacher won't always be the most popular but will be among the most widely respected.

Q *My son's grades dipped in his junior year. Is that going to be a problem?*

A It depends on how far the grades dipped, what he did to correct the problem, and where he thinks he wants to go to college. Whenever admission committees see irregularities in a student's program or performance, they need to know why this has happened. If there is a valid reason (injury, extended illness, distractions at home, etc.)—not an excuse—then he has a story to tell. The more selective the college, the more important it is that he demonstrates that he can rebound well from setbacks and makes sure that his story is told.

Q *When do we get to see the letters of recommendation?*

A You probably won't have that opportunity. Keep in mind the contract here is between your student and the teacher or the counselor. When your student asks for a letter of recommendation, he must indicate whether he is going to waive his right of access to the letter. While it might make him (and you) uncomfortable to do so, he should waive his right of access.

More than anything, admission officers look for a candid, balanced, and insightful perspective from the writer. When a teacher knows that his student will be reading the letter before it is submitted, he may be less inclined toward candor and insight. Instead, he might write what he knows you want him to write—and lose his credibility in the eyes of the admission committee. That's why your student needs to give those who will write on his behalf an opportunity to get to know him so they can be effective champions of his cause.

Q *Our school doesn't provide a rank in class. Is that good or bad?*

A Class rank provides admission committees a shorthand interpretation of the student's standing relative to his classmates. In large student populations that feature a wide range of academic ability, the class rank is helpful. In smaller academic environments where the difference between the first student and the one in the middle of the class in terms of ability and performance is miniscule, then the class rank is not useful to the admission committee. The only students favored by a rank in such scenarios are those at the very top of the class.

Q *If a school doesn't rank its students, how can a college make critical distinctions between them?*

A Schools that do not rank often provide alternative means of helping the admission committee understand subtle differences in performance. Some will attach different values or weights to the courses to indicate various levels of rigor. Others will report a given student's performance on a distribution of grades for the entire class.

Q *What is a good number of recommendations to submit?*

A The best answer here is "the number that the college requests." The only exception to that rule would be the situation where a potential recommender is able to provide unusual insight in the student's work habits, passion for learning, potential to grow, and ability to deal with setbacks. Letters from politicians, clergy (unless he is applying to faith-based colleges), and important alumni simply add to the weight of the application.

Q *I've heard that a lot of students use the Common Application® or applications that they can download from the Internet. Is it okay to use these applications or should my daughter complete the application sent to her by the school?*

A In theory, it shouldn't matter. The generic form can be completed once and copied to multiple colleges. It's a great time saver. In reality, though, the application your daughter uses might make a difference. While members of the Common Application® group agree not to discriminate against the users of that application, they *can be* sensitive to yield—will the student enroll if admitted? If an admission committee is trying to determine the yield-ability of a candidate, and they find that the student has not visited the campus, has had very little contact with the admission office *and* has used the Common Application®, they see a "ghost" applicant—one who is not really there.

Q *When is the best time for my student to apply?*

A The best time to submit an application is during the two- to four-week window *prior to the deadline*. The point here is that your student should take precautions against having his credentials get caught in the last-minute avalanche that will engulf most admission offices. By getting things in slightly ahead of time, he beats the rush, reduces the likelihood that information will be lost or misfiled, and gives the folks who process his application a chance to notify him (in a timely manner) of any missing or incomplete materials.

Q *My student is applying to a number of universities that have similar but slightly different essay questions. Can't she just use one of her better essays for each of the colleges?*

A She can do that, but it is probably not a good idea. When colleges create their applications, they often craft essay questions in order to elicit certain types of responses from students. When a student "re-purposes" a good essay written for one college and submits it to another, she risks falling short in terms of producing the impact desired by the second college.

Q *How do colleges factor learning differences into a student's performance? While my student has compensated well, he has still struggled at times and his grades show it. Is this something that colleges want to know about?*

A I would err on the side of self-disclosure. If a college is otherwise interested in your student but is concerned about an erratic record, they want to know why the struggles have taken place. Absent an explanation, admission officers will have to guess. More often than not, they are not too charitable in their guessing. By self-disclosing, your student provides needed insight into his performance. If that becomes a point of discrimination against him, then perhaps the college is doing him a favor. It probably would not have stepped forward to support him in times of struggle as an enrolled student.

Q *I have heard that some colleges provide application fee waivers for students who visit the campus or apply online. Is this on the "up and up?"*

A Sure. Just understand what is going on. Colleges that make those offers are recruiting your student's application. It can seem very flattering and convenient to be able to complete the application in this manner. Make sure your student is not lulled into a false sense of achievement—the notion that the "game" is in hand. After all, he hasn't been admitted yet.

Q *My student was involved in an accident several years ago that caused him to miss a fair amount of school. As a result, his grades have suffered. Will colleges care about this and, if so, how can we make sure they know what has been going on?*

A You have just described a situation that provides important context for understanding your student's performance. In effect, the accident and the rehabilitation process help to frame his story. Admission committees *do* need to know about situations that have an impact on performance. He should talk about it in an interview. He needs to make sure that his college counselor includes a discussion of the trying circumstances in her letter of recommendation. And he it wouldn't hurt for him to address the situation in his personal statement or an additional statement that he can attach to his application.

Q *My son is very excited about a university and I am afraid he will want to apply Early Decision. This worries me because I am concerned about our ability to cover the cost. I don't want to break his heart, but what should I do?*

A Generally speaking, you need to make sure that any deal-breakers that you may have been harboring are put on the table. If you know that there will be financial or travel constraints, for example, now is the time to talk about them. Let him know of your concerns and offer to meet with a financial aid officer at the college to see if that person can give you a better sense of what your EFC is likely to be as well as strategies for managing your out-of-pocket expenses.

Q *What is the right number of colleges to which a student should apply?*

A If the objective of finding a good fit involves putting him on the right "playing field" or in the right competition, then he shouldn't need to apply to more than six colleges. This will allow him to take a shot at one or two schools that might be stretches for him—the playing field is somewhat above the place where he might compete most effectively. The rest, however, should be colleges or universities that match his credentials—places where the odds of getting in are at least 50/50.

Q *Is it possible for a student to get into a very selective university through an academic program that might not be quite as hard to get into and then transfer into the program he really wants after a semester or two?*

A It is not uncommon for students who aspire to highly selective universities to look for the easiest point of entry. You need to discourage the "back door approach"—the attempt to scheme one's way into the university through the least selective program. Should your student get into that program, he will be expected to stay in it. His only way out will be to transfer. Transferring in general can be difficult. Transferring between programs or colleges *within* a university that is managing its enrollment tightly is no different.

Chapter 14

Behind the Scenes with the Admission Committee

Mystery. Intrigue. The college fate of thousands of young people has long been shrouded in a secrecy that rivals papal selections! After months of diligent preparation, students turn their applications over to a selection process run by the "admission committee." It is behind the closed doors of the committee in the dead of winter that their college futures are divined.

This chapter unveils the mystery by taking a look at what happens to applications after they are submitted—how they processed, who reads them, and how decisions are made. First, though, we will take a look at the credential review within the context of the enrollment management objectives that are established at each college and university. In place before any applications are received or considered, these objectives provide the framework for what is to come.

Enrollment Objectives

Each new application season brings with it the opportunity for colleges and universities of all sizes and prominence to build communities that reflect their institutional missions and values. In doing so, they are driven by the need and/or desire to:

Between the Lines

Retention
Managing the retention of students through graduation has become a point of major interest to colleges. Not only is the retention rate a point of scrutiny in the college ranking process but the ability of an institution to retain students at a high level eases the pressure to bring in larger numbers of new students, thereby allowing for greater selectivity in the admission process.

- Meet absolute enrollment goals.

- Generate the necessary tuition revenue to secure the institutional operating budget.

- Determine the capacity of each applicant to meet the institution's academic expectations.

- Assemble a student body whose individual and collective talents are most highly valued by the institution.

- Build the class in a manner that brings distinction to the institution.

While the first three objectives are common to all institutions, the last two accrue to places that enjoy greater levels of selectivity. Each provides a strategic reference point to the admission committee.

The enrollment goal is the ultimate beacon for decision makers who must achieve a certain overall enrollment by the time classes begin. Arriving at that goal requires a delicate balancing act involving the enrollment of both new and returning students. Because the number of departing students, either through graduation, approved leaves of absence, or withdrawals, is fairly constant from year to year, the requirement for new students is constant as well.

The overall enrollment goal is driven by the need to secure the institution's operating budget. While most institutions are able to draw operating funds from their endowments, annual giving (gifts from alumni, parents, and friends), and the government, they are "tuition-driven." The bulk of their funding comes from tuition dollars. In projecting enrollments, colleges anticipate an average tuition contribution per student. For example, "X" number of students bringing "Y" number of dollars (on average) will result in total tuition revenue of "Z."

In achieving its enrollment goals, an institution must make certain the students it admits are capable of meeting its academic expectations. Despite a high level of self-selection on the part of applicants onto the right "playing field," some candidates are simply not good fits academically. In its initial review of candidates, an admission committee must make certain the students it will consider further are capable of performing at an acceptable level in the classroom. Colleges that are inundated with qualified candidates will choose carefully in assembling a student body whose individual and collective talents they value most highly. This orientation to admitting students is increasingly prevalent as your student moves up the Pyramid of Selectivity.

Finally, colleges and universities will, when possible, build their classes in a manner that brings distinction to their respective institutions. When you reflect on our earlier discussions of the "Hidden Agenda," though, you begin to understand where this may be coming from. Colleges and universities that are determined to secure and/or advance their positions in the pecking order will do what they can to make sure the statistics that describe their new students, as well as the selection processes that yielded them, reflect well when presented to the public. Fully aware that future rankings might rest on the outcomes, they want their numbers to look good.

As you can see, an institution's enrollment objectives play a large role in shaping its selection process. The larger and more selective the institution, the broader are the needs and the more complex is the process. The manner in which a set of credentials is regarded or valued will depend on what the institution needs at that particular moment in time.

Putting It Together: The "Doors of Enrollment"

Let's take the contextual discussion a step further. Remember, we are looking into the minds of enrollment managers on college campuses to develop a better understanding of how and why they do what they do. And let's agree that the "agendas" as well as the employment of certain decision-making logic correlates with an institution's standing on the Pyramid of Selectivity. For example:

- The need to consider a greater range of credentials in filling the class and meeting the budget becomes *greater as you proceed down* the Pyramid.

- The pressure to make fine distinctions between candidates and, in doing so, maintain a competitive selection profile *increases as you go up* the Pyramid.

Not surprisingly, many colleges are caught in the middle. While each might want to hold a higher ranking among its peers, it continues to feel some of the more fundamental pressures associated with filling the class. Such a college wants to lower the admit rate, improve the yield, and produce a higher test score profile while generating sufficient revenue to pay the bills. Keep these agendas in mind as we take a look at how the "Doors of Enrollment" provide strategic solutions to enrollment managers.

Now, let's assume that selective institutions (with deadline admission) typically enroll new first-year students through at least three different "doors"— Early Decision, Regular Decision, and Wait List. Each door is distinguished by the anticipated yield rate (percentage of admitted students who enroll) that can be attached to that "door" based on past performance.

At "College X," a fictitious institution that aspires to improve its competitive position while maintaining a stable operational profile, the yield rates we plug in are consistent with actual yield rates from past years. While somewhat arbitrary in this exercise, they are proportionate to each other and come close to reflecting the reality at many aspiring institutions that admit one third to one half of their respective applicants.

	Sample Yield Rates for "College X"		
	Early Decision	Regular Decision	Wait List
Typical Yield	very high	low	high
	(95–98 percent)	(18–22 percent)	(65–75 percent)

Note: *This chart does not reflect the percentage of applicants accepted for each category.* (Note further that improvements in yield *will* contribute to greater selectivity.) Acceptance rates are generally higher for students applying ED than for students who apply Regular Decision. We'll talk about the Wait List later.

Marching Orders

Imagine that you are a member of the enrollment group at College X. Before you look at a single application, you know that your college wants to become more selective while improving the yield. If you admitted 50 percent of your applicants last year, the pressure is on to admit 45 percent this year. If your overall yield was 27 percent, you need to get it up to 30 percent. (And make sure you improve the SAT profile by 10 points, but don't spend any more money on financial aid or scholarships!)

So, how do you make this happen? As you can see from the chart, history tells you to expect a yield of almost 100 percent on Early Decision. (Yield rates do not vary much from year to year.) The yield rate on offers through Regular Decision, though, is much lower. It would stand to reason, then, that College X might improve its yield and become more selective simply by taking a larger portion of its class through its Early Decision (ED) program. Let's take a look at why that might be the case.

Between the Lines

Calibration

In addition to being an important enrollment management tool, the Wait List also gives the Admission Committee an opportunity to fine-tune the class. Whatever needs (such as special talents) are not fully addressed through Early Decision or Regular Decision can be met strategically from the Wait List. The Wait List also allows the Committee to award its remaining financial aid dollars in much smaller increments.

For each offer of admission through ED at College X, you should expect a corresponding enrollment. If you admit 100 ED candidates, for example, you can expect nearly all—about 95 percent—to enroll. On the other hand, the yield on Regular Decision applicants is about 20 percent. If you want to enroll 100 students through Regular Decision, you will need to admit about 500. If you want to enroll 1,000, you will need to admit about 5,000 and so on.

Your marching orders at College X are to increase yield and become more selective. One solution is to increase the number of ED students you enroll from 150 to 200. If successful, the enrollment of 50 additional ED candidates in the current year would reduce by 50 the number of students to be enrolled through Regular Decision—and thus reduce by 250 the number *to be admitted* through Regular Decision in fleshing out the class. By admitting and enrolling 50 more ED candidates, the net reduction in the number of offers made is 200. When the dust settles, the yield will be higher and the college will appear to have become more selective.

If all of this seems like risky business, it isn't really. As I mentioned earlier, colleges can predict their yields on offers with a high degree of accuracy because they have history on their side. They can refer to years of results that afford them highly predictable trend lines. And if they come up short, they maintain Wait Lists as high-yield "insurance policies."

For example, if the actual yield is off by 1 percent on 4,000 offers of Regular Decision admission at College X, you are suddenly short of your class by 40 students. That's the bad news. The good news is the opportunity afforded by the scores of eager and qualified students on the Wait List. After all, the candidates on the Wait List are on the competitive bubble—they were near misses in terms of gaining admission through Regular Decision!

So, instead of having to admit 200 additional students at the yield rate (20 percent) through Regular Decision, the Wait List gives you the opportunity to fill the class with students who can be targeted for acceptance. (We'll talk more about the mechanics of that process in the next chapter.) At a yield rate of 65–75 percent, you can admit 60–65 students to get the 40 you need to round out the entering class.

Given your "marching orders," you might be looking at the 65–75 percent yield rate on students from the Wait List with curious temptation—as in, why don't we just plan to admit more students from the Wait List. If so, you are right on target! Many selective colleges *plan to admit a portion of the class from the Wait List*! Think about it. If College X can comfortably enroll 40 students by admitting 60–65 from the Wait List, then why not admit 200 fewer (yield rate of 20 percent) through Regular Decision? The net effect would be to reduce the overall number of offers made—become even more selective while improving the yield—under the cover of having to make difficult admission decisions.

This decision-making dynamic has become commonplace as institutions seek to preserve or advance their competitive positions. Some places that historically admitted more than half of their applicants have improved their selectivity by as many as 20–30 percentage points in just a few years, not by becoming much better academic places but by manipulating their respective enrollment processes.

Making Sense of Early Decision

Given the discussion thus far, it is easy to see how young people and their parents can become confused about how to approach the application process. Because of the media attention directed at Early Decision and Early Action, there is a tendency to think that applying "early" somewhere is the best strategy for getting in. I can't tell you the number of times that students *and parents* approach me with the assertion that they need to find colleges to which they can apply early. "I don't know where, but we need to find a place for my daughter to apply ED."

Be careful about slipping into that mindset. Yes, the stats say that it is easier to get into most selective colleges through ED programs. And, yes, by getting the application process out of the way early in the senior year the pressure will be off.

But, NO, applying Early Decision is not the panacea that it would appear to be. If admission to a highly selective institution was a long shot to begin with, it remains so for the ED candidate. And, frankly, the strategy might backfire. The number of students who are admitted ED to one of the "car sticker" schools but LEAVE in the first or second year because they are unhappy, or ill-fitted to the place, is troubling.

True Love

Choosing a college is a lot like choosing a partner for life. Just as you want your child to be discriminating in the choice of a partner for life, you should encourage her to be careful in the selection of a college. She should be diligent in getting to know everything there is to know about the place. She needs to see it at its best—and at its worst. She needs to be convinced beyond a shadow of a doubt that it is the best place for her.

Early Decision should be reserved for the students who have found the absolute best fit in a college. You need to make sure that you and your student are honest with each other about the root of her passions for a place. She may love it, but you need to make sure that her passion is well founded. If you see that emotions are running wild—that all objectivity has been lost and the college is, perhaps, not the absolute best fit for her—you need to throw on the brakes with regard to ED.

The key to this decision is really quite simple: Has your student fallen in love? Or is this a brief romance or flirtation? ED is a serious business and it involves a contract. It's nothing to play around with. As a parent, it is your job to be sure that the love is true and not fickle – and that *you* are not being a party to a potential "shotgun marriage."

It is through the "true love" metaphor we can illustrate the difference between Early Decision and Early Action (EA). You'll remember that, at a handful of colleges, EA enables your student to get early, but nonbinding feedback to her expression of first-choice interest. Whereas ED is binding, much like marriage, EA allows the student and the college to test their feelings for each other without a commitment. A successful EA experience has the effect of putting the two parties in a situation of saying: "This was good. Let's keep talking."

In a nutshell, don't push ED or EA unless you are convinced it is the right thing for your student. In other words, can she demonstrate why the choice makes good sense? "But Dad, I *really* like it," may be enough to melt your heart, but does it really form the basis of a lasting commitment?

When True Love Isn't Reciprocated

If your student elects to proceed with an Early Decision application, she will be greeted with one of three responses by the school to which she applies: 1. Acceptance—let's do this! 2. Denial—it isn't going to happen—ever, or 3. Deferral—maybe later.

Clearly, the student who is applying ED is banking on the acceptance. And colleges, particularly those with agendas to improve yield and selectivity, tend to look optimistically at ED applicants: "If we *think* we *might* admit you later, we will admit you now." That logic doesn't apply to the ED program at every college, though.

You need to be ready for this uncertainty. Few things can be more devastating to a young person than being spurned by the university that is her true love. Even if she is guarding herself against disappointment, anything less than good news could cause a meltdown. If you have watched her break up with a boyfriend, you can measure the emotional recoil on a similar scale! It won't be easy, especially as some of her friends are likely to be accepted at their ED colleges. In the event that an ED application doesn't go well, here are a few thoughts that might help the two of you find the silver lining and move beyond the feelings of utter disappointment and rejection.

Keys to Rebounding for Success

1. **Encourage your student to stay focused academically** and to provide as much new information as possible about her performance both in and outside of the classroom. Deferred candidates will be evaluated again in the Regular Decision Process.
2. **Avoid the "let's just wait and see" mistake.** Her ardor might be rewarded—or it might not be. Help her move on to her next choices. The odds are she will need them.
3. **While denial may feel harsh, she will at least have time to regroup and focus on other options.** It would be, harder to do this later if the bad news were to come at the end of the Regular Decision process.
4. **Admission committees can be awfully arbitrary and they don't always get it right.** She shouldn't stop feeling good about herself. And you certainly must not give her the slightest hint that you are disappointed in her. You may not like the decision, but your love and support can never be regarded as conditional in this process.

5. **A college's decision to defer or deny is a reflection of where its admission officials see her credentials relative to those of other candidates.** She is still a bright and talented young person. Discovering this reality about "fit" should help her calibrate further as she considers her other college options. There are scores of other schools out there that will *value her for what she does well!*

A Fly in the ED Ointment—Financial Aid

A "deal killer" for many students who have found true love in a college is the cost of attending. It may be easy for your student to find colleges that, in the abstract, fit her well. She will meet people she likes. Mesmerized by the institution's culture, she will love the buildings and immediately find the environment to be cozy. (She may even be persuaded that the academic program has something to offer.) Just when nothing could be more perfect, the question of "how in the world are we going to afford all of this" rears it ugly head. She's making plans to outfit her new dorm room. You're calling the accountant! You don't want to disappoint her but are panic stricken at the thought of facing college costs that rival the payments you make on your car—or your house!

What do you do? Call it all off? The last thing you want to do is disappoint her. On the other hand, these are big dollar signs you are looking at. Could she possibly get financial aid? And how would raising the question affect her chances of getting in as an ED candidate?

Unfortunately, the responses to these questions vary as widely as the colleges of which they are asked. Just as each maintains its own posture with regard to admitting students, it does the same with regard to administering need-based or merit-based financial aid. You will hear things like:

1. "We don't award financial aid in the Early Decision process. If receiving aid is vital to your enrollment, then you shouldn't apply ED." (They want to look at all of their aid applicants together in order to determine where they want to invest their money.)

2. "We treat all of our candidates, ED and Regular Decision, the same when it comes to awarding need- or merit-based aid." (This is often the case. As soon as any school offers a financial aid award, though, it has begun to spend down its budget for aid.)

3. "We award financial aid to ED candidates who need it." However, the college may elect to "low-ball" its offer on the assumption that your student wants to be there so badly she will accept a lesser award in order to enroll.

Whether your student needs financial aid, deserves scholarship recognition for her achievements, or you simply would like a gesture of support from the college to which she wants to pledge herself, you need to resolve these issues before she applies ED—anywhere! Remember, her ED application is a statement of commitment. If accepted, it is expected that she will enroll. Period.

Further complicating the situation is the fact that many institutions that do offer financial aid to ED applicants may not provide offers until *after* the enrollment deposit is due. Even then, they are likely to provide tentative awards that require verification of your family's income for the most recent year through the submission of tax forms. Nonetheless, if admitted ED, your student will be required to confirm her commitment by submitting a *nonrefundable* enrollment deposit. This is a situation you need to get your arms around early in the process if you hope to see a happy ending.

Solving the Money Problem for the ED Candidate

Act early to size up the money situation. Have the money conversation with your child before her passion for a place is overwhelming. If you *know* that a university is not affordable without assistance, there is no sense pretending otherwise. On the other hand, make sure you have all the facts from the financial aid office at that school before writing it off completely. Find out if you can afford it. You owe it to your student—and yourself—to discover what the real cost to you will be.

Normally an ED agreement can be cancelled if the financial aid award is not adequate. "Adequate" doesn't mean that she gets what you *want* her to get. Rather, "adequate" means that the university has met your financial *need* as determined by the FAFSA and/or PROFILE.

Things to Consider as You Advise Your Student Regarding Early Commitments

- Make sure you are familiar with the NCAA rules regarding commitments at the level at which she would like to compete. Do this by the end of her junior year.

- Remember that your student may be an active Early Decision candidate at one college at a time. If she is deferred or denied at her first ED school, she becomes a "free agent" and may pursue another ED application at a new first-choice school.

- If she applies ED to one university, she would be well-advised to submit applications for Regular Admission to several others in the event that her ED application is not successful. If she is admitted ED, she will be required to withdraw all of the other applications immediately even though she may not have received decisions from those schools.

- It is possible for a student who has applied Regular Decision to a college to change the status of that application (convert) to Early Decision. If this possibility is raised with your student by a recruiter, make sure that her response is consistent with her priorities and her preparation to commit.

- Colleges and universities share lists of admitted students. This is especially true of close competitors and/or institutions that participate in consortium activities. Such schools will know if a student has applied to ED to more than one place at a time or that an admitted ED candidate has not withdrawn her other applications.

- Be wary of pre-application scholarship offers or guarantees of admission. Read the fine print. While the offers may be valid, they may draw your student (and you) into a premature emotional response that precludes her consideration of other options.

- Early Acceptance is an option that some universities extend to students who wish to leave high school at the end of the junior year. Such acceptances are conditional on the high school's approval and stipulation that the first year of college will satisfy any remaining requirements for high school graduation.

The Race to Become More Selective and Improve Yield

As colleges and universities manage their enrollments, they draw from a range of tactics to become more selective, improve the yield, and, quite often, produce higher measures of student performance (higher SAT/ACT scores, stronger profile of GPAs, etc.). In addition to the creative use of Early Decision and the Wait List, don't be surprised if your student encounters the following tactics.

- Application fee waivers offered to students who visit campus or apply online—the more students applying, the greater the selectivity.

- Promises of special opportunities (scholarships, preferred housing, etc.) for an early enrollment commitment.

- Mailing of "likely" letters informing her that her chances are looking good in advance of formal decision letters.

- Tracking of demonstrated interest ("if we accept her, will she come?").

- Offers of special enrollment opportunities overseas or at other universities for the first semester. This enables institutions to draw more "on-the-bubble," "full pay" students into the overall enrollment without having to account for them or their credentials on published profiles of entering students.

Between the Lines

Winning the Fame Game
Many institutions operate from the perspective of "what we have is not good enough if we want to maintain our standing among our peers." By manipulating their enrollment processes, they have not substantially changed anything qualitative about their learning environments. They haven't become "better." To the extent that selectivity is equated with quality, though, they have changed the perception of quality in order to win points in the "fame game."

Application Life Cycle

Armed with an appreciation for the strategic orientation admission officers bring to the credential review, let's take a look at how they actually get the job done. We move forward with the caveat that, just as priorities vary across institutions, so do the credential review processes. Consider, then, the life cycle of an application *after* your student has put the finishing touches on it.

The day the application is received by an admission office, often with thousands of other pieces of mail, it is checked for completeness and processed with other applications. Applications with fees attached are matched with other credentials already on file such as letters of recommendation, transcripts, test scores and notes taken from meetings or interviews with the student. Applications without application fees or an approved fee waiver are separated for appropriate follow-up.

A card or e-mail is sent to the applicant acknowledging receipt of the application and informing her of any required materials that might be missing. It is possible in the case of electronically submitted applications that notices of missing materials are sent when in fact the "missing materials" are simply arriving a day or two later via snail mail. Should your student receive such a message, she should double-check the dates when she mailed the "missing materials" before putting out an "all points bulletin" in search of the missing goods.

Soon after the application and related materials are processed, a file is created for the application contents. Any later-arriving information, including new grades and test score information, will be added to the file. Some colleges will immediately scan the application documents into a digital file that can be viewed electronically. In either case, a candidate evaluation form is typically added to the file onto which reviewers will later record their comments. Institutions that have tracked the contacts initiated by your student over time will also quantify her demonstrated interest and campus visit information in some way in the file.

As soon as the applications are complete and ready for review, they are submitted to an initial screening. Depending on the size and complexity of the institution, candidates may be grouped by high school, or the academic degree program for which they are competing, or the scholars program for which they are being considered. At universities that are large and/or highly selective, the screening is often computerized using values derived from test scores, classroom performance, and strength of academic program. Students whose credentials are either not qualified or not likely to be competitive are pulled out of the competition and marked for denial. Some highly selective institutions use a numeric index to indicate the relative strength of each candidate. Applicants whose index scores fall below a certain point are screened out of the competition at this point as well.

The Admission Committee

The actual composition and organization of the Admission Committee vary from school to school. When eyes first meet paper (or the file on the computer screen) at most schools, they belong to members of the admission staff—full-time professionals who have been engaged in other aspects of planning and recruitment throughout the year. There is a good chance that one of them will be the staff person who is responsible for recruiting in your region.

Faculty members may join the review of candidates who are competing for entrance into their respective degree programs and may contribute to the assessment of candidates for scholarships and honors programs. At highly selective schools, additional readers are employed on a part-time basis during the heart of the credential review season. The objective: Identify from a pool of well-qualified candidates those who will best enable the institution to satisfy its various agendas.

Admission Committees vary in size from 3 to 50—and they don't always resemble committees! Some credential reviews feature a small group of readers who review applications together, debating the merits of each and arriving at a consensus with regard to who should get the nod. Other committees are staffed by individuals who read assigned packets of credentials in the privacy of their offices or even their homes where they independently develop perspectives about each candidate that are compared with those of other readers until a consensus is reached.

The more complex and competitive the candidate pool, the more decision-making "filters" are employed. In relatively open selection processes, the review of a single reader might suffice in moving the applicant through to an offer of admission. Conversely, a successful candidate at colleges near the top of the Pyramid may be reviewed by as many as 3 individuals *and* a committee charged with sorting out cases on the "bubble" before gaining acceptance.

However they are organized, application readers typically try to establish a bias with each application they pick up—a bias that can then be proved or disproved by quickly reading through the balance of the application. Some readers are predisposed to finding something to like about the candidate. At the more selective schools, though, it is easy to become jaded when wading through a seemingly endless supply of applicants with superstar credentials. (A single reader at such schools may participate in the evaluation of more than 1,000 applications over a three to four month period.) After a while, these readers find themselves looking for reasons to deny applicants!

Hotspots and Hooks

A reader's orientation to the application is influenced by the matrix of variables that emerge from her institution's agendas for enrollment. Although a typical application might include fifteen to eighteen pages of supporting material, an experienced reader can develop a strong and pretty accurate bias in less than a minute. She can do this can scanning half a dozen or so "hotspots" on the application for evidence of "hooks."

Hooks are good things. They are the talents, perspectives, and experiences—gifts, if you will—that set your student apart from her peers. Count academic achievements among the most important of the hooks. Readers at the most selective universities often start with the transcript in establishing their biases. If they don't see evidence of rigor and high achievement, it will be a short read. Let's take a look at some of the other possible hotspots frequented by readers.

Sample Hotspots

- Student's home and/or school address—either might provide an indication that the student will bring a unique perspective rooted in the cultural experience of her geographic background.

- The student's selection of an academic interest may indicate that she is eager to study in a discipline of the college that might be underpopulated.

- A student's family background provides interesting perspective and context for many of the events and achievements in her life. The fact that she may be related to someone who attends or attended the institution, though, makes her a legacy applicant and may give her an advantage. Except for schools at the top of the Pyramid—those accepting fewer than 25 percent of their applicants—the legacy factor is often a tie-breaker—or more—in a close competition.

- The section of the application featuring academic honors and extracurricular activities and achievements is your student's resume. It is her opportunity to provide an orientation to her gifts or what she has done to "fill her canvas."

- The personal statement or essay provides an interesting canvas in and of itself. While most students shrink from this assignment, some will leap at the opportunity to use that space to create a hook for the reader.

If, in perusing the "hotspots," a reader discovers what might become a "hook," he will then look to the rest of the application for consistency and to the letters of recommendation for validation. It's easy for students to make claims or overstate their involvements and achievements. An experienced reader will look for evidence of depth and consistency in what the student reports. And when a teacher attaches an independent testimonial—*that* speaks volumes to the admission committee.

The Application Life Cycle Continues

As the winter months advance, so does the application life cycle. Decision making becomes more intensely difficult as the realities of supply and demand hit home. There are simply too many good candidates for the available places. Tired but undaunted, the readers press onward until all of the fine distinctions have been made. This could take four weeks or four months depending on the size of

Between the Lines

Special Case Admission

As coaches and others make their pitches for candidates on the bubble, it is not uncommon for the dean of admission to respond with the following qualifier: "Give me evidence that she is *that* good and evidence that she will enroll if admitted and then we'll talk." Special case students can find admission into places where they may be off-profile academically if they can provide compelling evidence of their talents as well as their desire to attend.

the applicant group. With each round of discussions, though, the scrutiny intensifies around those candidates who remain standing.

A critical determinant among the selective colleges at this stage of the process is the student's performance in the senior year. Looking for the slightest indication that a talented student is losing focus in the classroom, admission officers take this opportunity—at the end of first semester of the senior year—to contact high schools for updates on the student's performance. Woe be unto the student for whom senioritis has begun to set in!

Near the end of the credential review, usually sometime in early March, the Committee will step back and take stock of its class. It will also hear presentations on behalf of students on the academic "bubble" whose hooks or gifts may not have been fully quantified earlier. This is when athletic coaches, music directors, and the alumni officers make impassioned pleas for their favorites and when committees will make sure students of underrepresented ethnic and cultural groups have been given appropriate consideration.

The "Hidden Agenda" also looms large in the latter days of the decision making as questions of "What are the chances that she will enroll if we admit her?" and "Can we really afford to commit $25,000 to a student on the bubble?" need to be answered. This tinkering with the edges of the class can cut both ways. While it might result in opportunities for some, it can also mean that some candidates with strong academic records might be reassigned to the Wait List in order to make room for the flashy talents. Remember, the Committee is not obligated to admit a student simply because she is well qualified!

By the end of March, most schools are ready to mail their decision letters. As you can see, what might begin as a fairly systematic and "fair" review process is now something far more subjective. This is inevitable given the ever-changing and heavily nuanced institutional agendas. Mix in fatigue, cynicism, and a few bad days on the part of readers here and there and you find a process that is far from precise. Just when your student is banking on fairness and logic in the determination of outcomes, they prove to be most elusive.

And it all happens in silence. The seemingly incessant recruitment banter that brought her to the brink of applying will be gone as the decisions are being made. Admission officers won't be calling with periodic updates. They won't drop your student a note to gauge her level of interest or to find out if she really needs $25,000 of financial aid. Instead, she will be enveloped in silence.

Your role as a parent at this time of the year is to keep her spirits up while maintaining her focus on her school work. Be careful not to bug her with the usual questions: "So, what do you think they're doing now?" "Do you think we should ask your Uncle Seymour to write? After all, he went there." "When do you think we'll hear from them? It's been a long time, you know."

Believe me, she knows! Now, *you* need to get ready to manage the eruption of emotions that is bound to flow when the decision letters begin to arrive in your mailbox.

Chapter 15

The Envelope, Please

"*Congratulations! We are pleased to offer you a place in the class . . .*"
The long awaited "thick" envelope has arrived. After months, if not years, of preparation and anticipation, your student gleefully reads the good news that he now holds in his hands. These words are sure to put a smile on any student's face—and a warm glow in his parent's heart.

As the countdown to college continues, this is the scenario you hope will unfold. Having read this far, though, you are no doubt hesitant, if not cynical, about forecasting outcomes. Your caution grows in direct proportion to the selectivity of the colleges to which your student has applied. You have seen how arbitrary the process can be and know there is little assurance that even great credentials will be rewarded justly. Anything can happen. You can only wait—and hope.

The last days of the college admission process are also a time of high anxiety—a time that requires a parent's calming presence. Nobody needs to tell you what is at stake. You will see constant reminders in the media. It will be the topic of daily conversation at home, at school, and at work.

"Have you heard yet?" "Does he know where he wants to go?" "Did you hear about Molly—can you believe she didn't get in?!"

As the days drag on, the angst and speculation mount for your student. The "what ifs" and "why nots" abound. You will learn that there is no middle ground. As the competition comes to a close and the decisions become known, emotions drawn tight over weeks and months of waiting are suddenly let go in shrieks of excitement and wails of despair. Even students who are admitted to one or more schools will be disconsolate when the places they *really* wanted turn them down. It will be up to you to keep the highs from getting too high and the lows from becoming too devastating. The answers *will* come.

Between the Lines

Choose ONE!

Multiple acceptances often mean difficult decisions. It is imperative that your student choose only one college. Despite the temptation to submit enrollment deposits to several universities so he can decide later, choosing such a course of action can backfire. Institutions need to get a handle on their enrollments and will compare enrollment lists for precisely this reason. Students found to have deposits at multiple schools will often be required to forfeit all enrollments.

Acceptance

This is the good news—and it does indeed come in the "thick" envelope with letters, forms, and invitations to this open house and that reception. The meaning, though, is clear. That college wants *your student*! He has a place to go. Deservedly happy, he can relax now—and breathe! And you can pop a few buttons as well!

But what does this mean? Is this an offer of admission to the college of his choice? Or is he still sorting that out? If he applied Early Decision, the game is over. He has landed right where he wants to be. If he did not apply ED and this is his first acceptance letter, the waiting will continue until all of the verdicts are in. At least he knows, though, that he has an opportunity. Hopefully, the rest of the decision letters will yield good news and more options.

Options are good as they afford him the opportunity to choose between the colleges that fit him best. As his options become clear, the next step will be for him to narrow them down by refocusing on the priorities he established earlier in the planning process. They can be an effective roadmap for him at this stage. If he already knows where he wants to go and the road is clear of potential financial "land-mines," then he's in good shape. All he needs to do is complete the enrollment agreement and submit it with his enrollment deposit. Be prepared, though, for a mixed bag of results as the decision letters roll in. The odds are that your student will be admitted to some, turned down at a few, and placed on a Wait List at one or two others.

Wait List

Ah, the Wait List. The owner of many identities—few of them fair or accurate—the Wait List is an outcome that students rarely embrace. Regarded as admission purgatory—the student is neither in nor out—or evidence of a polite denial, the Wait List actually holds much greater promise to those who read the fine print.

Between the Lines

Rules for Overtime

As colleges move to fill their classes from the Wait List, they will:

1. Act quickly and efficiently. They will call with offers that require immediate response. Make sure your student knows how he will respond if called.

2. Move strategically. They will take stock of unfilled needs in the class already enrolled and look for opportunities to fill those needs.

3. Follow the cash. Students who do not need assistance are more attractive at a time when the overall financial aid picture remains unsettled. Students with need may be called later when it is determined that sufficient funding is available to accommodate them.

4. Be discrete. Even though they may plan to use the Wait List in completing their enrollments, they will do so quietly.

Much like the congratulatory letter of acceptance, a Wait List letter might start off "We are pleased to offer you a place on the Wait List . . ." While this hardly sounds like a vote of confidence, the college in question is really saying, "There is a lot to like about your application. We can't take you now because we are rolling the dice on a higher yield on our regular offers of admission. If we come up short, though, we'll need more students. *Hang in there*, we might be able to admit you later."

There you go. The Wait List message is a definite maybe. As you saw when we discussed the "Doors of Enrollment," many places are reluctant to admit any more students than is absolutely necessary. After all, why take hundreds of students at a yield rate of 20 percent when you can take a fraction of that number at a rate of 70 percent!

Beginning in the middle of April, enrollment managers will do two things on a daily basis: monitor their new enrollments and manage the information they have about the "active" Wait List. By checking their enrollment patterns against those of past years, they can tell whether they are "yielding" according to plan. If they seem to be running short, they will scramble their staffs to begin calling Wait Listed students with offers of admission.

Wait Lists *will be* active—you can book it—especially at colleges that have a lot at stake in preserving if not improving the measures of their selectivity. So, urge your student to hang in there. Point out that the letter doesn't say "We don't want you." On the contrary, it is saying, "This may not be the news you wanted, but it isn't over yet." In the lines that follow the seemingly hollow greeting, he will find instructions for the students who wish to *remain active* on the Wait List.

In many ways, Wait List status signals the beginning of another round of play. The game has gone into overtime. Those who choose to play still have a chance at winning. Conversely, the candidates who feel betrayed and assume there is nothing more to be gained—who walk away from the game as it goes into overtime—have no chance at all.

Denial

There is little ambiguity about the thin envelope bearing a short message. No matter how pleasant the tone or sincere the attempt to portray the candidate pool as "the most competitive ever," the words ring hollow. "Denied." "Rejected." "Turned down." They all say the same thing to the once hopeful recipient.

Unfortunately, the quick translation is "They don't want me." Or, "I'm not good enough." When this sort of rhetoric begins to surface, you need to help your student find perspective. The hard truth is that the selection process is the *institution's* opportunity to identify the students who would best fit its agenda. Disagreeable as the outcome might be, it is what it is. If he did his homework before applying, he knew what the odds where from the very start. In the end, he wasn't regarded as a good fit. That might not feel very good and it might not even be fair. It is real, though.

How often is it the case, though, that when one door closes, another opens? It's time to start focusing on "plan B." There are plenty of places that *will* value him for what he does well. Those are the places with great programs that, while they may not have been prominent on *his* radar screen, would be thrilled to be able to engage him in their learning environments.

The even better news is that, rotten as he might feel at the moment, this outcome doesn't change the person. Don't let the bad news affect his sense of self-worth. Give him a hug and let him know that this turn of events doesn't change the way you feel about him. He's still number one in your book!

Next Steps

When all of the decisions are in, your student needs to take stock of his next steps. Finishing this process well is just as important as getting it started on the right foot. Whether he has five clear options, two that are clear and two that are still outstanding, or just one offer of acceptance, he needs to collect himself in order to make a deliberate, well-reasoned selection that will serve him well over the next four years. The following are steps he should take in response to various scenarios moving toward a final decision.

When he has been admitted to several schools, including one or two of his favorites, he should:

- Plan visits to each college. Many colleges offer open house programs for admitted students. If he can't attend an open house, urge him to schedule a visit on his own. This is his opportunity to give each school a thorough "once over" before deciding. When possible, he should stay overnight, attend classes, and talk with professors. He needs to take advantage of this opportunity to soak it all in—to watch and listen. In the end, his selection may boil down to a "gut" feeling. He needs to let his gut go to work for him.

    Note to Parents: You need to disappear. If you are traveling together, take advantage of this time to go shopping, see the sights, or visit with friends in the area. You need to give your student space to do his thing.

- Talk with upperclass students and recent graduates. They are in a better position to objectively assess the school's strengths and weaknesses. They can also speak to and, hopefully, validate from their own experiences the value-added components touted by the institution's literature. On the other hand, first- and second-year students can be loose cannons. While they are certain to share enthusiastically—their perspectives will make "good copy"—they are still finding their own ways through the college experience.

Note to Parents: Avoid name-dropping or revealing strategic anecdotes from your own sources to your student. He is trying to arrive at his own points of validation. However well intended your insights might be, they will do more to raise questions in his mind than to provide answers. He will ask for your thoughts—and those of others—when he is ready.

- Get expert advice. If he is focused on a particular career academic program or career track, it won't hurt for him to pick the brains of one or two professionals in those fields. They will let him know what they valued most about their own academic preparation and will have informed opinions about the college options he is considering.

Note to Parents: College rankings do not qualify as expert advice. They might have been useful at one point in giving your student a general direction, but their usefulness has come to an end. You are now helping your student find the best school for him, not the "best" according to a published ranking list.

When he has been admitted to several schools, none of which were ranked among his favorites, he should:

- Be reminded that he hasn't failed. After all, these are the colleges that value him most. If they reached his short list because he regarded them as good "fits" for him, then he may well be on the verge of finding a wonderful college match!

Note to Parents: Reinforce the positive aspects of your student's situation. He is in a good position if he is holding offers from one or more of the colleges that he included on his short list. It really is not acceptable for him to say "but I really don't want to go there" in response to one of these places. When that happens, it is usually an indication he is listening to voices that tell him the "grass is greener in other pastures." Resist the temptation to declare a "failed search" in order to look for new options *unless* his circumstances have truly changed (your family is moving, there are health issues, etc.).

- Follow the procedures outlined above for addressing the colleges that have admitted him. The sooner he becomes engaged in these activities, the easier it will be for him to remove the sting of the disappointing news from the other schools.

When he has been admitted to several schools, but has been offered Wait List status at one or two that he really likes, he should:

- Contact the schools at which he has been offered Wait List status to let them know of his continued interest *if he wishes to remain active on their Wait Lists*. His communication must indicate his desire to attend if admitted and include:

  *New grades (if they show improvement)
  *An updated resume
  *Changes that might have occurred to your family's financial situation
  *Current contact information (include personal cell phone number)

Note to Parents: This message needs to be personally conveyed by your student. Refrain from writing letters or placing phone calls on his behalf—unless you are writing to verify that you no longer need financial assistance. If this is the case despite an earlier indication of demonstrated need, you need to be prepared to indicate the source of the funding that will cover his expenses for the next four years.

- Be mindful of the timeline as outlined for admitted students at the colleges that have placed him on the Wait List. While he may not yet hold an offer of admission in his hands, he will not be given much time to decide if/when such an offer does arrive.

- Be sure to show the universities that have admitted him some love (see above). IF the Wait List situation doesn't work out, he will need to embrace one of them as his college home. He cannot afford to become distracted by the Wait List situation to the extent that he fails to productively come to grips with the offers he has in hand.

Between the Lines

"The Call"

Implementation of the Wait List strategy will vary from school to school. In most instances, though, the targeted student receives a call that begins with a verbal inquiry into his level of interest. If the response is positive and enthusiastic, the caller will then make a conditional offer: "The place in the class is there if you want it. But if you don't want it or can't commit now, we will need to offer the place to someone else." It is only after the student says, "Yes, I'll take it" that a formal letter of acceptance is generated. The enrollment deposit may be required immediately unless the May 1 Candidate's Rely Date has not been passed.

- Understand that there is no timetable for colleges when it comes to moving the Wait List. The calls might come anytime from the middle of April through the middle of June. He needs to be prepared to commit to one of the universities that admitted him in the event that he doesn't receive a call from one of the Wait List situations.

- Keep all colleges informed of his decisions. If he chooses to hold a place at one college while actively pursuing admission from the Wait List at another, he needs to notify the former (and forfeit his enrollment) should he accept an offer of acceptance from the Wait List at the latter.

When financial aid is a determining factor, he should:

- Compare the cost of attending or Estimated Family Contribution (EFC) for each institution. This is the final discounted price—the amount your family will need to cover after all of the need-based aid, scholarships, and loans have been factored in. He should not compare financial aid awards or the amounts of scholarships received. This is all ego food. Taken out of context—without regard to the list price or the comprehensive fee that may include another $2,000 to $3,000 in related fees—a relatively large scholarship at one school may still leave more out-of-pocket expenses than a smaller scholarship at a school with a lower price tag.

- Reconcile the differences in the size and composition of financial aid awards at comparably priced institutions. It is possible that a school will match the offer of a competitor. This happens when an institution either misreads his need analysis or deliberately "low-balls" him in an attempt to secure his enrollment with the lowest possible investment. Some schools will entertain, if not encourage, an appeal; others will not. He has nothing to lose by asking.

  Note to Parents: Most successful appeals are driven by data, not emotions. If you do become involved, remember that you are seeking clarity and fair treatment. You cannot, however, expect or even insist that your student is entitled to anything more.

- Take a close look at the composition of the financial aid award. Some institutions are clever about putting together a combination of loans and work study that dramatically inflate the perceived value of the award.

- Assess the value of each opportunity relative to the cost of attendance—and this is a conversation that should include you. By assessing the value, he is able to arrive at a justification for how much of the cost your family is able/willing to absorb. For example, your family may be willing to take on a higher out-of-pocket cost at one university if he is persuaded that there is a great benefit to attending that institution. In assessing value, he should focus on the priorities—and elements of a good fit—he established earlier in the college search.

Note to Parents: Resist the temptation to play the cost card (i.e., "If you choose the less expensive school, I'll have enough money to buy you a new car."). That's dirty pool! Such an offer unfairly equates the value of a new car with the cost of an education—who wouldn't find a new car attractive! By appealing to his emotions, you distract him from making the best decision about his educational future. Ironically, the new car won't hold its value—and certainly not its novelty—as long as a college education.

If he doesn't get in anywhere, he should:

- Take a step back to assess the situation. What may have contributed to this set of outcomes? Did he over-value himself? Had he been careful to discover schools that would *value* him? Shutouts like this are not random occurrences. If he can determine why he is without options, it will help him to begin planning an alternative course.

- Revisit his priorities with an eye toward identifying a group of schools that possess the same qualities as those he initially targeted but are somewhat less selective.

Note to Parents: Remember, these outcomes are not a reflection on your son or your family. He has not failed nor is he incompetent. You must not let him feel that way. He must also be reminded that finding the best college for him is a process and not an event. Each student arrives at his/her point of discovery by different means and according to timetables that are peculiar to each. He's no different from anybody else. He'll be okay.

- Talk with his college adviser to determine which schools among those that might now be of interest to him are willing to accommodate late applications.

- Contact these schools directly to inquire about the possibility of a late application. He needs to be prepared to present the application, often in person. In many cases, a potential offer of admission will be contingent on his willingness to commit to the school. He should not be surprised by such a condition and would be wise to consider his response in advance.

Tidbits to Tuck Away

- Colleges do share enrollment lists. Your student does NOT want to end up on more than one list! He needs to be prepared to honor the commitments that he has made.

- Colleges are serious about the senior year. In fact, the more selective the college, the less inclined it will be to continue a student's enrollment if he fails to live up to the condition of his acceptance. *Colleges do check grades through graduation.* Much as your student might feel that he has earned the opportunity to relax at the end of the senior year, his actions over the final two months could put his status as an enrolled student in jeopardy.

- Colleges make budget assumptions for four years. In other words, they assume that your family will maintain the same level of financial support (EFC) through graduation. As a result, it would not be wise for you to pool your resources to make it appear as though your student will have no "need" only to surface with a substantial need in subsequent years. While colleges will be sympathetic to changes in circumstance (unusual medical expenses, changes in employment, etc.), they are much less inclined to respond to your sudden poverty owing to a money management choice on your part.

- Every year, nearly 2 million students enter college. A vast majority of them attend institutions that don't appear prominently in the media or near the top of the Pyramid. And most of them are happy with their choices. They learn and grow through their experiences on their way to becoming productive members of society. Your student's future fortunes will hinge less on where he goes to college—and more on what he does with the opportunities present at that college.

Final Thoughts

You are discovering that, even at the latter stages of the college admission process, your student is likely to encounter the unexpected. The good news is that the final decision making shouldn't take more than a month as most colleges and universities require enrollment deposits by the Candidates Reply Date (May 1). (The notable exceptions are the students who might be receiving late offers of admission.) The bad news is that the thirty days of decision making can feel like utter chaos!

The end of the college admission process is marked by poetic irony. A time of great anticipation, it is the culmination of years invested in achieving the right outcome. It is also a time of happiness and a time of tears—of dreams realized and of near misses. Stay focused and don't panic. If you have gotten this far, the end is in sight. Besides, good plans are bound to produce positive results!

Epilogue

"Don't worry, Dad. You and Mom have done a good job. I'm going to be fine."

They came out of nowhere—words of comfort to an anxious parent. How could she have known, though, about the knot that had formed in my stomach as we finished packing and then tightened as we headed down the highway? Was it the contemplative quiet that filled the car during our early morning drive? Or the distant look in my eyes?

I thought I had hidden it well. After all, this was supposed to be an exciting time—her time. Heidi—the same young woman who less than a year earlier wasn't sure college was on her radar screen—was now reassuring her dad that everything would be fine, that he had done "a good job." Everything would be fine.

I looked over at my daughter and smiled. Words weren't necessary. She was right, though. Maybe it had been my job to worry, to think of the next steps, and to anticipate what might lay around the corner. Dads do that. Yet, somehow she knew that it was time for me to step aside—to give it a rest. Now it was her turn. She was ready to begin writing the next chapter of her life. The calm in her voice said it all. She would indeed be fine—and so would I.

You Will Survive!

It will be over before you know it—and probably before you are ready. After years of anticipation and planning, the college process will blow through your life like a twister. You see it coming and brace yourself. Then, as though punched by high winds and slammed by rising waters, you are overcome by the elements. Order gives way to chaos for what seems like eternity. Nothing can prepare you for the onslaught of late-night editing, the panicked rush to beat deadlines, the "forced marches" to college campuses, and the constant wrangling over what to do and how to do it.

And then it's over. In a flash, the college process becomes history—an apt metaphor regarding your lives together. One minute you speculate with your student about the "what if" and "wouldn't it be nice" scenarios. The next, she's on her way. With very little time to adjust, your role will be reduced to that of long-distance spectator. You give the better part of your adult life to making sure she has these opportunities—and then, in an instant, it happens. All you can do is watch.

This is a long way of saying you *will* survive the college process. She will emerge as the young adult who is ready to move out of your shadows and onto the center stage of opportunity that she has defined for herself in life. And, while you will never stop wanting the best for her and worrying that she has what she needs, you'll be able to step back and enjoy the "becoming" of this young person about whom you care so deeply. So, yes, you will both be fine. Having gone through this wringer three times and having learned something from each experience, I would offer three bits of advice in an attempt to ease this passage for you.

One, smile and relax—on both the inside and the outside. This process is too important and life is too short for this process to be taken too seriously. The opportunity to pursue a college education is one of the greatest gifts you can give your child. Give it unconditionally. Give it with love. And celebrate the occasion.

Two, recognize that the gift you are extending is that of an opportunity, not a place. Much as you might want to see your student at one place or another, you can't expect this process to work out according to your formula. If the outcomes match your expectations, that's great. If not, the giving continues. Be careful not to attach a value to your student that is a reflection of where she may or may not have gotten in.

And three, don't try to tinker with the genetic code. She is who she is. Don't try to make her into something else so she will get into the colleges you have in mind. I run into lots of parents who set high expectations for their kids and then are disappointed when the expectations aren't met. While it is natural to have such expectations—and to feel disappointment—you need to remember that the feelings are yours. Handling them is your problem. It is unfair to burden your child with the weight of failed expectations. As parents, we forget too easily that growing up is a process. It happens in different ways at different times for each of us. She'll be fine. She just needs to know that you have her back.

Best Wishes!

When I started this book, my intent was to contribute to happy endings. I wanted to share what I had learned about an increasingly complex process so that young people might give themselves the best opportunity to experience the college options they deserve. Many titles on the subject are targeted at students who are college-specific in their searches. As you have no doubt realized, this book does not contain the formula for admission to any school in particular. I have not provided summer camp suggestions, lists of essay topics, or questions to ask in an interview.

In truth, authors don't get kids into college. Neither do consultants or special summer programs. Kids get themselves into college. I have attempted to teach you and your student how to think about the process so you can support her in making productive choices—choices that will give her access to colleges that value her for who she is. I trust the information and insight included in these pages has given you a new perspective on the process. All the best!

"If the process of college admission were a maze, this book would be the map to help navigate through it. With its helpful insights on how to keep organized, interviewing tips, essay writing tricks, and guidelines for Mom and Dad, this book will help the family 'team' avoid dead ends."

—Alissa Belcastro, high school senior

"*Winning the College Admission Game* makes even the daunting task of applying to college seem less intimidating. Keeping organized will be easy with the season-by-season chart of preparing for college throughout high school and checklists for course selection and campus visits."

—Alexandra K., high school senior

"Peter Van Buskirk's strategy of applying to college emphasizes an individual's fit with a college, not a college's ranking in a magazine. *Winning the College Admission Game* gives a comprehensive and succinct overview of the nerve-wracking college admission process."

—William Mackey, high school senior

"What I found most useful about this book is its pragmatism toward college admission. It explains what colleges, as businesses, are looking for but don't tell potential applicants. *Winning the College Admission Game* will help students realize what they are looking for in a college."

—Thomas Batcho, high school student

"*Winning the College Admission Game* provides two interesting views of the college 'scramble.' By dividing the book into parent and student sections, Van Buskirk allows both parties to benefit from an easy-to-understand guide to the college admission process. This book was very educational!"

—Anisha Singh, high school junior

"With humor and understanding, Van Buskirk leads students through the college admission process. He tells you what college admission counselors don't want you to know and breaks down classic stereotypes to help students find the perfect college fit. Van Buskirk brings the whole admission process to a less stressful and almost enjoyable level."

—Sara R. Eckert, high school senior

Winning the College Admission Game

STRATEGIES FOR STUDENTS

Peter Van Buskirk

PETERSON'S

A **nelnet.** COMPANY

PETERSON'S

A (n)elnet. COMPANY

About Peterson's, a Nelnet company
Peterson's (www.petersons.com) is a leading provider of education information and advice, with books and online resources focusing on education search, test preparation, and financial aid. Its Web site offers searchable databases and interactive tools for contacting educational institutions, online practice tests and instruction, and planning tools for securing financial aid. Peterson's serves 110 million education consumers annually.

For more information, contact Peterson's, 2000 Lenox Drive, Lawrenceville, NJ 08648; 800-338-3282; or find us on the World Wide Web at www.petersons.com/about.

Editor: Wallie Walker Hammond; Production Editor: Susan W. Dilts; Manufacturing Manager: Ivona Skibicki; Composition Manager: Linda M. Williams; Interior Design: Greg Wuttke

ISBN-13: 978 0 7689-2491-6
ISBN-10: 0-7689-2491-X

Printed in the United States of America

10 9 8 7 6 5 4 3   09 08

First Edition

Dedication

Over the course of my admission career, I had the good fortune to meet thousands of bright and eager young people as they approached their college careers. Among them were authors, inventors, adventurers, leaders, thinkers, actors, musicians, and athletes. Each had a passion to pursue and a story to tell. No story was more compelling or inspiring, though, than that of the homeless student whom I met late in the application season.

While it didn't take long for the picture of Greg's life circumstances to become clear, the facts remained. Despite demonstrating unusual compassion, fortitude, and insight into the human condition, the glaring inconsistencies in his academic record seemed to beg the question: "Why bother?" Looking for a graceful exit from the conversation, I looked at Greg and asked, "What can you point to that suggests that we should go any further with this?" Without hesitation, he responded, "I just want a chance. *All I want is for someone to believe in me so* I can get an education that will give me a chance to go back and make the city a better place."

These powerfully poignant words from someone who had nothing carried an undeniable message. All he wanted was an opportunity, through education, to change his life—and the lives of others around him. Suddenly, it was hard to imagine that rules and bureaucracy could or should stand in the way. To make a long story short, Greg was admitted. Not only did he have an incredible impact on campus life, he graduated with a degree in literature. He has since received a master's degree and a Ph.D. and is now a teacher/administrator at a neighborhood high school not far from where he grew up.

This book is dedicated, then, to this young man and the thousands of other young people who dream of college and whose simple goal may be to have someone believe in them. It is my sincere hope that there is something in these pages that will provide hope, encouragement, and guidance to each of you as you continue to live the dream.

I would also like to dedicate this book to Jennifer, Heidi, and Kyle. Not only are they my children, but they're also pretty cool people! We have traveled down many paths together, including those that led to their respective college destinations. The ride hasn't always been easy or predictable, but we have persevered *together*. Now they are young adults finding their respective ways in life. I am proud of them for the persons they are and continue to become. I cherish their uniqueness and value their friendship and support. Without them, this book would never have materialized.

Contents

Contents

Introduction

You are bright, talented, and about to embark on one of life's great adventures—the pursuit of a college degree. If you are like most young adults, the prospect of striking out on your own is pretty exciting. As good as life has been up to this point, you're ready for change. It's time to create your own space and begin writing the script for the rest of your life.

College gives you the opportunity to do this. Whether you have a well-defined career interest in mind or you are still waiting for that inspiration to hit you, your college years will lay the foundation for future success and happiness. Embrace them with gusto and you will emerge a new person ready to make your mark in the world.

Getting there, however, is the trick. The road to college is lined with myth, legend, and high-minded rhetoric that is bound to confuse and discourage even the most focused and resourceful of students. Sorting through the noise that surrounds you to find the best place for you, then, requires thoughtful introspection and careful research. You'll need to learn a lot about the college admission process and you'll need to figure out how you can work with your parents as they are likely to have thoughts on the matter as well.

Prepare, Compete, Win!

Winning the College Admission Game gives you the tools and insight to navigate the college selection process. The objective is to put you in the best position to "win." Winning means having options and, in this process, you want to have the option, not only of choosing college, but choosing which college you will attend. In order for this to happen, you must first compete with hundreds, if not thousands, of other young people who want the same place at the same college. And, just like you, they are good. They can do the work and deserve a chance to enter as students.

In order to compete successfully, you must prepare well. You need to understand the competition, the politics of the places you want to attend, and the variables that affect the selection process. You also need to know yourself so you can make good decisions about where and how to apply. Unlike many other books on the subject, this one begins with the assumption that you, not the colleges, are central to the conversation. It is most important, then, to identify a destination that makes sense for you.

Finding a place on the right "playing field" gives you a reasonable chance of getting into an institution and of doing well once enrolled.

So, what can you expect from this book? While there are no guarantees or "magic bullet" solutions for getting into the college of your choice, I will share with you insights and strategies you can use to give yourself a competitive edge as you apply to college. For example, this book will:

1. **Give you a roadmap.** The college process can be pretty stressful and confusing. There is a lot to consider in getting from point "A" to point "B." We'll look at how you can develop a plan or roadmap that will help you arrive at point "B" with your sanity intact!

2. **Help you establish ownership.** It's really important that *you* own the process. If all I did was talk to your parents about the college process, they would be even more inclined to take it over and make decisions for you—and you don't want that to happen! You need to be in charge!

3. **Reveal the logic and motives of the decision makers.** You are more likely to tackle this project head on if you have a better understanding of what's going on than if the process remains mysterious and elusive. By getting inside the heads of the decision makers, you can better anticipate the actions you need to take to win in this competition.

4. **Help find the best college *for you*.** Finally, the ultimate objective of this book is to help you get it right. If you get into a college that fits you well, you can have an amazing experience that prepares you for years of happiness and success.

Chapter 1

Getting from Where You Are to Where You Want to Be

Do you want to go to college but aren't quite sure how to get there? Unfortunately, there aren't any quick and easy solutions. You can't snap your fingers and make it happen. No wave of the wand or genie in a bottle will get you there. Even though you may have done everything within your power to make yourself a worthy candidate, you still don't have the elusive piece of paper that says, "Congratulations, you're in!"

In order to achieve that objective—to receive the "good news" letter—you must compete with hundreds, if not thousands, of other young people whose credentials are a lot like yours. Success in this competition is predicated on your ability to size up the situation strategically. In this instance, knowledge is power. By knowing who and what you are up against, as well as focusing on the assets you might bring to bear in the competition, you can chart your way to success.

That's what this book is all about. It will give you insight into how admission officers approach the selection process so you can prepare yourself to compete effectively, and it will guide you through a reflective

self-assessment so you can be well armed with an awareness of how and where you should be able to compete most effectively. Just as important, it will set you up as the person in charge. After all, you are the one going to college (parents tend to forget!).

The process of exploring college options—deciding where to apply, preparing credentials, and, finally, choosing where you will enroll—is all about you and your future. You need to own it. Your parents are understandably interested in what's going on, but sometimes their enthusiasm can get in the way of good decision making on your part. I'll work on that in the other half of the book. I'll also give you "tools" that will help you make good decisions and prepare you well to compete for admission. Ultimately, the objective is to help you achieve your educational goals—to get you from where you are to where you want to be. If this sounds good, read on . . . .

The "Game"

The college admission process really isn't a game in the way you think about most games. You won't find fan-packed stadiums cheering you on. There are no game clocks, scoreboards, or mascots. One is even hard-pressed to identify rules (more like guidelines) or recognize any type of officiating. Here, the playing field is more figurative than literal and, oddly enough, it is one on which each player can emerge a winner.

The college admission process *is*, however, one in which you must compete. You submit your credentials into a competition in which there will be many more good candidates than can possibly be admitted—a competition in which the outcomes are far from predictable. Consider the numbers. In the United States alone, nearly 2 million students apply to college each year. They come from more than 23,000 high schools. That translates to 23,000 valedictorians and more than 200,000 who rank in the top ten in their respective classes. That's a lot of talent!

As you can see, the demand for higher education in this country extends well beyond your school, your city, and your state. And most of the students who look forward to taking that next step educationally have credentials that will make them competitive at some level. Unfortunately, not everyone will be admitted to her/his favorite or first-choice school. On the other hand, there is room for everyone among the 3,600+ colleges and universities in this country. The question for you with regard to college, then, is not "if" but "where?"

Selectivity

Who gets in? Where? How? Why? All are good questions. If "getting in" is akin to winning, you must compete. You know from experience that you can't expect to win simply by showing up or, in this case, applying. You wouldn't expect to do that at an audition or tryout. Yes, you are a strong and viable candidate. That won't always cut it, though. You must compete with the other candidates of equal strength—folks who have just as much right to a place in the class as you do.

And don't delude yourself with the notion that this is a fair competition! Forget the notion that "Good work deserves just praise." As you apply for admission, anything can and will happen—thus giving rise to the likeness of a game in which there are no guarantees. Admission committees at colleges around the country must make fine distinctions between strong candidates every day in competitions that affect everyone, not just the students who aspire to the most elite institutions. For perspective, let's take a look at the Pyramid of Selectivity.

The Pyramid of Selectivity

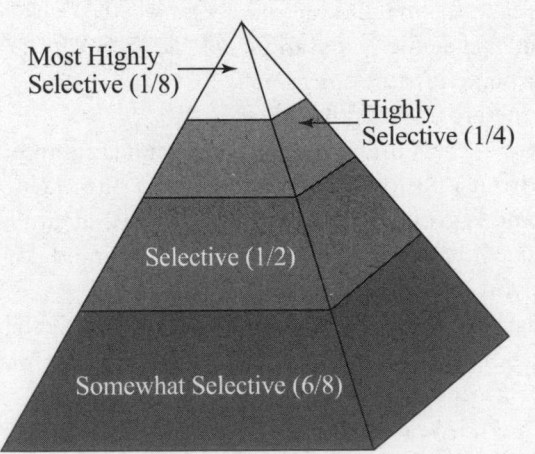

(Fractions approximate the odds of getting in at each level of selectivity.)

Each college in the country occupies a place on the Pyramid according to its "level of selectivity," or the percentage of applicants it is able to admit. (When you hear people talk about "how hard it is to get into College A" they are talking about the selectivity of College A's admission process.) The number of colleges becomes fewer as selectivity increases. The more intense the competition for admission, the higher its placement on the Pyramid.

It is important to note that this is *not* a "Pyramid of Quality." Don't assume that the schools at the top of the Pyramid are the best and those at the bottom are not as good. In reality, there are great schools everywhere. Yes, many of the schools at the top of the Pyramid have superb academic reputations—but so do many of the colleges and universities that are far less selective. Keep in mind that, by definition, selectivity is a function of popularity and not quality. The more popular the school, the more applications it will attract (and the greater the number that must turned down).

It is easy to imagine factors, other than academic reputation, that might make institutions popular and, therefore, selective. For

Between the Lines

Determining Selectivity
You can determine the selectivity or admit ratio of a college by simply dividing the number of applications it receives into the number of acceptances it offers. The lower the result, the harder it is to get into the school. At universities that admit by college or degree program (engineering, nursing, arts and sciences, etc.) look for the numbers that describe selectivity for the program that interests you. This information is typically available on institutional Web sites and guidebooks.

example, the success of an athletic program has catapulted more than one university from a position of respectability to one of elite standing. In fact, a rather famous group of schools now draws its identity from the name of its athletic conference. If you like to be around high-profile athletic programs, you understand the phenomena.

Similarly, location seems to be a big draw. Early in her college search, the only schools my daughter would consider were places that sent her literature featuring palm trees, pools, and beaches! She eventually chose a college in a cold-weather climate, but many others find the attraction to warm weather climates or other exotic locations to be compelling. And I can't tell you how often I hear students declare that they *need to be in* an urban environment. More specifically, they want to go to Boston. They haven't quite figured out which school in Boston just as long as they end up in Boston! I know Boston is a great college town, but come on!

You get the picture. Quite a few colleges and universities have benefited from factors outside of the classroom to become incredibly popular. Just keep this in mind as you look at colleges and resist the

temptation to conclude, "It probably isn't very good because I've never heard of it and it's not that hard to get into."

The Pyramid and You

When a college can say "no" to any candidate, whether the number is 100, 1,000, or 10,000, it is selective. The admission process and selection elements remain the same. The process just becomes more intense and the focus on the elements is more microscopic as you aspire to colleges that are higher on the Pyramid. For example, the same academic record that might win you admission and a scholarship at one school might fall short in the competition at another.

Let's personalize this point. Imagine that you are haunted by a bad grade (that you really didn't deserve!). It may be the only blemish on your record but now you worry that you might not be able to get into a "good school." Everything else on your record might be flawless, but you are still sweating out that one bad grade. So, what's the deal? Are you truly "toast" in the admission process?

The answer lies in the Pyramid. If you are defining a "good school" as one that is at or near the top of the Pyramid (not the best or most accurate definition of a "good school"), your chances aren't very good. Keep in mind, however, *they weren't very good even without the bad grade*! That has nothing to do with you or whether you are a good person or a strong candidate. It is much more a reflection of the competition.

Given the ratio of applicants to available positions, the more selective schools are looking for reasons to turn students down. A bad grade will almost surely eliminate you as it won't pass through the many filters that are in place to help discriminate among excellent candidates. The bottom line: you have to be very good *and* very lucky in order to find success in the upper ranges of the Pyramid.

On the other hand, if you are focusing on many of the great schools that are not quite as selective (further down the Pyramid), then you've got a shot—even with the bad grade. Schools that don't have to be so picky can actually be more forgiving of credentials that might not be perfect. They understand bad days and bad semesters. Rather, they are more interested in how you responded to adversity. They don't have to filter you out because of that credential and can afford to value you (remember those words) for all that you have done well.

The Pyramid of Selectivity will be instructive as you move forward in preparing your applications. Questions such as, "How important are . . . (fill in the blank—SATs, senior year grades, etc)?" can be addressed within

the context of the Pyramid. The initial answer will be: "It depends." It depends on where you aspire on the Pyramid. If you are targeting schools near the top of the Pyramid, each factor is scrutinized under a microscope—with multiple filters! As you descend the Pyramid, though, the number of filters becomes fewer and the opportunities for you become greater.

The Competitive Edge

Going forward, the objective is to put you in a better position to compete—to help you find a competitive edge in the admission process. Before you get too excited, though, understand that we won't be talking about shortcuts or secret insider information or, for that matter, a blueprint that guarantees

Between the Lines

Filters

One way the Pyramid can give you perspective on competition is to imagine the filters that might be applied to the various levels of selection. Filters are the different application requirements (courses, grades, scores, writing samples, etc.) *and* the performance expectations that are attached to each. (We'll get into this more as we talk about "What Colleges Want.") The more selective the school, the more stringent are the filters. Your objective as an applicant is to pass through all of the filters that have been imposed.

success. Rather, you will find a candid orientation to the manner in which admission officers evaluate credentials. The underlying premise is rather simple: If you know how and, more important, why decisions are made, you can then take action to help yourself.

This is a competition in which you must stand tall. You are the one who is going to college—not your parents or your teachers or your counselor. This one is on you. If you have decided that this is really what you want to do, you've got to go for it! You give yourself a competitive edge by preparing well and putting yourself on the right playing field.

As you try to imagine yourself in competition at places of varying levels of selectivity, you can appreciate the importance of preparing well in order to compete. None of these schools is going to hand you anything because you are good. They can't. They don't have room to accommodate all of the students who deserve to be admitted. Instead, they want to see how competitive your credentials are with the rest of the applicants.

It is essential, then, that you put yourself on the right playing fields—places where you have the best chances of getting in and where

you should do well academically if given the chance. Preparing to compete involves knowing yourself, understanding the competitive arena, and having a game plan for success. Attempting to compete on an inappropriate playing field reflects a lack of good planning and can be incredibly frustrating. There are hundreds of interesting and viable playing fields for you on the Pyramid. Find those that are right for you and you will put yourself in a much better position to achieve your educational goals.

Chapter 2

The Best College Is a Good Fit

The Right Playing Field

A key to success in any competition is making sure you are competing at the right level. You know this from your own life experiences. Wherever you compete, whether on the field or the stage or in the classroom, you have the best chance of finding success when your skills are competitive with those around you. Simply having knowledge of the fundamentals and a passion for the game will not advance you very far in the competition—if you are not on the right playing field.

The same is true of the college process. As you have seen, getting into college is like a massive competition. Students must compete for admission at colleges up and down the Pyramid of Selectivity—some that are not that selective and others that admit fewer than 10 percent of their applicants. The intensity of competition on these "playing fields" runs the gamut. It's your job to find the right playing fields on which to compete for admission.

The Best Colleges

Your college selection process is set against the backdrop of another high stakes competition (let's call it the "fame game") that is taking place between colleges and universities around the country. The "fame game" got started more than twenty years ago with the publication of college ranking lists. Perpetuated by guidebook and magazine editors, it's a game that preys on institutional insecurities and a growing consumer desire to know or have the best.

Between the Lines

A Good Fit

A college that represents the right playing field is one that is not only reasonably accessible to you through the admission process, but also is a place at which, given the opportunity, you should be able to find success academically. Such a college or university represents a good college "fit" for you.

The premise is really quite simple. Tap into a consumer mentality that is already sensitive to the "best" in whatever category—cars, vacations, school districts—and establish a ranking system that identifies the "best colleges." No sooner were rankings published in the 1980s than families began to attach values to institutions and clamor for the "best."

As a result, colleges and universities began to quietly take steps to improve the measures that would preserve or enhance their positions relative to their peers. In the end, the potential to carry the label of "*Best* Research University" or "*Best* Regional Liberal Arts College"—or even "*one of the best*"—became the incentive to invest in what has been likened to an arms race among colleges and universities. The school that is number "one" doesn't want to lose that position, while the number "three" school will do what it can to reach the top spot.

So, what can we learn about the "best" institution in the country? Can you name it? Is it a college or university? Can it be found on the West Coast or the East Coast—or someplace in between? The fact is such a place doesn't exist. The "best" can't be objectively measured. While there are many superb places of higher education, none can really carry the mantle of "the best."

In truth, there are several places that could legitimately vie for the title of best. The context is different, though. These are the schools that would be *best for you*. They are the places that will give you what you need—they will help you learn and grow. They will teach you skills and

help you define your future career path. In short, they are the places that will fit you best.

Finding the Best College Fit

The quality options that emerge on your radar screen will be the colleges that are most compatible with you and your priorities. Not only will you be happier at such colleges, the odds are you'll have a better chance of getting in. A good college "fit" is one that will:

Between the Lines

Fool's Gold

Be careful about attaching too much value to what you read or hear with regard to ranking guides. By and large, the rankings are derived from a recipe that includes sound data about entrance credentials and college outcomes mixed with a strong dose of editorial flavoring. In the final analysis, it's the opinion of the editors that colors the rankings. You can be sure those opinions will change from year to year—the demand for books is much too high to allow for predictability.

- Offer a program of study to match your interests and needs

- Provide a style of instruction to match the way you like to learn

- Provide a level of academic rigor to match your aptitude and preparation

- Offer a community that feels like home to you

- Value you for what you do well

As you consider colleges, how do they measure up against these rules for a good fit? Be sensitive to inconsistencies between what is offered and what you want as they will likely become sticking points for you later on. Don't settle for a college that only meets one or two criteria.

A Good College "Fit" Will . . .

OFFER A PROGRAM OF STUDY TO MATCH YOUR INTERESTS AND NEEDS

If you know what you want to study in college, it makes sense to target places that will accommodate your interests and support your strengths. For example, if you want to pursue chemical engineering, focus on schools that offer it. The same is true with business, elementary education, or graphic design. If your passion is film studies and a college doesn't offer a

very substantive program in that area, then it's not a good fit. Look into colleges that offer strong programs that meet your needs.

On the other hand, if you are still searching for some direction, don't worry. It's difficult to know at your age what you'll do for the rest of your life, so relax. You've got a lot of time to figure it out. If you want to have some fun, ask your parents to talk about their career aspirations when they were your age. The odds are they had vastly different ideas back then about what they would be doing at this point in their lives!

Find out what influenced their thinking if and when they discovered new interests. What, if any, changes would they make? Just as most people of your parent's generation followed pathways to success that they couldn't imagine when they were your age, you need to be flexible in finding and following your path. A good college fit is one that will encourage you in this direction.

Between the Lines

What Do You Want to Study?
What do you want out of college academically? Training for a specific job? An opportunity to learn about lots of things? Both? If you are not sure, you should opt for the latter! Colleges are very different in their orientations. If you are not sure about your future directions, the best college for you is one that will encourage you to explore.

Did You Know . . .

- You will probably change your major in college. Most college students do at least once.

- Most students enter college "undeclared" with regard to a major.

- The odds are that you will change jobs at least four times and change careers twice.

- Many colleges report that 80 to 90 percent of the people who graduated more than twenty-five years ago are now in careers that did not exist when they graduated.

PROVIDE A STYLE OF INSTRUCTION TO MATCH THE WAY YOU LIKE TO LEARN

Before you begin looking for a good college "fit," take stock of your learning style. The more you know about your learning style—how you like to learn—the easier it will be to make critical distinctions among the learning environments of different colleges. Just as each student might have

a slightly different learning style, colleges offer different styles of instruction. Each delivers education in a slightly different manner.

For example, some will teach biology in seminars that include 25 to 30 students, while others teach it in lecture halls of 500! Others will attach labs to the instruction or offer research opportunities. In each case, the material is the same—bio is bio—but the experience is different. How would you function in these different environments?

If your approach to learning is to take good notes, read diligently, and prepare carefully—all in the relative anonymity of the back row in the auditorium, then you will function more comfortably in a larger instructional setting. On the other hand, if you like the engagement of a small classroom where you can ask questions—where you can challenge and be challenged—then the seminar format will be more productive for you.

Imagine, however, that you really like the engagement of the small classroom but find yourself in large lecture halls all the time. Or that you prefer to operate in relative anonymity—but most of your classes put you front and center around the seminar table! Are these learning environments going to bring out the best in you? It's doubtful that you'll get the most out of your abilities if you find yourself in an environment that is ill-suited to the way you learn.

Think about the following questions. Be particularly attentive to "*why*." As you reflect on your answers—especially the "why" part—you come to better understand the characteristics of a learning environment that would be the most appropriate for you in college.

- Who is your favorite teacher—and why?
- What is your favorite class right now—and why?
- In which type of classroom setting (i.e., large group lectures, seminars, etc.) are you most comfortable—and why?
- With what kinds of people and personalities do you enjoy exchanging ideas—and why?

I asked these questions of my daughter, Jennifer, as she was looking at colleges. After some reflection, she concluded that, "Choosing a college is one of the most important decisions I will make in my life. In order to make a good choice, I need to know myself a little better."

Provide a Level of Academic Rigor to Match Your Aptitude and Preparation

How comfortable are you around water? Are you a strong swimmer or do you struggle to keep your head above water? Are you comfortable venturing into the deeper water or do you prefer to wade in as long as the

bottom is visible and the footing is certain? Most people expose themselves to water and swimming situations with which they are most comfortable, no more, no less.

The same is true of academic work. While most students have the basic aptitude and preparation to perform in a range of college environments, some are better equipped than others to meet challenges at higher levels. They have both the aptitude *and* the preparation (through exposure to a regimen of demanding courses in high school) to find success in more rigorous environments.

That said, a lot of students look at colleges where their current skill sets are not good matches for the rigor that will greet them in the classroom. They may have the

Between the Lines

The Right Rigor

Look for academic environments where your aptitude and preparation are good matches for the level of academic rigor—colleges that will challenge you in appropriate ways without overwhelming you. The best sources of insight regarding your preparedness to meet the academic rigor of various colleges and universities are your high school teachers. Their familiarity with your capabilities will be invaluable in identifying the colleges where you will be well served academically.

ability but are not well equipped to find success. Even "getting by" academically will be a struggle as they will be "in over their heads."

Conversely, some students who are immensely talented and accustomed to achieving at a very high level will choose environments that do not provide much of a challenge. They may enjoy the easy pace for a while, but like strong swimmers in a wading pool, they quickly become bored.

It's likely you will be able to do the work at most of the colleges you consider. You have the necessary aptitude and, in many cases, the right amount of preparation to make the grade. Your ability level is not always an indication, though, of a good fit nor will it necessarily get you in. Rather, it's an acknowledgment of a possibility—an option. It's an indication that you have an essential aptitude or, to borrow from the swimming metaphor, you can handle yourself around the water. The best college fit will challenge you at the right level given your aptitude and preparation.

Offer a Community That Feels Like Home to You

Very often when students believe they've found the college of their dreams, they're hard-pressed to explain the attraction, except to say, "It's a gut feeling. It feels right—like I would be at home." As you think about living apart from the comforts of home, finding your niche is vitally important—as is an understanding of the factors that define your future happiness.

What gut feeling do you hope to find as you look at colleges? You probably want to find people with similar backgrounds, interests, and loyalties—students with whom you'd like to hang out. It might be nice to meet professors who immediately engage you. And you might be excited by elements of the campus culture or architecture that are particularly welcoming.

What evidence can you find, though, that a given college will

Between the Lines

The Teenage Paradox
Do you ever feel the urge to shout, "I can't wait to get out of here!" And "here" is wherever you are—home, school, community. You're ready for a new look, a change of pace, for independence. Ironically, I suspect there is a quiet voice inside you that periodically says something like, "I don't want to go. They feed me and let me drive their car. My friends are right down the street. I actually like it here." If this sounds familiar, know that it's a good sign (you are well-rooted)—and you have lots of company. In choosing a college that feels like home, the odds are you will experience the same laments as you prepare to graduate in four years!

stretch and support you through various aspects of your college experience? Who will encourage and support you as you continue your journey of self-discovery? Can you identify anyone who will broaden your perspective—get you to take risks, to think outside of the box periodically? Will anyone know if you are struggling? Will anyone care? Are you considering a college that will tease the best out of you—make you a better student, a better citizen, a better person?

The answers to these questions will help define the ideal college community for you. Be careful not to react impulsively, though, as you consider your college "home away from home." Until you experience such a place and come away with a "gut feeling," it only exists in your imagination. At a time in your life when you may be aching to get away and have a different experience, it's vital that you "land" well when you get to college. Be prepared, then, to visit campuses—*and revisit and revise*

your list—as your college search continues until one day the feeling hits you.

VALUE YOU FOR WHAT YOU DO WELL

When the dust settles on your college search, there should be abundant evidence that the college you have chosen is excited that you will be joining its number. More than *just* another face in the freshman directory, you are someone who will be valued in that population for the things you do well.

Think about your close, personal relationships. A relationship works because both parties are equally invested in its success. Each side values and respects the other. Problems arise when the degree of investment in the relationship is not even. Despite the determination of one party to make things work, one-sided relationships are often doomed to failure.

The same is true of your pending relationship with a college or university. Your investment in the relationship would seem clear. You know what you want out of your four years and you know what you are prepared to do in order to achieve your goals. On the other hand, what type of investment in you can you expect from the institution? Where is the evidence that it is prepared to help you achieve your goals?

Be discriminating as you look for this evidence. At some colleges, the offer of acceptance may be the only indication that you are valued. How far will that letter carry you when you need financial assistance or want to pursue a special independent study opportunity? In all likelihood, you'll be left to figure these things out on your own. Contrast that with the colleges that go out of their way to:

- Give you personal attention throughout the recruitment process
- Answer your questions about housing, registration, and payment plans in a timely manner
- Provide financial aid to meet your need
- Recognize your talents with scholarships and/or special academic opportunities (i.e., study abroad, internships, research, etc.)

As you will see when we talk about "What Colleges Want" (Chapter 7), the decisions to admit students and give them financial aid are extensions of this very point. They are decisions based on the values orientations of each institution. Doesn't it make sense, then, to want to spend time at a place that values you? The best college for you, then, is the one that proves it is investing in your success by putting you first.

Priorities—and the Importance of Getting It Right

A college education is an important lifetime achievement. During your college years, you will meet new people, prepare for a career, and learn more than you could ever imagine. The payoffs are both immediate and long-term. That's why families are willing to make the investment. Unfortunately, the investment can prove costly when college plans go awry.

When you consider that barely two thirds of starting freshmen return for the second year and that about 40 percent fail to graduate from any school in four *or five or six years*, you know there must be a problem somewhere. Every year, thousands of students fall short because they find themselves at colleges where they are ill suited to find success. Some are not adequately prepared academically, while others labor with seemingly insurmountable financial burdens. Many leave college prematurely simply because they did not systematically address matters relating to a good "fit" as they initially looked at colleges. They bought into one or two elements of the good fit and assumed that everything else would work out.

When you're not able to finish what you start, your family loses the money it has put into tuition and other college expenses. You also lose time toward completion of an undergraduate degree and the opportunity to gain an advantage in the job market. If you return to the classroom after being away for a while, or transfer to a different school, the cost is significant. Not only must you absorb the cost of an additional year or so of education (due to credits lost in the transfer process), but you must also wait to take advantage of your new earning potential.

It's important, then, to invest in some soul-searching before you make any commitments. Why are you going to college? What do you want out of the next four years? Do you want independence? Good times? An education? Intellectual enlightenment? Career training? And what are you prepared to do to produce results?

As you consider the possibilities, you take an important step toward identifying your priorities. Your priorities are the "must haves" of your college experience. Keep them in focus as you look for colleges that offer the best fit for you and you will put yourself in the best position to find success both in admission and the years that follow.

The Best College for You May NOT Be . . .

Before we sign off on this chapter—and only because you now appreciate the importance of getting it right—it might be worth touching on a few factors that more often than not lead to tales of woe.

For example, *the best college for you is not the place that your love interest attends*! The college-going process happens at a very inopportune time for many young people. Just as you look forward to graduating from high school and moving on to college, you are likely to find yourself in a relationship that is very important to you. The notion of having to spend four years apart at a time when you are swearing allegiance for a lifetime is hard to take. How can you possibly manage the separation?

It won't be long before you've worked out plans to see each other on weekends and to call and IM in between. Then, in a burst of sudden clarity, you declare that you'll go wherever she goes (if you can get in!). It will be a wonderful beginning to the rest of your lives together. Or will it?

Before you get too far along in the planning process, you need to know that the odds of maintaining the relationship are not in your favor. It's true. Most high school romances break up before the end of the first year of college. So, think about it. Does it make sense for you to commit to four years at somebody else's college *just so you can be together*? The odds are that before the end of the first semester she'll find other attractions and you'll end up being a spectator on her campus. Would you call that a good fit?

The same logic might apply to the tendency of some students to follow their friends. While you are ready to graduate from high school, you might not be ready to leave the people with whom you hang out. As a result, the whole gang heads off to college together—in many cases, site unseen. When asked why you chose to attend that college, your response is "my friends go there."

Now, how much sense does that make?! One or two of your friends have it figured out. They know the program and have made considered decisions. The rest of you just want to hang out. Now, you are on a campus that is strange to you except for the guys you want to hang with. A good fit?

The next example of *a potential bad fit is the place that either of your parents attended or want you to attend*. This can become uncomfortable as your parents are probably pretty proud of their alma maters. You can tell because they couldn't wait for you to start looking at colleges: "Son, I had the best four years of my life there. I met wonderful friends and had amazing professors. I think we should go take a look."

You're now in an awkward position. You don't want to disappoint your parents. On the other hand, you want to find your own place. After all, you are different people. What worked for them might not be the best for you. If this happens, you need to find a diplomatic solution to this situation early in your search. The longer you allow your parent's alma mater to linger prominently in the picture, the harder it will be to extricate yourself from it later in the process—that is, assuming you truly want to look in different directions.

The best college for you is not likely to be the place that won the national championship. Everybody likes to be around a winner and there is something to be said for body painting and the crowd frenzy on crisp Saturday afternoons in the fall. Just remember, though, that whatever colors you bleed, you still need to be a student Monday through Friday.

Finally, *the best college for you is not necessarily the place that will give you the most impressive car decal*! In our world, that's a metaphor for prestige. Consider how the events unfold. The "Committee of We" has been involved in an exhaustive college search process. I guess I shouldn't have to explain that mom and dad are integral to this committee! ("When are *we* going to get started?" "When are *we* going start visiting schools?" "When are *we* going to get the applications finished?" "When are *we* going to hear?") Does this sound familiar? One day in late March of your senior year, the letter from XYZ, a very prestigious college, arrives in your mail slot. A committee member is home (not you because you're in school) and finds the letter. Unable to find restraint, this committee member opens the letter to discover the good news—"We're in!!" Before you know it, this unnamed person pulls the XYZ car decal out of a drawer (where it's been in safe keeping *just in case*), puts it on the car and begins to drive slowly through the neighborhood so everyone can see where "we're going to college!"

This is an exciting time for the entire family because, of course, "we" got in. And good for you—if this is truly the place that you want to attend. Unfortunately, a lot of students and their families get caught up in the rush for "gold." The process is more about winning the prize or receiving the "yes" letter then it is finding the best fit. You may have "won" the car decal and all the bragging rights that go with it, but do you have the right college? Maybe, maybe not. You need to remain reflective throughout the process—and even a little selfish—in order to make sure a university, especially a high-profile place, is the right one for you.

College choices based on emotion are often regretted. They just don't "fit" you well in the long run. As you move forward, resist the

temptation to act impulsively or run with the herd. You must be able to live with your choice for the next four years and it needs to work for you in the years that follow. Invest in learning more about places that might be right for you, not your parents, or your best friend, or the people in the neighborhood. In doing so, you are more likely to be accepted and much more likely to have a successful four-year college experience.

Develop Your Options

Ownership

Like most important undertakings in life, getting from where you are to where you want to be with regard to college requires a plan and a good roadmap. In this case, you are both the cartographer and the navigator. As the one most directly affected by the outcome of the journey, you need to give the plan direction and guideposts that will help mark your progress. You must own it.

The alternative is to let your parents do it for you. You know, they can read through the literature, do the Web research, and schedule all of the appointments. They can tell you what you need to know and keep you on task. They're probably starting to do that anyway. Don't let them!

If you had the opportunity to own a new car, wouldn't you want to do the shopping? You might not be entirely comfortable with all the technical aspects of the process, but you probably would want to have input into things like the model, the color, and the amenities. Does it have a sunroof? What about a CD changer? Is it an automatic or will you have to

learn to shift gears manually? You can let someone else do the shopping and the buying, but then you are stuck with what that person has decided is best for you. Much as you might like having a car, the one that is chosen for you may not be what you had in mind!

The same is true with the college search. At the end of the day, you will be moving into a new home. For four years, you'll have a new place to live, to play, and to study. Do you want to leave that selection to chance? Doesn't the notion of putting your college search in the hands of someone else make you feel just a little bit anxious?

The intent of this chapter is to equip you for the task—to give you tools and ideas that will enable you to approach the process both qualitatively and quantitatively. The qualitative assessment focuses on the factors that are important to you while the quantitative will help you sort out your chances of getting into a given school. In the end, you should be able to draw from what you have learned to make good decisions that position you to compete effectively for admission.

What Are Your Priorities?

If the mail from colleges has not already begun to arrive, it will soon. In a very short period of time, you will be deluged by sound bytes and images from countless colleges and universities, each of which is carefully crafted to attract your interest. Before long, your awareness of colleges will go from one of excited curiosity to mild annoyance. While sorting through a seemingly endless stream of materials can be tiresome, take advantage of this opportunity to begin sizing up the possibilities. This exercise can be especially productive if you are able to first identify a set of priorities through which you can filter the information.

Before trying to make value judgments about colleges and universities based on initial impressions, take time to reflect on what is important to you. What are your priorities? More specifically, *what are the three or four things you want to make sure you have accomplished when you cross the stage at graduation*? This question goes to the core of your personal values system and forces you to focus on the things that are absolutely essential to defining a successful college experience.

Do more than "think about" your priorities. Write them down. In fact, create a spreadsheet that lists each priority across the top. Then, enter the names of the colleges that you would like to consider down the side. As you get to know each college, use the spreadsheet to note how it

is able to address your priorities. You might even create your own rating system. Consider the following:

- What do you want to achieve academically and intellectually?

- How would you describe your learning style (engaged or quietly absorbent, self-reliant or work best with structured expectations, prefer small or large classes, etc.)?

- Do you want to be challenged in a rigorous academic environment (i.e., did you take a majority of honors, AP, or IB courses in high school) or will you function better in a less pressured academic environment?

Between the Lines

Hierarchy of Needs
As you research your options, differentiate between factors that are "essential," "important," and "would be nice" with regard to your selection of a college. Having such a hierarchy of needs can help you stay focused on what is most important in the face of emotional pulls to less important factors. Theoretically, an "essential" factor would hold a place among your priorities.

- How do you weigh the importance of social opportunities versus a focus on academics?

- Are you an adventurer or risk taker who enjoys a lot of change or do you prefer a stable, predictable environment?

- Do you want to spend the next four years with people like you or do you want to meet people from cultures and backgrounds very different from your own?

- What do you do well or care about deeply? What interests, talents, or skills do you want to pursue while you are in college? How do you want the school to support these interests?

Armed with this insight, research as many colleges as possible. Visit campuses. Talk to recent graduates about their experiences. Ask professionals in your community for opinions about career tracks that interest you. Don't try to find the best absolute fit right away. Rather, make sure that you know enough about a range of schools that you can continue to make informed judgments.

Separate Fact from Fiction

As you process the information you receive from colleges, be careful to separate fact from fiction.

It is a rare college, for example, that will volunteer its weaknesses to the students it is trying to recruit. Most will do their best to either cleverly disguise—or ignore—their shortcomings altogether. That said, you would be well served by a healthy dose of cynicism. Observe the following to make sure you know what you are getting after you take off the "wrapping."

1. Check the numbers. You are bound to hear about small classes and impressive student to faculty ratios as you learn about schools. Make sure you know what these numbers mean. Ratios and averages are only useful in comparing schools if the methodologies for reporting them are the same across institutions. In reality, local interpretations are heavily nuanced, making it difficult to find good comparative data.

For example, an average class size can be found by dividing the total number of students by the number of classes offered. Some colleges inflate the number of classes while reducing the number of students. Imagine the impact on this statistic if independent study projects are included as classes and the students counted include only those who are full-time and degree seeking (rather than all students enrolled regardless of status).

A good question to ask is: "What percentage of the classes include 20 or fewer students?" Or, better yet, find out the percentage of under-graduate classes taught by tenured faculty. If you are concerned about the student to faculty ratio (not to be confused with average class size), ask if teaching assistants or nonteaching administrators with academic credentials are included in the faculty count. You get the picture. Make sure you understand the numbers you are given.

2. Who gets the perks? Every institution wants to give the impression that its students have access to enhanced learning opportunities. Internships, independent study, study abroad, and research with faculty are examples of such activities. While these opportunities usually do exist, the question to ask is: "For whom?" Find out what is required in order to participate. What percent of students take advantage of such opportunities before they graduate? Ask to see lists of completed projects. If a perk sounds good in a college's presentation, look for evidence that it can become a reality for you.

3. Understand course availability. Most undergraduate programs expect students to take twenty-eight to thirty-six courses (depending on how they define course credits) in order to graduate. Toward that end,

colleges will attempt to impress you with the breadth of their curricula and the amazing range of academic experiences. In order to determine how well you will be served by this curriculum, you need to dig further. For example, what will happen if you change your mind about a major? How easily can you move from one program or college to another? Will you lose ground in your progress toward graduation? How often are upper-level courses in your discipline taught? And how accessible are interesting courses that are taught outside of your major?

4. **Who graduates?** The choice of a college should represent a four-year investment of time, energy, and talent that results in a bachelor's degree. Look for evidence that schools will actively support your progress toward graduation. Who will notice if you have difficulty or need assistance? What is the availability of summer school? What are the graduation rates for students in four years? Five years? At some institutions it is not possible for a student to complete a full program of undergraduate study in four years due to inaccessibility of required courses. You need to factor this into your decision making. The financial consequences will be obvious in terms of tuition expectations. Be sure to consider the cost of your lost income opportunity as well.

5. **Outcomes** What happens when you graduate from college? You will hear lots of promising rhetoric. Make sure it is grounded in reality. Ask the career counselors at the colleges where you are interested for information about their placement activities. How do they help prepare soon-to-be graduates for the job market? Do they facilitate internships or provide alumni mentoring programs for their students? What support is there for applicants to medical or law school?

And what are the results? Career counselors at each college should be able to produce information about job placements by major for a five-year period. Look for patterns of quality and consistency. Consult independent studies that show baccalaureate origins of Ph.D. recipients, medical school placements, and business executives. Most of that information is available through the institutional research offices of the colleges you are considering.

Essential Data Checklist

As you process college materials, it will be helpful to create an informational spreadsheet (not to be confused with your personal priorities spreadsheet!) that you can use to chart critical information about each

college and university. Much of the information can be found in the literature provided by the colleges or on their Web sites. List the categories across the top of the page. Then, moving down the left side, create rows for each of the colleges in which you develop an interest.

1. **Application fee/deadline** Enter deadlines for both Regular Decision and Early Decision. On separate lines, note the amount of the fee (as well as conditions under which it can be waived) and indicate whether you can apply online.

2. **Interview** Is it offered and where (on campus or off campus with a staff member or alumnus)? If off campus, note the location and necessary contact information.

3. **Required tests** Beyond the SAT Reasoning Test and/or ACT that most schools require, know which other tests (SAT Subject Tests) you need to be prepared to take. Create at least three lines on which you can list the dates for the tests that are required. Be sure to highlight schools that are test-optional in their requirements.

4. **Location of school (urban, suburban, rural)** Each has its advantages. Make sure you know the type of community (and neighborhood) in which the school is located.

5. **Size** Styles of instruction and opportunities for involvement vary dramatically with the size of an institution. Enter the size of the undergraduate population.

6. **Housing options** Is housing available? Where? For how many years? Are the residence halls gender-specific or gender-neutral?

7. **Type of support (Public, Private)** Another factor that is often underestimated as it often speaks to institutional mission and variances in cost.

8. **Structure (College, University)** Schools vary in their complexity—and can offer programs that are similar in name only but feature styles of instruction as different as night and day. Again, there are advantages to each.

9. **Student/professor ratio** These are important numbers that tell a lot about the accessibility of faculty. Make sure the ratio reflects undergraduates only as well as the professors who teach them.

10. **Academic program** Record the availability of key majors or programs in which you are interested. Note the relative strength of the program that interests you.

11. **Admit ratio (a.k.a. Selectivity)** Note the admit ratio for the college or program of study in which you are interested. This stat will help to define the appropriateness of the playing field for you at that school.

12. Cost Sooner or later, you will need to deal with issues of cost and affordability.

13. Availability of financial assistance Know what you might expect in terms of need and merit-based assistance. List required financial aid applications and scholarship requirements.

14. Distance from home (travel time) Travel time is more relevant than "miles to be traveled" if considering great distances.

15. Travel costs Estimate roundtrip expenses. Make sure you know what it will cost to make the trip several times a year.

You are now ready to absorb lots of information. Armed with the Essential Data Checklist, you can organize the data strategically. Patterns will become clear and critical distinctions between colleges will emerge. You will quickly learn that not all colleges and universities are alike. In fact, they can be very different. A few will have the right educational package for you.

The Pyramid of Selectivity and You

As you research colleges, take time to become familiar with their academic profiles. Where do your credentials fit? At which colleges do you have a reasonable chance of competing for admission—where are you likely to be on the "playing field?" In order to make this assessment you need to know your best SAT verbal and math scores (or highest ACT result) as well as your rank in class and grade point average (if your school does not rank).

Next, compare your results with the admission profiles for schools you are considering. Look at the score ranges for the middle 50 percent of their enrolled students. This is where the real competition takes place. To get a reasonable approximation of your chances of admission, plot your test score (SAT or ACT) aggregate on the continuum. If your scores are:

- In the middle 50 percent, then you are in the competition (Competitive).

- In the top 25 percent, you should be very competitive (Probable).

- In the bottom 25 percent, you should regard that college as a "reach." You need to do all the little things well, prove that you have something unusual to offer—and be incredibly lucky! (Reach)

The same is true of your grade point average. The best combination would be for both your scores and your GPA to be in the top 25 percent of those reported on the profile. Even then there are no guarantees. The

further up the Pyramid you advance, the more your credentials will shift toward the competitive and, then, reach categories.

The Pyramid of Selectivity

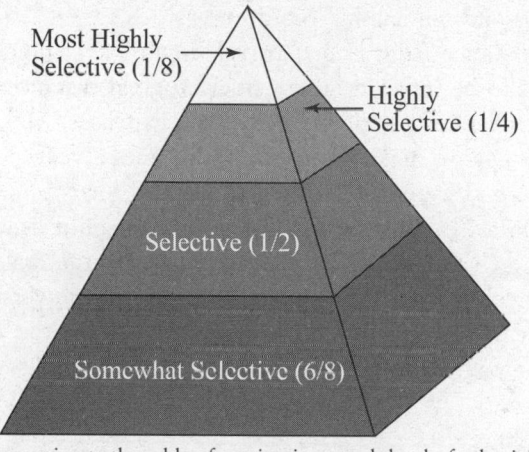

(Fractions approximate the odds of getting in at each level of selectivity.)

The following chart offers a rough approximation of your chances of getting into a college based on its selectivity and where your credentials fall on its profile. The chances or odds of admission are expressed as ratios (i.e., 1:4, 1:2, 3:4, etc.).

	Selectivity (acceptances/applicants)	Where Your Credentials Fall on the Profile		
		Top 25%	Middle 50%	Bottom 25%
	1/8	1:4	1:8	1:16
College	1/4	1:2	1:4	1:8
Admits	1/2	3:4	1:2	1:4
	6/8	9:10	6:8	1:2

For an initial frame of reference, assume your scores and your GPA fall at the same percentile on the admission profile. If your GPA and your scores fall in different percentile ranges, you'll need to split the difference to get a rough approximation of the odds. For example, if you are considering a school that admits one out of four (1/4) and your GPA is in the top 25% (odds are 1:2) but your scores are in the bottom 25% (odds are 1:8), then your overall chances are closer to 1 out of 4.

The data are never as clear-cut in real life as they are in this chart, so you would be unwise to treat this exercise as a precise forecast of your admission outcomes. There are no guarantees for applicants anywhere on

the Pyramid. Even the strongest candidates—the statistical "probables"—must compete against long odds in those environments to gain admission. *The point here is not to offer any assurances but to help you understand how you might use what you know about your credentials to self-select into competitive situations that make sense for you.*

A Competitive Twist

It is common for universities to apply different standards to their various degree programs due to the varying levels of demand for them. For example, the competition to get into the engineering program may be much more intense than the competition for nursing program. The College of Arts and Sciences might operate under yet another set of expectations.

Make sure you understand the admission profiles for the specific programs of the schools that interest you. The standards will not only be different, but the required application elements may be different as well. And resist the temptation to scheme your way into the university through the back door (least selective program). Should you get into that program, you will be expected to stay in it. Your only way out will be to transfer—and transferring between programs or colleges *within* a university that is managing its enrollment tightly can be very difficult if not, at times, impossible.

List Management

As you consider your options, allow your list of colleges to grow—and keep track of the information about each school on your spreadsheet. Highlight your impressions of the *essential* variables at each college. Make note of the selectivity. Then, process each college against your list of personal priorities in search of the best fit. By the time school starts in the fall of your senior year, you should be at the point where you can focus on a short list of six to eight to which you will apply.

Tips for List Management

- Keep an open mind as you get started. As you look for colleges that meet your personal and academic criteria, become familiar with a range of options. There are no "bad" colleges. Some, though, will prove to be better fits than others.

- Don't confuse personalized letters and handsome brochures with indications that a school really wants you. These ploys are all part of sophisticated marketing campaigns. Tens of thousands of students arc getting the same letters from the same schools.

Between the Lines

Be Careful About Making Assumptions

Colleges at the same level of selectivity may boast very different entry standards due to the high degree of self-selection into their applicant pools. While your credentials might be competitive at one college, they may not be on the playing field at another despite similar admit ratios.

- Keep a guidebook or two handy for easy reference as you learn more about colleges. Understand what you are buying, however, as many guidebooks will attempt to seduce you with comparative ratings or provocative reviews. This type of information can be incredibly distracting when you need to be making critical choices based on your own research and priorities. Remember, there are no reliable shortcuts in the college search process.

- Visit college campuses. Experience firsthand the campus culture of any college you are considering. Take tours. Visit classes. Whenever an interview is offered, take it! Talk with students and faculty. Ask questions. You should try to visit at least once before you apply.

- Don't buy on impulse. Sleep on your feelings as long as you can. If they are strong, they won't go away. Decisions driven by emotions are those you are most likely to regret.

- Take an honest look at affordability. Ask your parents what they can or are willing to afford. It is better to know up front rather than finding out after you fall in love with a school that your family cannot afford it.

- Make note of how you are treated. The way an institution responds to you is a good indication of how that place will treat you once enrolled. Look past the fancy literature, the telemarketing, and the staged visits. What happens when you write for specific information or call with a question? How are they treating you?

- Don't assume that, because you believe a college would be great for you, it will value you in the same manner. Use the Pyramid of Selectivity as a guide to the "playing fields" that are best for you.

Make Effective Use of College Planning Resources

As you think of your college goals—and how you get from where you are to where you want to be—where will you turn for guidance? How will you sort through all of the noise that engulfs the college-going process? It seems everyone has an opinion they'd like to share—or sell! Good advice, though, will help you achieve your goals. What may have worked for someone else may not be appropriate for you. Be discriminating, but don't hesitate to rely on those who know you best.

This brings us to the need for good and open communication with your parents. *Seek their advice.* Let them know how you feel about the process. Your parents will have good insights with regard to the interests and concerns that need to be addressed as you look at colleges. In the end, they will be your most important resources—and partners—as you make your way to a happy and successful college experience.

Seek Advice from Teachers and Counselors

The most reliable sources of advice are the people who know you well. They watched you grow. They understand what you like and how you learn. They are familiar with your intellectual abilities and your academic skill set. They have seen you respond to adversity and appreciate your passion for learning new things. They are your teachers, counselors, and advisers—the people to whom you will eventually turn for letters of recommendation. They are your champions. Let them help you.

Start now to take advantage of the guidance these folks have to offer. Find time to meet with a teacher when you can focus on your future. Share your dreams and ambitions. Reflect on strengths, weaknesses, and factors that may have limited your ability to achieve. While this teacher knows you well from extensive in-class experiences, give her the "rest of your story" so she can be an effective mentor to you. Start early (before the senior year) to allow time for a truly expansive conversation.

ACTION STEPS

- Make a list of the things you want your teachers to know about you. Ask for advice to determine how you might best present yourself as a college applicant.

- Prepare a resume that you can share. It will be a good exercise for you and it will give your teachers and counselor an easy frame of reference in talking with you about the future.

- Write a brief statement explaining why you want to go to college and

what you hope to accomplish. Share it with those who will write your recommendations.

Are Independent Educational Consultants in Your Future?

If you are getting started in the college process, you and your parents may be thinking about engaging the services of an Independent Educational Consultant. Independent consultants (a.k.a. private counselors, educational consultants) are individuals who provide a range of college planning services, independent of the school setting, for a fee. Many developed their skills and perspectives through earlier careers as counselors, teach-

Between the Lines

Is a Consultant Right for You?
You need to involve yourself in the conversation with your parents before they hire a consultant. Once on board, that person will be working directly with you. You must be in agreement that the consultant is needed and how he can be helpful. And you must be able to trust him. Otherwise, the experience will be a waste of your time and your parents' money.

ers, or even college admission officers—and are quite good at their work. They are diligent about staying abreast of developments regarding the admission process and often visit several dozen colleges a year.

It is important to note that consultants cannot "get you in" anywhere nor should they do your work for you. While consultants may legitimately offer a range of services from test prep to essay writing support to college list development, *you* must own the process and the outcomes. Don't be taken in by promises. In fact, if a consultant makes a promise with regard to outcomes or seems to be telling you what you want to hear, run!

ACTION STEPS

- Interview prospective independent consultants. Jot down three questions you want them to answer to your satisfaction.

- Describe what your responsibilities would be in the relationship with an independent consultant. What would the consultant's responsibilities be?

- Identifying specific needs with an independent consultant can be helpful.

Get the Most from Web Sites

Web sites offer creative and inter-active college search engines pro-duced by guidebooks, lending institutions, news media, test prep organizations, consultants, and authors. In fact, you will find excellent information on the Web sites of the colleges themselves. The best sites not only answer your questions but also expose you to more questions and answers than you could have imagined. They can take you from start to finish in the college planning process.

Between the Lines

Print It Out

Print out the admission profile pages from the colleges' Web sites. File them with the information you are keeping about each college as they will be useful tools later in the process as you try to determine how well you fit in the admission competition.

Some sites, both independent and college-sponsored, guide you through a self-assessment that reveals more about your aptitude for certain types of career tracks—and then give you links to colleges that offer compatible programs. Most provide an orientation to the admission process (what counts? where? and how much?). Other Web sites focus on strategies for test taking and essay writing. Savvy surfers can complete most of their applications through online connections.

It won't surprise you to know that quite a few colleges now offer access to online chat rooms. While they can be valuable sources of the inside "scoop" on colleges, process what you hear carefully. When one or two voices dominate the conversation, the perspective you gain will be limited if not very one-sided.

ACTION STEPS

- Be clear about what you hope to learn from Web sites.
- When you find a Web site you like, bookmark it!
- Look for value-added qualities. In addition to the basic "stuff" about college admission, what do they have to offer? Chat rooms? Blogs? Newsletters? Scholarship searches?

The College Planning Calendar

The college search and selection process will happen very quickly—and can overwhelm you if you aren't prepared. We will address the application process in the following chapters; however, it might be helpful for you to see the entire timeline in one sequence. Make notes and plan well!

9th Grade	
All Year	Establish good habits in the classroom. Set goals for personal and academic achievement. Follow your passions and interests, not the crowd. It is not too early to prepare for your future!
Fall	Begin to think about the things you like to do or would like to try. Take steps to "test the water" and become part of the action. Try out for the team. Audition for the play. Run for office. Join a club. Volunteer in the community. See what works for you.
Winter	When it is time to choose courses for 10th grade, remain focused on moving to the next level of challenge. If you are in a college-preparatory program, most of your courses will be determined for you. Follow your "tracking" but also stretch yourself.
Summer	Take advantage of enrichment opportunities (sports, performing arts camps, travel). Start a folder that includes brief journal descriptions of your accomplishments.
10th Grade	
All Year	Push yourself academically and grow with your extracurricular involvements.
Fall	Follow your passions. Do the little things that keep you engaged and allow you to grow in the areas that interest you. Take the PLAN if the ACT is the dominant test in your area. Consider taking the PSAT in October just for practice.

Winter	In planning courses for 11th grade, look for ways to move to the next logical level of rigor. Avoid the temptation to focus on courses you might want to pursue in college. Colleges want you to keep your academic base broad and to wait until college to start your major. The exception to this rule is if you are planning to pursue a vocational or specialty program after high school.
Spring	Take any year-end examinations for accelerated courses you have taken. The results will validate your performance as well as the strength of your school's program.
Summer	Continue to pursue enrichment opportunities. Get a part-time job. Begin to think about what you want to do after high school. Take advantage of family vacations and business trips to visit college campuses. Develop a system for organizing the admission materials you will receive/collect from colleges. Fill in your personal calendar with registration deadlines and test dates for the PSAT, SAT, ACT, and SAT Subject Tests that will take place during your junior year.
11th Grade	
All Year	It is time to bear down academically. Expectations continue to grow and the pressure to perform will be greater. If you haven't found your stride academically, it's time to look for it! Colleges are eager to see how you respond as the "bar" is raised.
Fall	Begin a conversation with your parents about what you want to get out of college. Don't worry about the details (what, when, where) just yet. And don't feel that you must be absolutely certain about what you want to study. That will follow. At this point, simply get the conversation started.

11th Grade (continued)	
	Take the PSAT/NMSQT in October. The official practice test for the SAT, the results also determine qualifiers in the competition for National Merit Scholarships. Results will arrive at your school in December. If you are going to pursue test prep, now is the time to explore your options and get registered somewhere.
	Attend college information sessions with visiting admission officers at your school as well as school meetings for juniors that deal with selecting and applying to college. Keep an eye on opportunities to attend college nights and college fairs as well.
	Ask good questions about colleges, careers, and the different routes you might take in defining and then achieving your goals.
Winter	Take stock of your priorities for college. Why do you want to go? Develop a list of possibilities. Ask your parents for their opinions. Map out a plan to take the SAT, SAT Subject Tests, and ACT that extends through your senior year.
	Choose a senior year course load that continues to stretch you. If you want to compete for admission to selective colleges, you must make your senior year count!
Spring	Plan college visits during your spring break. Open House programs can provide very helpful introductions to a college for you and your parents. Attend a college fair in your area if you haven't done so already. Take the SAT or ACT as well as any appropriate AP tests.
	As you plan summer activities (jobs, camps, youth conferences, etc.), be sure to include college visits.

Summer	Continue college visits; interview wherever possible. Register for fall SAT/ACT examinations. Investigate community-sponsored scholarship opportunities.
	Late in the summer, *after your college visits*, begin to narrow your list of colleges. Start your senior year with a "short list" of six to eight colleges, including colleges in each category of selectivity (Reach, Competitive, Probable).
	Become familiar with the application requirements for each college on your list and orient yourself to the essays you need to submit. Start a journal. Write an essay to yourself entitled "Why I want to go to college."
12th Grade	
All year	Prepare for a busy year. The college application process will seem like another course or two on top of everything else on your schedule. Continue doing the things you love. Assume leadership roles where appropriate. Stay on top of your grades!
Fall	By the end of September you should 1.) meet with the teachers who will write letters of recommendation for you, 2.) notify your counselor of the colleges to which you may be applying, AND 3.) complete good drafts of your essays. Familiarize yourself with your high school's procedures and deadlines for processing application materials, including transcripts, mid-year grades, and counselor recommendations.
	Prepare supporting material (portfolio, tape, CD) that speaks to your special talents. Continue to attend college information sessions at your school.
	Plan an overnight visit at a college where you might apply Early Decision (ED) AND at another of your favorite colleges. Compare your impressions of each before completing any ED forms.

12th Grade (continued)	
	Take the SAT/ACT at least once between September and December. Plan to take the SAT Subject Tests necessary to satisfy the requirements of the colleges to which you are applying.
	In October, provide your counselor with your final college list and application due dates. Release test scores to colleges if you are applying Early Decision or Early Action (EA) by October 15. Complete forms for ED/EA applications by October 31.
	Give your parents a copy of the deadline list in the event one of them will be writing the checks to cover application fees.
	File the College Scholarship Service (CSS) PROFILE if appropriate. The PROFILE is typically required of privately supported institutions to determine your eligibility for assistance from the college itself.
Winter	In early December, finish applications that are due between December 31 and February 15. If you applied ED and have been admitted, withdraw all of your outstanding applications.
	Complete and submit applications with pending due dates. Take the SAT, SAT Subject Tests, or ACT if necessary. Make sure your mid-year grades are submitted to the colleges where you have applied.
	File the Free Application for Federal Student Aid (FAFSA) as soon after January 1 as possible. The FAFSA will determine your eligibility for government assistance.
	From early February through mid-March, consider returning to some of your favorite colleges to stay overnight and attend classes.

Spring	You should begin to receive final admission decisions from late March to early April. Financial aid awards will typically follow after a week or so.
	Attend receptions/programs for accepted students. Ask lots of questions! Be prepared to declare your commitment by May 1.

Chapter 4

Road Trip!

Seeing Is Believing

At the risk of stating the obvious, there is a good chance your college education will represent one of the most significant investments in your life. Whether you choose a place that costs $40,000 or $140,000 over four years, that's a lot of money—and four years is a big chunk of your life! When you consider everything that is at stake, how much are you willing to leave to chance?

The question, then, is, how are you going to do your shopping? You could learn everything you need to know online and make your purchase there. Or you might prefer to buy from the catalog—guidebooks certainly give you that option. After all, you can buy pretty much anything you want from the comfort of your home.

That said, do you really want to order your college experience sight unseen? Would you buy a car this way? Not likely. You would want to sit in it, test all the options, and see how it handles on the road. So, why not give the colleges you are considering the same treatment? Get out and see

their campuses. Talk to their students. Experience the classrooms. Check out their dining halls. Get up close and personal with the places you are considering so you can make informed choices.

By investigating college campuses in person, you reach beyond the marketing propaganda to make firsthand evaluations. The college is there for you to discover on your own. You can replace the preconceived notions (biases introduced by family, friends, the media, and promotional brochures) that define your initial level of interest with your own filters. Now is the time to begin working on your gut feeling.

The following are common observations made by students upon finally visiting a college or university campus. Imagine how these revelations affected the thought process for students as they made decisions about where to enroll.

Things They Wouldn't Have Known Without Visiting the Campus

The Good . . .

- "The professors are amazing. One of them even gave me a tour of her lab."
- "The students were very outgoing. Everybody asked if we needed anything."
- "I really liked the energy. It seemed like there was a lot of life on campus."
- "It's a beautiful campus. I liked the architecture and wide open spaces."

The Bad . . .

- "Security was everywhere. I didn't realize it was in such a bad section of town."
- "The people are nice but I wouldn't want to have to live in their dorms."
- "The people weren't very friendly. Everybody seemed *so* serious."
- "There was a lot of graffiti and the campus was actually pretty dirty. It didn't seem like anyone really cared about how the place looked or felt."

The Better to Know Now Than Later . . .

- "There were a lot of hills. I don't know if I can deal with all the up and down."
- "It's much bigger than I had imagined. Getting to class could be a hassle."
- "When I finally found the beautiful fountain that was in the viewbook it was dry and covered with leaves. It made me wonder about other pictures I had seen."
- "I really didn't get a sense of a campus per se. It was just a group of buildings scattered around the neighborhood."

When you approach the college selection process as a consumer, the value of the campus visit becomes clear. Each place you visit *could* become your home for four years. Spending time on its campus gives you an opportunity to check out the merchandise before buying. In many cases, the

campus visit also gives you the opportunity to accomplish two other important objectives: demonstrate your interest in the institution and tell your story.

Demonstrate Interest

In Chapter 7, you will learn more about the Hidden Agenda and factors (beyond the credentials you submit) that can influence admission decisions at some schools. One of those factors is the likelihood that you will enroll if accepted. The best indicator of your interest in a college is the fact that you have gone to the trouble of visiting its campus. Therefore, you should make sure you are on the "radar screens" of the schools on your short list.

Don't wait, as many students do, to see where you are accepted before making plans to visit. For schools that are trying to gauge your level of interest through the campus visit, it will be too late! Whenever possible, plan to visit places on your short list *before* you apply. And when you visit, make sure you check in at the admission office—or some place where you can sign in to document that you were indeed there!

Between the Lines

Are You Undocumented?

The odds are that you have already been on the campus of at least one college or university that you really like—but nobody knows it! You are undocumented! You may have visited a friend for the weekend, gone to a ballgame, or attended a concert—but the time you spent on the campus was never recorded. To the person reviewing your credentials there is no context for your application—no way of knowing that you have a relationship with the school in question. You can ill afford to have an admission committee put you on the Wait List because it isn't certain of your interest!

Tell Your Story

If a college offers the opportunity of a personal interview while you are on campus, take it. The interview gives you a chance to develop a relationship with someone who will later be involved in the credential review process. If there are things that need to be made known regarding your academic performance or your life experience in general—interpretations or explanations of unusual circumstances—this is also the time to tell your story. Admission officers need to understand what's going on contextually, but they aren't mind readers. They can't make it up and you

don't want them to start guessing. So, you need to ask yourself, "What do I have to lose?"

The prospect of having to talk with a stranger for half an hour or so may not seem too appealing. That you'll probably be expected to talk about yourself or that this conversation might have a bearing on your admission outcome doesn't make the task any easier. The good news is that nobody ever died in an admission interview! It's safe—and relatively harmless. It's not a test. In fact, the people you meet are really decent human beings who are simply interested in getting to know you better. Give them the chance.

As an interviewer, I always looked for opportunities to learn something new with each encounter. This led to fascinating conversations about the mental preparation actors go through as they take on other personas, theories regarding the convergence of parallel lines in space (way over my head!), and the politics of poverty. I learned how to sail, followed the hand of an artist as it covered fresh canvas, and watched the sun in its early morning ascent from the top of Mount Masada through the eyes of students who had been there.

For me, each interview was an opportunity to meet with and understand a young person from a perspective that wasn't scripted anywhere. I could not have otherwise known the circumstances of the political exile who was understandably reluctant to reveal her family's story or the homeless youth who came to my office with the simple plea: "All I want is a chance. I want someone to believe in me so I can get an education that will enable me to make a difference in the world."

Interview Tips

- Dress comfortably. Don't let your attire distract interviewers from the opportunity to get to know you.

- Take advantage of opportunities to become familiar with campus life. Check out the school newspaper or a calendar of activities to get a sense of what's happening.

- Relax. Smile. Extend a firm handshake. Maintain good eye contact. Don't slouch in your seat. You demonstrate your respect for the interviewer by your posture and mannerisms.

- Eliminate the conversational "hiccups" ("like," "well," "you know") and stow the gum!

- Be prepared to talk about your passions. Many interviewers are eager

to learn something new. You never know when something you enjoy might lead to a broader conversation.

- Have a resume handy but don't be surprised if the interviewer puts it aside to focus on you.

Between the Lines

No Such Thing as a "Drive By" Visit!

You need to do more than drive by or through a campus in order to get a handle on what it has to offer. You've got to get out of the car, walk around, talk to people, and feel what it's like to be on that campus. There is no such thing as a "drive by" college visit!

- Be prepared to ask one or two thoughtful questions that relate to your areas of interest. For example, why not find out about opportunities for independent study or study abroad?

- Tell your story. If circumstances beyond your control have influenced your performance, now is the time to bring them to light.

Make the Most of Your Visit

Plan to visit colleges as early and often as possible. Talk with your parents about combining college visits with business trips, family gatherings, and vacations. See as many places as possible early in your search. Even if a college does not appear on your initial list, spending time on its campus will give you a valuable perspective for more informed decision making later in the process. Besides, you may discover things at a previously unknown college that may impress you. More than a few students have chosen such colleges that emerged from random visits.

You are likely to run into a range of visit opportunities that include:

- **Personal Interviews.** Many colleges offer personal interviews on weekdays throughout the year. Call six to eight weeks in advance to schedule the date and time that works best for you.

- **Group Information Sessions.** Institutions that welcome large volumes of visitors provide information sessions one or two times a day, including Saturdays. The sessions are typically an hour in length and offered in tandem with campus tours.

- **Campus Tours.** Student guided tours are usually offered several times

daily on weekdays throughout the year and on Saturdays during the academic year. Some colleges and universities offer additional tours of featured academic (arts, sciences, etc.) programs.

- **Open Houses.** Colleges tend to offer open house events at times of the year (breaks in high school calendars) when large numbers of students are likely to visit. These events provide good opportunities to hear student panels and meet with faculty.

- **Overnight Visits.** At some point you will want to have a comprehensive, overnight experience. Admission offices can help arrange these visits with volunteer hosts.

- **Meetings with Professors/Coaches.** With enough advance notice, you can arrange, through the admission office, to meet members of the faculty. You may need to contact the athletic departments directly to schedule informational meetings with coaches.

VISIT SEQUENCE

Ideally, you will have visited the college at which you enroll *three* times. Each visit serves a different purpose as you become acclimated to the college search and advance your interest in specific schools.

1. **Look/See.** This is the initial survey visit. Take a tour. Attend an information session. If the college is far from your home and an interview is offered, take it. The purpose of this visit is to determine if you want to add the college to your list. Visit as many colleges as possible. Resist the temptation to make emotional commitments right away. You may find yourself falling in love with a place, but there is much more to learn before you are ready to rule out other options. The best time to make this visit is during your junior year or the summer prior to the start of your senior year.

2. **Investigate.** When you have determined your short list of colleges, begin planning a second round of visits. The point of these visits is to learn as much about the place as possible—from the insider's perspective. Visit when the college is in session, preferably in the fall or winter of your senior year. Try to achieve immersion. Become a student on that campus for 24 hours. Talk with students, meet with professors, and, if possible, stay overnight on the campus. Get inside the culture of the place—especially those elements of campus life that are important to you (athletics, music, theater, volunteerism, etc.).

    If the cost of attending will be an issue, you and/or your parents should meet with a financial aid officer. Many financial aid officers

will review costs as well as sources and methods of payment. Some will work with your parents to determine your expected family contribution.

3. **Time to Buy.** You have been accepted—hopefully, to several colleges—and now it's time to "buy." Assuming you used your priorities and the five points of a good fit as a compass bearing thus far, you need to rely again on your gut feeling in making a final decision. Attend programs for accepted students. Stay overnight—again. Imagine yourself in the classroom, the residence hall, and the dining hall every day. How does it feel?

In the final analysis, visiting college campuses is probably not at the top of your list of things to do right now. Every day you spend visiting campuses is time away from school, rehearsals, work, and just hanging out with friends. Multiple visits to colleges that are geographically removed from you can represent a major disruption in your schedule.

If the trips take place during school time, make sure you communicate well with your teachers. You need to stay on top of your work. Colleges are not likely to cut you slack if your grades slip while you are visiting campuses.

On top of it all, you will be spending more time than usual with your parents. As you may know from experience, there will be good days and days when you might want to go back to bed! The last thing you can afford, though, is to allow any kind of tension to persist. Stress and frustration are pretty transparent to an interviewer. Whatever may be going on behind the scenes, you need to stay composed when going "public."

That said, there is no reason why you and your parents shouldn't enjoy this experience. This is a big deal for them, too. They are proud of you and eager to see you achieve your goals. That's their prerogative. In all likelihood, they will bear the brunt of the cost over the next four years. Smile and indulge them in the questions and well-intended suggestions that are bound to pop up along the way.

Checklist for a Successful Campus Visit

1. **Plan ahead.** If possible, schedule your visit at least two weeks in advance. At some colleges, you may need to call two months in advance for an interview appointment. This will be especially true over the summer and around holidays.

2. **Prepare well.** Read the information you have about the school. While on campus, you will want to test your impressions. Know why you are there. See how you fit. Think of good questions to ask. They should reflect your understanding of the place and not be designed to trick anyone. Get a good night's sleep before your visit.

3. **Arrive early.** Give yourself time to stretch and walk around before you make an official introduction. Find a snack bar or some place where you can comfortably take in campus life. Take advantage of opportunities to introduce yourself to the people you encounter. Listen to their stories. When its time to check in, *you* take the lead.

4. **Take advantage of everything they have to offer.** Interview if you can. Take a tour. Visit an academic department or program area in which you have an interest. Ask thoughtful questions that reflect your interest. This is your chance to learn—and to make a good impression.

5. **Get more than one opinion.** A campus visit that features an interview, or an information session, and a tour, limits you to the perspective of two people: the interviewer and the tour guide. Don't be content with what they have to say. Casually engage other students in conversation as well. Ask questions like: "What do you like most about your experience?" "How would you describe the academic environment?" "How is this college helping you to achieve your goals?" "If you could change one thing about your experience, what would it be?"

6. **Record your visit.** Make notes as soon as you are able. Take pictures and collect post cards. The more colleges you see, the more they will run together in your mind. Record the visit in a timely fashion to avoid confusion later.

7. **Follow-up.** Your campus visit gives you a chance to collect impressions and establish relationships. Be sure to thank people for extending themselves to you.

8. **Absorb it.** Resist the impulse to come to immediate judgment, one way or the other, on a campus visit experience. Sleep on it. Process what you have learned. Weigh your impressions against those you have of other schools. Your first reaction is bound to be emotional. In the end, you need to remain as objective as possible.

Get Your Testing in Order

Standardized tests. You know these guys—the dreaded SAT, the ACT, the SAT Subject Tests. I have found few students who have anything positive to say about the tests. They're long and grueling exercises. And they're scheduled on your day off—what a way to kill a weekend! Sitting for the ACT or the SAT is clearly not something you do for enjoyment. Rather, you do it because you have little choice in the matter.

So, what's in a test and why does it seem to carry so much weight in determining your future options? Who gets the advantage and why? Do colleges really pay attention to test results? After the pain and suffering, is there any possible good that can come from taking these tests?

A Little Background

Standardized tests were established generations ago to provide a standard measure of assessment for students coming from a wide range of academic environments and to help colleges determine which students had the

capacity to find success in their first years of college. Produced by different test-making companies, the ACT and the SAT are as different as "night and day" in terms of content and orientation. Whereas the SAT gauges your ability to reason in areas of reading, writing, and math, the ACT measures subject-based achievement.

The logic behind the testing begins to unravel, though, with the realization that test results have a marginal effect on the ability of colleges to predict the success of students in the first year. In other words, as diagnostic measures, the SAT and ACT are not terribly useful in most situations because:

- Factors such as courses, grades, grade point average, essays, and letters of recommendation are, in the aggregate, more reliable predictors of student success.

- The high level of self-selection of students into applicant groups at colleges across the country means that most students applying to most colleges have effectively prequalified for admission at those places.

- The tests can be coached. The fact that improvement can be achieved through test prep lends an air of superficiality to the results and lessens their value as diagnostic tests.

Together, these factors greatly reduce the predictive value of standardized tests and render test results virtually meaningless in the decision-making process. This is a troubling notion if the purpose of the tests is to provide colleges and universities with a measure that will help them make better decisions about whom to admit.

So, if test results are not that useful within the context for which they are intended, why all the angst? Why do they still hang over you like a dark cloud? Surely, there must be some good reason why colleges and universities continue to require the submission of test results. The following are five possible rationalizations for the use of standardized testing beyond predictive diagnostics.

1. **Scholarship Qualification and Recognition.** The PSAT serves a dual role as the practice test for the SAT and the qualifier for students in the National Merit Scholarship competition. (Colleges are discouraged from factoring these results into their decision making.) Your SAT and ACT results also factor prominently as colleges, universities, and community organizations administer their own scholarships.

2. **Scores Level the Playing Field.** Standardized tests have been regarded by many in education as "levelers of the competitive playing field." With students applying to college from all types of academic backgrounds across the country, these tests provide information about applicants that is standardized. In theory, if every student takes the same test, the results will indicate who is better prepared for that first step into the college classroom at colleges up and down the Pyramid of Selectivity. That sentiment has abated, however, with the realization that other factors are better predictors of academic success and the test results indicate little more than how well a student has mastered a particular testing format! It can also be argued that the playing field is not so "level" when many students cannot afford the advantages of test preparation.

3. **Test Results Are Competitive Credentials.** Colleges and universities are very sensitive to what the testing profile will look like for each entering class. In fact, many admission and scholarship selection processes treat test scores as competitive credentials—the higher, the better! To the people who "keep score" on college campuses and in the media, it seems test results are an indicator of how intelligent an entering class might be. They wrongfully assume, for example, that score improvement from one entering class to the next is an indication that "we enrolled more smart kids." A more accurate assessment would be, "we enrolled more test-savvy kids."

4. **Big Business.** College entrance testing and all of its ancillaries have become very profitable enterprises for the test-makers. In addition to selling seats for each test administration, the testing companies sell the names of test-takers to colleges and universities that are trolling for applicants. (You are asked if you want to receive information from colleges when you register for each test.) The test-makers have also gotten into the business of test preparation and curriculum development (in high schools) on the premise that students can be prepared to achieve better results. Given what is at stake financially, it is little wonder that the test-makers aren't inclined to concede to the assertion that the tests may have outlived their usefulness.

5. **Test Results Help You Find the Best College Fit.** The flip side of the "trolling" by colleges is that, armed with test results, you are afforded a point of reference in finding a good college fit. After all, you know your scores. Why not look for places where they fit into the range of acceptability. Be careful, though, not to make too many

assumptions regarding admission outcomes. While your scores might project you onto the playing field, they will likely be factored with all of your other credentials to determine whether you get in. At the more selective institutions, your scores must compete with thousands of others—that are just as good.

The Testing Line-Up

The following are brief descriptions of the tests you will encounter as you make progress toward completing your college applications.

ACT®

The ACT it is a four-part test that measures your general educational development in English, mathematics, reading, and science. Scores range from 1 to 36. The optional Writing Test measures your ability to plan and write a short essay.

SAT® Reasoning Test

The SAT Reasoning Test (a.k.a. the SAT) provides an assessment of a candidate's preparedness to meet the academic challenges and expectations in the first year of college. The test assesses critical reading, math problem solving, and writing (including a written essay)—each on a scale of 200-800.

PSAT/NMSQT®

The PSAT is really short for PSAT/NMSQT or the Preliminary SAT/National Merit Scholarship Qualifying Test. The PSAT/NMSQT is cosponsored by the College Board and the National Merit Scholarship Corporation. Patterned after the SAT Reasoning Test (but without an essay), the PSAT can help you qualify for scholarships and serves as a practice test for the SAT.

PLAN®

The PLAN is a pre-ACT test offered to students in the fall of the sophomore year as a means of assessing current academic development.

SAT® Subject Tests

SAT Subject Tests are one-hour tests measuring knowledge and college-level preparedness in particular subject areas. Students may take up to

three tests on the same test date but may not take the SAT Reasoning Test and the SAT Subject Tests on the same date. Nineteen (19) SAT Subject Tests are offered six times a year.

You Have Options!

You don't have to absorb the on-rushing tidal wave of testing, and you don't have to turn yourself into a nervous wreck or testing geek into order to survive. You have options! For example, the tests are "coach-able." It has been demonstrated that you can effectively prepare yourself (test prep) for optimal results. Moreover, you can choose the test format (ACT or

Between the Lines

More Colleges Move to Test-Optional Admission

The number of colleges and universities that now make tests optional in the admission process continues to grow rapidly. Despite cynical taunts that they are merely engaging in public relations gimmicks, many will point to higher acceptance rates among "non-submitters" and more diverse classes overall as evidence that the test-optional environment is producing healthy results.

SAT) that most closely favors your testing orientation. And, finally, you may find yourself applying to colleges that will consider your application *without* test results. Let's take a look at how each of these options might play out for you.

You Can Apply to College Without Submitting Standardized Tests

Did you know that you can apply to many colleges without having to submit standardized test results? It almost sounds too good to be true, but approximately 25 percent of the four-year colleges in the country now welcome applications from students that do not include test results. The number of test-optional institutions now exceeds 700 and seems to grow daily as places at all levels of selectivity on the Pyramid have found they are comfortable making decisions without test scores.

I will never forget the day my former institution announced that it had become test optional. As an admission officer evaluating thousands of applicants each year, it was an incredibly liberating experience. I felt like my colleagues and I had emerged from the tyranny of numbers. We could now value students for their personal interests and strengths rather than their test results. The test results were truly no longer important in our deliberations.

If your scores are modest and you ever find yourself in a situation where an admission representative offers assurance that test results are "not that important" at his school, go to www.FairTest.org for verification. A Web site run by a watchdog organization concerned with the appropriate use of testing, FairTest.org lists all of the test-optional colleges and universities in the country. Schools that back up their rhetoric with action will be on the list.

Tips for Applying Test Optional

- If your scores are not in the top 25 percent of those listed on the college's profile for enrolled students, then you are a prime candidate for test-optional admission. Why risk allowing them to hurt your overall credentials?

- Do *not* request that the College Board or the ACT report your scores directly to the test-optional colleges to which you are applying.

- Be prepared to submit alternate credentials, such as portfolios or graded writing samples, in lieu of test results.

- Don't assume that because you have found a number of test-optional colleges that you don't need to take any standardized tests. The odds are that somewhere along the line you will want or need to consider a college that requires a test submission. Better to be safe than sorry in that instance.

Most Colleges Will Consider Either the SAT or the ACT

Most colleges in the country (99 percent) welcome either test result in their admission process. But there is a very good chance that you have grown up with an awareness of and loyalty to one "flavor" of testing or another. If you live in the Midwest, you've come to know the ACT and PLAN very well, whereas the SAT has been the coin of the realm on either coast. The notion of switching or mixing and matching when it comes to the tests for which you sit is not foremost on your mind. If the SAT is the dominant test in your area, the reasoning goes, why complicate your life by taking a test that not many people seem to know about?

Consider the following scenario. You have applied to XYZ university—a place that admits 40 to 50 percent of its applicants. By most standards (courses, grades, extracurricular activities), your credentials are very attractive to XYZ—except for your SAT results, which are relatively modest in this competition. The folks at XYZ like what you have to offer in general but get hung up on your test results.

"How will these scores affect our (college) profile?" is the unspoken question that lingers over your application. The people making the decision already know you can do the work at XYZ. They have conceded that your SAT result no longer holds any diagnostic value. It has become, however, a competitive credential. As such, how will it look on the profile?

If, however, they find you are presenting a respectable ACT credential as well, their attention will turn quickly to those results. Realizing that the public is not nearly as focused on the ACT as a measure of comparison among colleges and universities, the decision at XYZ might be to admit you on the basis of your ACT results. That way, they will have a viable score result for you (ACT) and can avoid having to report the less than favorable SAT score on the institutional profile.

MORE THOUGHTS ABOUT MIXING AND MATCHING

- Sit for at least one administration of both the SAT and the ACT. What do you have to lose? Rather than sitting for multiple sessions of either—more than two tend to provide diminishing returns—why not use one of those Saturday mornings to diversify your testing credential?

- Play to your strengths. If you are a strong test-taker, you should do well on either test. If taking tests is not your thing, then you are more likely to produce strong results on the ACT than the SAT. Remember, this is a reflection of test-taking savvy, not intelligence or achievement.

- Many colleges accept the ACT in lieu of SAT Subject Tests.

- The ACT is well known among colleges. In recent years, the numbers of students sitting for the ACT and the SAT are essentially the same.

The Tests Are Coach-able

Most colleges still require test results of some sort. That much we know already. If you are fortunate to have really high scores, you can tuck them away and move on to more important things. On the other hand, if your scores are at or below the average for your favorite colleges—or you haven't even taken tests yet—then you might begin to worry: "What if my scores aren't great? How will I compete?" If you believe that your current testing situation won't represent you well or you are not confident as a test-taker, then explore test prep options.

You *can* improve your scores through test prep, and your options range from well-established test prep companies to courses offered by your teachers at your school to a whole host of tutoring scenarios. You can participate in instructor-led programs in the classroom and you can engage in self-taught programs through test prep books and online courses.

Whatever the test prep looks like, you must invest in making it work, however. Just because your parents might be prepared to put money down on a test prep course to "take care of the testing problem" doesn't mean that your SAT results will automatically go up by 200 points! You have to sit yourself down and commit to the course in much the same way you commit to doing well in trigonometry or English literature or French IV. You can't "will" score improvement!

Guidelines for Approaching Test Prep

- Examine your motives for pursuing test prep. What impact will your scores have on your admissibility? Will investment in test prep detract from your ability to stay focused on other elements of your academic and extracurricular performance?

- Outline what you hope to accomplish through test prep. How will you measure success?

- Distinguish between test prep courses, test prep workshops, and practice tests. The courses are more intensive, include practice tests, and address both content and strategies. Workshops focus on strategies and may include a practice test. They tend to be less content driven. Practice tests are either actual tests that have been "retired" or are carefully constructed look-alikes.

- Good test prep courses will help you to relax by giving you an understanding of the construction, content, and pace of the test and by allowing you to practice on content that may be customized to address your areas of weakness.

- The best time to engage in test preparation is the period of two to three months immediately prior to the date of the test itself.

- Be wary of test prep companies that promise to improve your scores by hundreds of points. While they might have good products, the effectiveness of the product is dependent on your level of investment.

- When you measure progress through test prep, make sure you compare actual test results—your actual test results before test prep with those of the next test following test prep. It is not uncommon for test prep companies to use comparisons of actual tests taken prior to the course with the results of practice tests in reporting score improvement.

- Even without test prep, students often experience score increases from one test to the next (i.e., your scores may go up regardless!).

- Reading continues to be one of the best and least expensive strategies for maximizing score potential.

What to Do and When

Now that we have exposed some testing options for you, let's take a quick look at the basics: What do you need to do and when? First, plan to sit for tests of choice at least twice—once in the spring of the junior year and again in the fall of the senior year. You will have options in each season. May (spring) and November (fall) seem to work the best for most students, although you will want to be sensitive to your Advanced Placement exam schedule in the spring and Early Decision deadlines in the fall.

Taking the tests at six-month intervals allows you to absorb more of the traditional classroom

Between the Lines

Get Your Scores into Play

Make arrangements to have your scores sent to the colleges where you will be applying. You can take care of this when you register to take the test and you can ask to have scores sent to colleges after the fact as well. While many high schools routinely report score results on transcripts, colleges like to see official reports sent directly from the testing organization.

content while giving you a chance to prepare more systematically. The natural learning curve is likely to contribute to some score improvement even without test prep. Regardless, resist the temptation to over-test. More than three tests tend to fall in a very predictable range and there is usually no advantage to persistent test taking. If you feel the need to sit for a third, try the test you have yet to take. If you are otherwise SAT oriented, take the ACT and vice versa.

Check with the colleges and universities to which you might apply to determine their requirements for SAT Subject Tests. While these tests are not required by many schools, it is best to know which ones are required and where. The best time to take the Subject Tests is at the administration that allows you to complete as much subject-related course work as possible in school. For example, if you take biology as a junior, then May or June of your junior year would be the best time to take the Biology Subject Test. Similarly, if you take AP Biology in your senior year, you might wait until December to take the Biology Subject Test.

Finally, there is little value to taking any of these tests (except the PLAN, which is only administered in 10th grade) prior to your junior year. Some talent search programs such as the Center for Talented Youth use the results of SATs taken in 7th or 8th grade to determine eligibility for their programs. Otherwise, introducing you to college entrance tests

that early in your life is placing undue emphasis on the tests at the expense of other things you would normally be doing.

For more information about the SAT and the ACT, including access to online registration, go to www.collegeboard.com and www.act.org/.

Be Careful Not to Obsess About Testing!

The downside to spending so much time talking and thinking about testing is that we have already conceded more to the testing process than it deserves. Yes, you need to take tests to get into college. Yes, there are things you can do to help yourself and improve your scores. And, yes, it is possible to obsess on this part of the admission process to the point of excluding other important considerations. Among them is your need to have a life!

Regardless of their perceived value, standardized tests are clearly an integral part of the admission process. Keep them in perspective, though. Find the reality of each admission situation so you can determine how, if at all, your test results may be factored into the admission decision. Then, prepare accordingly.

Chapter 6

Challenge Yourself in the Classroom

The "Number One" Credential

Much of what you have accomplished thus far in school and in life is foundational. It establishes a base upon which you can build as you apply for jobs, leadership or cross-cultural opportunities, or admission to college. This is particularly true of your work in the classroom where your credentials have been taking shape since your first day in high school. Collectively, they define your capacity to respond to complex learning situations and to produce at higher levels academically. At colleges that can be highly selective, they determine your competitiveness as a candidate.

That you are able to "do the work" is a fundamental consideration for admission officers. If they're concerned about your ability to function successfully in their academic environments, they won't admit you. It won't matter that you might be immensely talented in other areas or that your family has a long-standing relationship with the school. You need to

be able to demonstrate that, if given the opportunity, you'll be able to find some level of success academically.

Demonstrate Your Passion for Learning

Colleges are always on the lookout for students who love to learn and whose passion takes them to the highest level of challenge and achievement. Students who are able, well prepared, and excited about learning routinely go beyond what is expected to find new opportunities to stretch themselves.

Highly selective institutions—those in the top half of the Pyramid of Selectivity—are especially interested in this sort of passion as they make fine distinctions between very talented candidates. Their tip-off to your passion: **the progression of courses you took in high school.** Specifically, have you moved to the next logical level of rigor in each of your years of high school?

Between the Lines

Breadth and Depth
Colleges want to see that you're well prepared across the curriculum. *At the very least*, this means taking four years of English and social studies and two years of math, science, and foreign language. Selective colleges want to see more. The higher you aspire on the Pyramid of Selectivity, the more likely it is that *colleges will expect you to take four years of each* (*starting in ninth grade*)—even though you are not required by your high school to do so.

Colleges can infer a great deal about your passion for learning from the way you use the curricular choices that are available to you in high school. In particular, they want to see evidence that you are continuing to stretch yourself academically across all disciplines. The choices you make tip off admission officers in this regard as they define your skill sets and establish your competitiveness.

For example, if you want to pursue engineering, it is imperative that you develop your math and science skills to the most advanced levels offered at your school. If you are inclined toward foreign language and cross-cultural study in college, then advanced exposure to a second foreign language would be a good idea.

Perhaps an even more compelling reason to choose well in planning your academic program is that selective colleges will use the strength of your academic program as a filter in determining your competitiveness. The farther up the Pyramid you aspire, the greater the possibility that an

element of your academic preparation could be the determining factor in eliminating you from the competition. A missing science class in the senior year or the appearance of less rigorous social studies electives in place of what could have been an advanced or honors course can be the proverbial kiss of death in tight competitions. In order to compete at highly selective schools, you need to move to the next logical level of rigor in each of your subject areas.

Finally, you need to get the job done. Having good ability is not enough as you compete at highly selective schools. What better way to show that you are *getting the most out of your ability* than to challenge yourself in courses that are progressively more difficult—and do well in them!

Between the Lines

The Choices You Make Affect Your Options

Not everybody is cut out for the most rigorous courses in each discipline. For example, if you are not very good with sciences or don't have a good history with foreign languages, your course selections might be skewed away from those areas. While this might not be an issue at less selective schools, the absence of breadth in your curriculum may limit your options among colleges that can be very picky. The best colleges for you, then, will be those that *value you for your successes* in the courses that you have taken.

The Most Important Year Is . . .

The most important year of high school is the year you are in! Each year is foundational. Whether you are in your first, second, or third year, your performance sets you up for new opportunities in the year that follows. If you are a senior, the premium on doing well is tied to getting into college and setting yourself up for academic success in your first year.

Whatever your year in school, it is vital that you get off to a good start and stay on top of your studies. Resist the temptation to put off assignments. The last thing you want to do is dig yourself a hole academically. You may have remarkable recovery skills but you will spend too much energy playing catch up, diminishing your ability to perform at your best in critical situations. Work toward mastery of the material on a day-to-day basis in order to develop the skills and confidence necessary to handle more difficult work later in the year. Do well today so tomorrow can count for something.

While each of your high school years is important, admission officers regard the senior year as a good indicator of where you have placed your passion and your priorities. Given options in choosing courses, how do you opt to stretch yourself? Admission officers can get a quick read on your passion for learning by checking to see if the degree of rigor in your senior year program is appropriate to your level of ability. The more selective the institution, the greater are the expectations.

Between the Lines

Keep Stepping Up

Which impression do you want to give colleges—that you are content to stay at the level of your junior year and just take what you need to graduate or that you are continuing to seek new challenges? Your best bet is to show you have the desire to better yourself in the classroom. In doing so, you keep yourself on the playing field that defines the competition for admission.

That does not mean you should try to take five Advanced Placement classes in the senior year—especially if AP is not the next logical step up for you in a given discipline. It does mean you should follow your academic tracking to take courses that represent the next logical step *up* in rigor or difficulty. If you are considering a highly selective college and are tracked to five AP classes, then you need to take them.

Senior Year Myths

Now, let's put all of this in perspective. The word on the street is that your senior year of high school is supposed to be unlike any other you experience. After all, it's your last year. And what a year it will be! Sure, you'll need to take care of getting college applications ready and you'll have to go to class most of the time. (Even though rumor has it that colleges don't really look at the senior year, the cameos can't hurt.) Otherwise, the plan is to have a great time!

The talk around your school is much the same. You've no doubt heard your friends, as they make plans academically for the senior year, say things like:

"I've already had four years of language starting in eighth grade so I'm done!"

"No more math for me—I've already satisfied my graduation requirement!"

"The sciences aren't for me. Chemistry just about killed me! That's it. I'm out of there!"

" . . .After all, colleges don't really look at the senior year."

Each of these statements reflects a choice the speaker is making—choices that students who want to go to selective colleges will regret. Think carefully about the choices you make. If you succumb to the notion that the senior year isn't that important—that you sim-

Between the Lines

Gain the Competitive Edge
The more selective the college, the more important the senior year performance is *as the deciding credential.* Many colleges wait to see what you do when you don't have to do anything. Give yourself a competitive edge with a strong senior year performance.

ply need to put in time until graduation—you are effectively limiting the range of options that will materialize when the decision letters are delivered in the spring of your senior year.

Let's personalize this even further. Have you ever heard or contemplated the question, "Is it better to take an easier course where I know I can get an 'A' or should I take the harder course where I can probably do the work, but it is more likely that I will get a 'B' or a 'C'?" The answer: take the harder course—and don't give up on the "A!" While that may be easier said than done, you really have no choice if you aspire to schools that fall on the upper third of the Pyramid of Selectivity.

Even if you take the hard course and get the "A," there is no guarantee that you will get into schools at the top of the Pyramid. If you take it and get a respectable grade, though, you will make a good impression on other schools that may not be quite as selective but will respond well to your determination to stretch yourself academically. Taking the easy course and getting the "A" doesn't tell admission officers anything about your ability to perform at high levels of rigor. Choose well, then, to keep yourself on the playing field that defines the competition for admission at the schools you are considering.

Assuming you do all the right things in setting up your courses for the senior year, you still have a major hurdle to clear. It will appear early in January of your senior year. The holidays are a thing of the past. Classes have resumed and the winter doldrums are about to set in. Despite the fact

that this is the time of the academic year when even the best student is prone to letting her guard down, it's perhaps the most important juncture for a student who aspires to a selective college or university.

Colleges that can, and often must, make fine distinctions between well-qualified candidates are eager to see what you do at precisely this point in time. Because they can be choosy, they wait to make final decisions until the middle of March in your senior year to see how your grades are holding up. It's another decision-making filter they can employ given the depth of their respective applicant pools and the knowledge that many talented candidates will take themselves out of the competition at this point.

Things to Keep in Mind as You Choose Courses

- The choices you make matter a great deal. If you are uncertain about what to do with course selections for your senior year, seek advice from the admission representative from one of your favorite schools who is recruiting in your area.

- Students who finish strongly in high school are more likely to find immediate success in college. Conversely, those who do not push themselves, who give in to "senioritis," experience a much more difficult transition when it comes to the academic experience in college. Your senior year effort is an investment in your future success in college.

- Don't over-schedule. It's vital that you understand and stay within your capacity to do work academically. Take courses that make sense given your prior experience and that will enable you to step up to the next logical level of rigor *for you*. Then, do well in them.

- Sprint to the finish! Your high school experience is like a mile race and your senior year is the fourth and final lap. If you are in the lead at the end of the third lap, you haven't won anything. Coasting at this point could be perilous as others are trying to overtake you. Sprint to the finish and leave nothing to chance!

Context Counts (Will They Know?)

It's not unusual for students and, more commonly, parents to express concerns about the different levels of difficulty across high schools. Schools are different after all and it is entirely possible that the same level of effort that produces a 3.6 GPA at one school might produce a 4.0 at another. While this can be very frustrating if you are the one with the lower GPA, take heart. Most colleges understand the differences.

Selective colleges in particular are careful to look at each candidate within the context of the learning environment at his or her high school. Before an academic transcript can be fairly assessed, admission officers

must understand the strength and breadth of program at the high school as well as the nature of the competition in the classroom. When possible, they talk with guidance counselors and review high school profile information to become familiar with curriculum descriptions.

They consider the performances of recent graduates on Advanced Placement examinations as well as their college placement records. They respect the strength of the International Baccalaureate (IB) program, as well as curricula that are indigenous to other countries, and have seen all sorts of permutations to "block scheduling" at schools in this country. Generally, much of this information is made available through your school in the form of a profile submitted with your transcript.

In the end, admission officers are pretty savvy regarding the differences between high schools. As they make fine distinctions between high achieving candidates, though, they go beyond the fact that you are getting the job done to understand "how" and where you are getting it done.

Commonly Asked Questions About Academic Planning

Many of the issues that arise for students as they make course selections must be considered within the context of their learning experiences as well as the competitiveness of the colleges to which they are applying. That's why it is difficult to provide "one size fits all" solutions.

For example, your school may have limited course offerings. Or there may be good reasons for you *not* to take advanced level language courses. Or you might not have the kind of preparation that would enable you to take some of the higher-level courses that might interest you. In each case, you need to make sure the admission committee understands the contributing circumstances.

Keep the Pyramid of Selectivity in mind as well. Each of the colleges and universities on the Pyramid will respond differently to questions about course selections and grades. The more selective schools expect more from you in terms of both program rigor and performance. As a result, they will apply more academic filters to the selection process. Occasionally, institutional responses will be rooted in the requirements of the programs you are considering. Good examples are specialty curriculums in the arts or technical programs.

The following are questions students often ask about matters relating to their academic programs. As you read through the answers, remember that a viable alternative in just about every case is "ask the expert." Contact an admission officer at one or two of the schools on your short list to get an expert opinion.

Q Colleges keep saying that I should take "rigorous" courses in my senior year. Isn't that a good time to take courses that connect to my career interests? I've been a good student and can't believe that colleges care that much about what I do in my senior year. What should I do?

A It really depends on where you want to go and what you want to do. Just be careful not to compromise your ability to prove that you belong on the academic "playing fields" at the schools to which you are applying. Your first objective is to get in—and, yes, the senior year is very much in play, especially at the more selective schools.

Q I am really into literature and the arts and will probably pursue a major in one of those areas when I get to college. Would it be okay if I dropped math and science in my senior year so I can take Advanced

British Literature and a writers' workshop my school has decided to offer? I've gotten really good grades in all my courses so far and want to go to a top university. Will making these switches hurt my chances?

A Good question. On the one hand, the courses you want to take sound rigorous and speak to your academic passions. If you take them, make sure the rigor is well demonstrated, especially for the writers' workshop. That said, you need to be careful about narrowing your course selections as you will be competing with lots of other talented students for limited places in the class—and many of them will have kept their academic programs broad by continuing to take math and science.

Q I am trying to decide whether I should take a third year of language to be competitive for admission at most colleges. My dilemma is even though I give Spanish lots of study time, try as I might, I cannot achieve high marks. I am strong in my other academic courses, but Spanish is the one thing I just don't seem to get. Would it be acceptable if I took another academic course, such as an additional history or science instead of Spanish III?

A If the burden of Spanish is weighing you down, such a switch into another program is probably a prudent move. Clearly, you want to put yourself in a classroom where you are more likely to find success. If you move out of the languages in this instance, it will be important to replace Spanish III with a course of equal rigor.

Q In order to continue playing in the orchestra (where I am first-chair viola), I will need to drop AP physics (that would be my next science course) in my senior year. I like physics and don't want to drop it, but I have been playing the viola for eight years and it would mean a lot for me to continue playing in my senior year. What should I do?

A There really aren't any good solutions here except to go with your gut. If you elect orchestra for reasons that are very good, then you need to make sure your choice is thoroughly explained to admission officers in your application and through the letters of recommendation you assemble. Whatever you do, make sure the reason for the decision is documented.

Q I didn't do as well as I could have academically during my first two years of high school. My junior year was much better and my senior year is off to a great start. I am taking challenging courses (honors and AP), so my question is "will I still be able to get into a good school?"

A Certainly. The only caveat is how you define a "good school." If you mean schools that admit less than one third of their applicants, then you remain a long shot unless you are able to present other credentials that somehow compensate for your academic record. On the other hand, you should be attractive to good schools that are admitting half of their applicants or more. While the ideal scenario is to do well consistently throughout high school, many places will interpret your strong finish as an indication that you are ready to tackle the rigors of college.

Q I have taken three years of French. Would it be acceptable if I switched to another language such as Latin or German in my senior year? Would it count as a fourth year of language, or would it set me back?

A If you *must* switch out of French, you would be better served moving into a higher level course in another discipline. If that isn't possible, going to another language is a viable option because it keeps you engaged with a field of inquiry and skill development (languages), albeit in a first year classroom, that is valued by colleges. The question that admission officers will ask, though, is "why are you switching?" Now, you have a story to tell. Make sure admission officers know why you made the switch. Don't make them guess about your motives.

Q I go to an insanely competitive high school where I work very hard to achieve a 3.5 GPA. I have friends at other schools where I know that I could probably get a 3.8 or 3.9 without working nearly as hard. Will colleges know this or am I going to be penalized for where I go to school?

A You should be fine. Colleges, especially those that are very picky, go to great lengths to make sure they know the schools from which their applicants are coming. You can be sure they'll know about your school and how competitive it is.

Q This is my junior year and I am taking two Advanced Placement classes. Do I need to take the exams?

A While you may not be required to take the AP exams, it is strongly recommended that you do so for three reasons. One, the exams are standardized. Your results will validate the strength of the course you have taken. Two, your exam results are your legacy to students who follow you. Admission officers are more likely to respect the AP course at your school if they see that students have done well in the past. And, three, scoring well on the exam can result in your receiving college credit and/or immediate access to advanced standing in college courses.

Q My parents are talking about sending me to a private boarding school because they don't think my high school is very good. They seem to think that going to the private school will help me get into some of the elite universities. I actually like my school and am doing well. How can I persuade them that I don't need to change schools?

A Most admission officers would agree that your success as an applicant has much more to do with *what you have done with your high school experience than where you have gone to school*. There isn't a school or an adviser or a curriculum in the country that gets kids into college. Kids get themselves into college.

Q Are competitive colleges looking at how I challenge myself or are they more interested in the final grade that affects GPA and class rank?

A Yes and yes. Colleges want to see how you challenge yourself—especially as you get to the higher level courses. Remember, the more selective schools want to see what you do when you don't have to take the challenge. Obviously, they'd like to see you do well. Getting high grades in easier courses, though, won't impress any of the more selective schools. You should try to expose yourself to academic rigor that matches your level of ability—and then do well!

Chapter 7

What Colleges Want

A Good "Fit"—From the College Perspective

As you work your way toward a short list of colleges (six to eight) to which you will apply, start thinking about what will happen when you finally submit your credentials. You know what is important to *you* in selecting a college. Soon, the "shoe will be on the other foot" as colleges take their turn at defining what is important to them and who best "fits" their needs. This chapter takes a look at the factors that influence the decision making of admission committees. Much of what is covered will seem familiar. It's what you don't know, however, that will surprise you.

A common assumption is that admission officers simply admit the good candidates and let the rest go. The problem with such an assessment is that most colleges attract many more applications from good candidates than they can accept. In fact, most (80 to 90 percent) of the applicants at most colleges are worthy of consideration. They have put themselves on the right playing fields academically. As a result, admission committees, including those at colleges that are less selective, are forced to

make fine distinctions between strong candidates. Whether the number is 10 or 10,000, they must say "no" to applicants who have demonstrated they deserve a chance. So who will emerge with the "yes" letter—who gets in?

The answer to that question at the colleges to which you apply lies in how those places define the applicant qualities and credentials that represent the best "fit" for them. The real question, then, is "where will you fit in the college's equation?"—an equation that includes factors that reach into and beyond the credentials you submit. So, what's out there? What kind of underlying institutional pressures and agendas are you about to encounter? What hurdles, seen and unseen, will you need to clear?

The definition of a good fit emerges from different places within an institution. Policy decisions (size of class, availability of funds, marketing orientation, etc.) come from the trustees and senior administration. These folks are concerned with both the financial and the competitive viability of the institution—the business side of the equation.

On the other hand, the faculty usually has a strong voice in determining the academic and personal characteristics that are sought in the entering student body. When you think about it, the professors have good reason to be interested in "fit." They decide what will be taught, how the material will be taught, and how students will be evaluated for their efforts. They "set the bar" academically. Given the opportunity, professors won't hesitate to remind the admission committee, "We want more students who are . . ." They determine the "Agenda" for decision making.

The Agenda

Generally speaking, the message to the admission committee from the faculty at most colleges is, "We want students who are . . ."

- Bright
- Motivated
- High Achieving
- Diverse in Background
- "Givers"

The more selective the college you consider, the more important it is that you demonstrate strengths that correspond with each of these areas. Let's

take a closer look at what colleges might be looking for in each category as they review your credentials.

Bright

What college faculty wouldn't want students who are bright—who have the capacity to learn at advanced levels of instruction? The professors are setting the bar in the classroom. They want to make sure you have what it takes to "clear the bar" in their academic environments.

Between the Lines

Social Engineering

Admission officers are often regarded as social engineers. After determining that candidates are qualified—bright, motivated, and high achieving—they turn their attention to selecting those students who would best comprise a community of diverse backgrounds, talents, and interests.

Motivated

Colleges want to know how you demonstrate your passion for learning. Do you ask questions and press for greater understanding? Do you "push the envelope?" Do you stretch yourself beyond the requirements of the classroom? Professors are genuinely excited when students pose questions for which there aren't easy answers. Motivated students energize the classroom.

High Achieving

Colleges want to know how you use the gray matter that is packed between your ears. They know you've got it because they understand that most students apply to schools where they can do the work. So, having "it" is not the question. They want to see how you use it.

Think about this scenario within the context of the Pyramid of Selectivity. While a lot of schools might be forgiving of temporary lapses in concentration or achievement, the further up the Pyramid you aspire the less tolerance you will find for "under achievement." If you have high aspirations but recognize under-achieving tendencies in your performance, you would be wise to find better focus in your daily work—or be prepared to readjust your college expectations.

Having passed through the first set of filters in the admission process, you've made it to the playing field—and the next round of scrutiny. Now, the question becomes: "What do we get if we take him?"

You've convinced the committee of your academic worthiness. Now, you must demonstrate that you have something to give—something that will set you apart from your peers. This is when the focus shifts from the academic to personal qualities, talents, and perspectives.

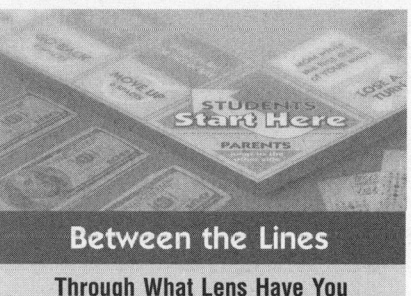

Between the Lines

Through What Lens Have You Seen Life?

We each see life through a lens that is unique to us. That lens can be shaded by many different factors that reflect our life experiences. What has shaped your perspective? *Every applicant has the capacity to bring an element of diversity to a college campus.*

Diverse in Background

Colleges want to know how your life experience shaped the person you have become. What perspectives are you able to share due to your ethnic background? Your social or economic background? How have your faith experiences influenced the way you see the world? Diversity speaks to the *different* perspective you might bring into the classroom and campus environment.

If your background has played a defining role in "who" you have become as a person and "how" you see the world, then you need to make that clear in your application. Don't assume that simply checking boxes related to ethnicity, gender, hometown, faith background, or academic interest will automatically get you in. While a checkmark might be enough to help get you into some schools, others will dig deeper for evidence that you will do things that will share your diversity with others on their campus.

Diversity in Academic Interest

An often-overlooked point of diversity in the admission process is tied to the academic program. Simply put, colleges and universities want to make sure that all of their academic programs are populated. Disciplines such as biology, political science, English, and psychology tend to be very popular and rarely face enrollment problems. On the other hand, a program that is consistently short of students, either because it is new or not terribly visible on the radar screen of majors, will have difficulty sustaining itself. Professors from such areas of study are constantly on the lookout for new students for their programs and will be more aggressively involved in support of the admission effort. If you find you have a *sincere interest* in

an under-populated academic program at a college, you may have an advantage.

That said, be true to your passion. Don't *discover* anthropology, for example, just to give yourself a better chance of getting into your favorite school. Such a strategy will backfire if you can't produce evidence you actually understand the concept! If anthropology has genuinely caught your attention and you can't wait to study it further, make sure this fact is not lost on the admission committee.

How can you know if you might hold such an advantage by virtue of your academic interests? Well, the first tip-off might be that not many people are familiar with the things you would like to study.

Between the Lines

The Niche Gift
For many students, the ability to think about or do something *better* than most is central to defining their respective gifts. Their talents are, by some objective measure, extraordinary. On the other hand, some students possess talents or interests that are extraordinary simply because they are different, perhaps even odd or peculiar. If everything else is equal, such "niche" gifts can carry the day in the competition for admission. This is especially true among the most selective colleges.

If your interests are seemingly obscure, the programs that serve them might be as well. Conduct searches relating to major and career possibilities on the Internet to identify college matches. Or check with your counselor and teachers. Counselors often learn about under-populated programs in their discussions with admission representatives or when they visit college campuses. Teachers with shared interests may also be familiar with strong programs you might explore.

Givers

Colleges want to know what your passions are. What do you like to do more than anything else? Do you sing? Act? Write? Lead? Take care of others? What talent or perspective do you enjoy that sets you apart from your peers? What do you have to *give* that will enrich the campus life of the college you choose to attend? What is your "gift?"

Your gift is reflected in your talents and passions. The best gifts are organic. They are talents and/or feelings that continue to grow, and their impact is realized in proportion to your investment of time and energy. The gift of talent can be found on the stage and the playing field as well as

in the functioning of organizations and the expression of ideas. It can be found in laboratories, soup kitchens, and wilderness clean-ups.

The strength of a gift, though, is relative to the competition that surrounds it. The greater the competition, the more common a gift might seem in the eyes of those rendering judgment. Again, the Pyramid is instructive. A gift that might stand out in the competition—and even help you win a scholarship at one school—might be passed over quickly in the competition at another. That is why you look carefully for colleges that will *value you for what you do well*—that will cherish the gifts that you carry with you.

It's not uncommon for students to struggle with this notion of giving and gifts. While gifts or special talents might be most apparent in the virtuoso musician, marquee actor, and star athlete, you might think your gifts are not that visible. Don't worry. You may not fully appreciate them yet, but you *do* possess gifts—passions, interests, and concerns—that define you and set you apart from your peers. Frankly, not all gifts will be headline grabbers. For example, you might be a gifted writer or thinker. You may have the uncanny knack of being able to influence the behavior of your peers—to move people to action. Or you might quietly demonstrate concern for the environment or care for the sick or elderly. Your gifts of compassion can make a huge difference in the world around you.

If you find yourself hung up on this notion of "giving," talk with your parents. They have known you for quite a while and might be able to lend a perspective that you hadn't anticipated. Once you make it onto the academic playing field, it is what you have to give that can make the greatest difference in the selective admission process. Find your gifts. Cultivate and nurture them. Allow them to grow so that you are in a position to reveal them to the colleges that you would like to attend.

More Thoughts About Giving

- Assess your talents and perspectives. Be sensitive to points of consistency or themes that begin to emerge. How do they define your niche? Be prepared to frame your credentials with a common theme or message that sets you apart.

- Colleges are seeking a broad range of talents in their student bodies. Not all colleges will have the same agenda, however. Some can afford to look for the best of the best or the most unusual when it comes to talent or interests. Others are eager to see that you have been meaningfully engaged in life outside of the classroom in any number of activities.

- Be yourself and avoid becoming gratuitously involved simply to build a long resume. College admission officers are adept at spotting "padded" credentials. Sing well, play hard, and give graciously—bring your commitment to life. The colleges that value you for these contributions will admit you.

- Project yourself as a contributor. You need to make a compelling statement that you intend to continue your involvement in college. Admission officers tend to be cynical. If they become suspicious that you are simply showcasing a talent that you are likely to abandon once in college, they pass right by it.

Between the Lines

Colleges Value Work Experiences
When colleges consider to whom they will award financial aid, they often look favorably on the students who are trying to help themselves. Think about it this way. Is it possible that colleges might find you to be disingenuous if you apply for financial assistance after taking an expensive trip during the summer to do volunteer work in Eastern Europe? What will your choices say about you?

Use Your Summers Productively

Be careful to discriminate between activities that are enriching and those that are chosen to impress colleges. Admission officers regard vanity programs somewhat cynically because students who participate usually can afford them and participating makes them think that they are doing something that will look good to colleges. Examples are academic programs on college campuses, leadership seminars for which you have been "nominated," and service trips to foreign countries.

In the abstract, such activities can be enriching. If they are natural extensions of you and your passions, then, carry on. However, you need to ask yourself: "Would I do this if I knew that it was not going to help me get into college?" If the answer is "no"—if you are considering a program in order to enhance your college application—save your money. Instead, think about how you might engage yourself in productive activity. Challenge your competencies. Invest in your passions. Broaden your perspectives. Learn to deal with personal responsibility. Get a job.

In short, use your summers to explore opportunities that will give you the chance to grow as a person. This type of activity can be good for

you. Read a book. Climb a mountain. Explore a different culture or experience the satisfaction of serving others. Colleges are watching to see what you do—when you don't have to do anything!

Putting the Agenda into Perspective

The factors we have reviewed thus far in discussing "what colleges want" shouldn't surprise you. Elements of the "Agenda" are found on transcripts and resumes. They are the subject of essays, interviews, and letters of recommendation. You should be able to see the importance of taking care of business in the classroom so you can establish yourself on the academic playing fields of the colleges that interest you. You also need to take care of business in life—do the things you love and do them well—so that when the question "what do we get?" is asked, the answer will be apparent.

There is more to this discussion, however. While we have considered the factors that put you on the playing field and influence your competitiveness—the stuff admission officers love to talk about—we have yet to touch on several of the key, yet little-known, variables that often influence final outcomes *after* the "Agenda" has been considered. This is the information admission officers do *not* include in their presentations. Let's call it the "Hidden Agenda."

The Hidden Agenda

An emerging reality is that colleges and universities must run themselves like businesses. As businesses, they constantly compete with each other for new investors (students, donors, research grants, etc.). This competition is especially intense among institutions that are either regarded among the "best" or aspire to be in that company, that are absorbed in the "fame game"—a phenomenon brought on by college rankings.

Before college rankings came into the picture, the Agenda was simple because most places were content to recruit and educate good students. Now, the emphasis at many colleges falls on *doing what it takes* (in the selection process) to burnish their images and push their rankings higher. At schools obsessed with achieving "more and better," the processes of admitting and awarding aid to students are a reflection of how they value each candidate. The "what do we get" question takes on new meaning in this context as institutions are very conscious about how their decisions influence their positioning among their peers.

As a result, the decisions to admit or not admit are often calculated business decisions. While the attention is focused publicly on all of the good stuff—courses, grades, essays, and extracurricular activities—more discreet conversations are taking place about whether you are a valued candidate. The final decision to admit or not admit, then, may well hinge on answers to such questions as, "How will this student's test scores look on our profile?" or "Is this someone in whom we want to make a $25,000-a-year investment?" or "If we admit him, what is the likelihood that he will enroll?"

The Push for More and Better

The concepts of selectivity and yield are important measuring sticks for institutions in the fame game and have a real impact in both the recruitment and the admission processes. One of the questions facing admission officers *before they begin their review of applicants* is: "How can we become more selective (admit fewer students) and improve our yield (get more students to enroll)?" As a result, colleges employ all sorts of strategies to attract more applicants, limit the number of admitted students to those who are most likely to enroll, and focus on increasing the yield.

You will see evidence of this well before you apply as your mailbox is inundated with recruitment material. You will find incentives to apply: coupons for application fee waivers if you visit the campus and invitations to apply online at no cost. Some places will provide two-part applications, including an easy-to-complete part one, while others will even give you partially completed applications.

If you are considering selective colleges, you may be encouraged to use the Common Application®, an application form shared by more than 300 institutions across the country. The advantage: you can fill out one application form and send copies to any number of member colleges. Since participating colleges promise to regard the Common Application as their own, this can be a great time-saver—and another incentive to apply. In all cases, the message seems clear: "We want you!" The greater reality is, "*We want your application*. We'll decide about you later."

None of this is bad. You just need to see it for what it is—colleges trolling for more applications. Don't be misled, though, about the depth of the interest in, or knowledge about, you. In fact, many admission officers regard the resulting influx of applications as a mixed blessing.

While they can point to greater applicant interest and subsequent selectivity, they still need to figure out who among the applicants is truly interested. "Ghost applications" need to be teased out of the process before they can focus on the "serious" applicants.

Between the Lines

Ghost Applications

Admission officers tend to regard generic applications as "ghost applications" if there is little accompanying evidence of the candidate's interest in the college. If you use Common Application, make your interest in the college known by visiting the campus and otherwise participating in recruitment activities whenever possible.

Strategies to Limit Offers of Admission

An important filter that has entered the deliberations of many admission committees is the question, "If we admit him, will he come?" It is a question that is asked over and over by admission officers who are vigilant about not admitting any more candidates, strong and talented as they might be, than are absolutely necessary. With this question, the emphasis moves quickly from the strength of your credentials to the likelihood of your enrollment. And you won't even know it. If they can't find evidence of your interest, they will simply find a place for you on the Wait List with the observation that, "If he's really interested, he'll show up later." Such a practice may not seem fair, but it's real.

Before you worry too much about this, take heart—you can help yourself. Quite simply, let the colleges you like *know* that you like them! Many of them are already discreetly tracking your contact with them. Make sure you are active on their radar screens. Attend information sessions, touch base with admission representatives who visit your school or attend a local college night, and visit college campuses. You might even contact the admission person assigned to recruit in your region for advice about your course selections. As you build relationships with colleges on your short list, make sure there can be no doubt about the sincerity of your interest. Eliminate questions regarding your level of interest and force colleges to focus on the good stuff in your application!

Standardized Tests: The Rhetoric and the Reality

As we discussed in Chapter 5, standardized testing is still a factor at most colleges and universities, but for reasons that you may not have anticipated. While each college uses the results differently, at many the test scores are pinned on each entering class as if to say, "Look at the really bright kids we are getting."

Contrast that sentiment with the feedback you might get from an admission representative early in the process: "Don't worry. Standardized tests aren't that important in our selection process." So, what's the scoop? You can tell if the scores really aren't that important by checking www.FairTest.org. If score submission isn't optional, then you are being fed a line so that you will apply. You can be sure of this, however: colleges that *do* require testing will want to report the best results possible! After all, big scores are important credentials in the fame game.

Between the Lines

Fill Out the Card!
Whenever you have taken the time to learn more about a college, make sure you get credit for it. **Fill out the inquiry card or registration form.** Even if you are already on the mailing list, filling out the card *again* demonstrates your continued interest in the institution.

The Money Factor

It isn't very comforting to know that money plays a role in the admission process, but it has become a very real factor in decision making at many colleges, even those that proclaim to be "need blind." This is an inevitable manifestation of the fame game. Institutions want to make sure they use their places in the class—and their resources—to secure the students they value most.

This practice can cut both ways for students on the competitive bubble. Candidates with marginal credentials who are self-supporting financially—who do not need financial aid—may find opportunities at some schools simply because they are "good enough" academically and it won't cost the institution anything to enroll them. They're "free." Conversely, the question may be asked about applicants who need large sums of financial aid, "Do we really want to invest in this student with these credentials when we might be able to get more for our money elsewhere?"

If the answer is "no," the application will be designated for the Wait List (for consideration if there is any money left over) or, perhaps, even denial.

If you are concerned that money may factor adversely into your admission outcome, the best solution is: get off the "bubble." You can do this by getting the kind of grades that will make you very attractive to a college. Similarly, your ability to make a strong case regarding your potential contributions of talent—your gifts—may establish you as a worthy investment by that college.

Another solution is to apply to colleges that value you for what you do well. Think about it. The more selective the college you consider, the more likely you will be on its competitive bubble.

If you need financial aid and

Between the Lines

The Pyramid and the Competitive Bubble

Applicants on the competitive bubble are good students who don't project to be among the top scholars once enrolled. Logic would suggest that, regardless of the strength of your credential, the farther up the Pyramid you aspire, the greater the likelihood you will find yourself on the competitive bubble. If you and your family are concerned about managing college costs, it would make sense to identify colleges that will embrace you for what you do well and demonstrate a commitment to your success.

are interested in colleges that offer rolling admission—they make decisions as the applications come in—apply early. Such colleges will begin to award their financial aid as students are admitted and will continue until it is gone. Apply early and get the first dollars, not the last.

The Hidden Agenda in the Rear View Mirror

The Hidden Agenda is an unpleasant reality of the admission process. If you work hard to put yourself on the playing fields at places that can be selective, the last thing you want is to lose your opportunity due to factors beyond your control. This is a good illustration, though, of why it is important to find and apply to schools that value you. In doing so, you reduce—if not eliminate—vulnerability to the Hidden Agenda.

Chapter 8

Reveal Your Talents

The "X" Factor—Your Gift

The importance of "giving" varies from school to school. Colleges and universities regard your potential to contribute outside of the classroom as integral to your personal development—and for good reason. You are probably happiest and most productive when you lead a full and rewarding life. Colleges recognize this. That's why they look for evidence that you are active. Even places that may not be so selective want to see that you are engaged and growing with your gifts.

The premium on giving goes up, though, as you consider colleges that are harder to get into. The farther up the Pyramid of Selectivity you aspire, the closer admission committees will look to find something special in your credentials that will be the "X" factor for your application. They are looking for the "best of the best" or, more likely, the student with an unusual or "niche" talent. In that competition, the strength of your academic record may get you onto the "playing field,"

but the strength and/or uniqueness of your "gift" can be the "hook" that elevates you above the competition and into the class.

Wherever you are in the college search and planning process, you need to get your arms around this part of your credentials. In order for your gift to become the "X" factor or difference-maker, you must be realistic in your assessments of both the qualities that define your gift and the extent to which the college to which you are applying might value them. You must also make certain that the qualities that distinguish your gift are well documented in your application.

Between the Lines

Feeling Passion-less?
If you are still searching for your passions and your place in the world, don't despair. You are actually quite normal as the revelations regarding gifts occur at different times in our lives. Keep looking inward and rely on what you find there to invest in becoming the best you can be. That "best" will eventually be evidence to a college or university that you are leading a full and healthy life. It might even be the hook that makes the difference in your admission status.

Discover, Cultivate, and Nurture Your Gift

What are your passions? Are there common themes to the activities you enjoy most with your friends? Do you worry about social issues? What would you do if you had 2 hours of free time and could do anything? If these questions bring positive thoughts to mind, the next step is to take action. Give focus to the things you like to do. Look for opportunities to invest in your passions. Take ownership in determining the quality of your life. In doing so, you will enjoy watching your gifts begin to emerge.

It is the overall body of work you present that will make the difference in your application. Just because you have achieved through well-defined passions, don't rest on your laurels. To many observers, the real story in giving lies in *how* and *what* you achieved as well as your capacity to *build upon* that achievement. That is why they look at your involvements to find evidence of substance. "One-year wonders" don't cut it. Consider carefully, then, opportunities to invest in advancing your skills and competencies.

TIPS FOR DISCOVERING AND NURTURING YOUR GIFTS

- **Be true to yourself.** A parent once observed that "I think I need to get my son involved in sports" in order for him to become a more competitive college applicant. My response was to urge the parent to support his student's theater involvement as that is where the young man's passions were rooted. There is absolutely no need to "remake" yourself as you prepare to apply to college.

- **Resist the temptation to be a "joiner."** If the primary reason for signing up for a club

Between the Lines

Jack of All Trades or Master of One?

The question, "Is it better to be well-rounded with several serious involvements or to do one thing really well?" has haunted college applicants for years. The answer, "It really doesn't matter." What matters more is how you invest in the one, two, or three things you care about most. Colleges are looking for all types of givers.

or an outing is "because it will look good on my college application," don't do it. If doing it seems easy, then it will lack credibility with the admission committee. Spend more time becoming better at the things you really enjoy than worrying about adding new activities.

- **Community service is nice, but do it for the right reasons!** Yes, colleges like to see involvement in community service. It needs to be right-spirited, though. Showing up for an hour or two every month to help at a recycling center is nice, but it's not going to turn any heads.

- **Grow with your talents.** Enhance your experience by taking on added instruction and/or responsibility. Four years on the team speaks to your perseverance. A year or two as a starter shows growth. Being named captain in the senior year demonstrates leadership.

- **Use your summers wisely.** Summer "experiences" are the rage these days. You can have an immersion in government experience in Washington, DC, spend six weeks in a cross-cultural exchange in Eastern Europe, attend a leadership program on a university campus, or participate in a "problem-solving for engineers" camp at another. While such programs can be wonderful learning opportunities, choose them for the right reasons. If one of them provides content that is consistent with your passions and you will truly learn from the

experience, then go for it. Otherwise, use your summers to do things that make sense given your interests.

- **Do what you love; love what you do.** There are no "right" or "wrong" answers when it comes to assessing your passions. If music is your thing and the clarinet is your instrument, stick with it. Even if oboe players are in demand, there is no sense abandoning the instrument that works for you. Make yourself happy. You can be sure there will be colleges that need good clarinetists, too. The next step will be to find them!

Identify Colleges That Will Value You for What You Do Well

As daunting as this task might seem, it can turn out to be amazingly straightforward. Just do two things. Be who you are and focus on the elements of a good college fit. With more than 3,000 colleges and universities to consider, the odds are good you will find more than a few that will embrace you and your talents. Do an honest self-assessment and then look for colleges that will value you for who you are and the things you do well. Find the right playing field for *you*.

Doing this can be relatively easy if your talents lie in athletics, music, theater, and the visual arts. These programs are usually integral to the branding of an institution. You know about XYZ school because, among other things, it has a strong theater program or a perennially-ranked lacrosse team or amazing studios and exhibit facilities for artists. You just need to find the appropriate level of competition or instruction.

On the other hand, finding the right playing field can be challenging if your interests are not so mainstream. For example, if you are looking for opportunities to write and read poetry or a place that will embrace your desire to engineer a radio show, you'll have to look a little harder. The same is true if you want to find a competitive debate program or you'd like to build robotic insects. Such programs and opportunities do exist. They just don't receive prominent billing at most colleges.

Take heart, though. For every interest you can imagine or gift you might possess, there are colleges and universities that will accommodate (quite well) if not embrace your desire to pursue it. The trick is finding those places.

Tips for Identifying Colleges Where Your Gift(s) Will Be Valued

- Identify individuals in your community who have common or shared interests with you. Quite often, such folks will be able to refer you to

journals or Web sites that might include articles or ads for schools that promote programs of interest to you.

- Talk to club advisers at your school or in your community. They should be able to refer you to directories of college programs and, perhaps, introduce you to other students who have already discovered opportunities like those you are seeking.

- Attend college nights or fairs at which you can ask the representatives about the availability of the programs you seek.

- Utilize search engines on the Internet to research your interests within the context of colleges and universities.

Between the Lines

Win an Advocate

When you present evidence of your performance, you put those who view it in the position of imagining what it would be like to have you in their programs. If you can convince them that you would make a difference—that you would add value to their existing efforts—you will win them over as advocates. While having a talent advocate does not mean you are sure to be admitted, it can make a big difference in a tight competition.

- Ask your college counselor. It is not uncommon for college counselors, both school-based and those who work independently, to learn about unusual program opportunities when they visit college campuses.

- As you develop your longer list of colleges (early in the process), send each a brief e-mail survey in which you ask them for information about program opportunities. You might also find it instructive to subscribe to the student newspapers on those campuses.

- Make careful distinctions between the fact that a program might be available and the degree to which it represents a viable opportunity for you.

Reveal Your Gifts

If you have a clear sense as to what you do well and have discovered colleges that are likely to value you for the things you have to offer, the next step is to make a strong connection with these colleges. This is especially true at colleges that must make fine distinctions between hundreds

of talented students. You need to make your gifts and talents known so when they ask the question, "What do we get if we admit you?" the answer is clear.

Bring your talent to life. If you are a musician, make a studio quality recording (tape or CD). Audition if you can. If you are an artist, attend portfolio days or assemble a slide collection of your work to submit with your application. This demonstration of talent will be required for entry into highly selective conservatory or specialty programs in the arts. It can also make the difference for you at schools that value the arts but are not professionally oriented. You do not need to have professional aspirations as an artist,

Between the Lines

What Are Your Talent$ Worth?
Many colleges and universities recognize unusual talent with scholarships. The most noteworthy examples are NCAA Division I athletic programs. If you can run, jump, or shoot better than most, you might win a scholarship. The same is often true for accomplished leaders, thinkers, writers, and artists. So, reveal your passions. Put yourself in a position to be rewarded at colleges that value you for these contributions.

musician, actor, or dancer in order for your talent to give you a competitive edge in the selective admission process.

By demonstrating your talents in this way, you go beyond the listing of activities and achievements on your application to reveal the nuances of tone and texture that distinguish your performance from the rest of the competition. Just as athletic coaches want to see game tapes to determine who will be competitive, music directors, drama coaches, and art instructors observe closely to identify those who will contribute to their programs.

Consider also how evidence of your gift(s) might give flavor to the overall presentation of your application. Take advantage of an interview or e-mail exchange with the recruiter in your area to talk about the things that excite you. Use the personal statement or mini-essays to expound upon them. Make sure the people who write on your behalf can bear witness to your personal growth and commitment through your passions.

You do need to be convincing, though. It is one thing to present an application that includes activities you have pursued extensively with listings of honors, awards and positions held. That type of presentation is important in validating your commitment. It is quite another when you

list every club for which you have attended at least one meeting! Students who do that are not unlike the kids who were somehow able to sneak into all the group photos that appear in your yearbook. It's clear they don't belong. Admission officers look for substantive involvement over time that is marked by achievement and leadership. It is up to you, then, to reveal your gifts in such a way that those who read your application are easily persuaded that your passion and commitment are real.

TIPS FOR REVEALING YOUR GIFTS

Between the Lines

The Coach Is Calling
If you are a serious athlete at any level of competition (Division I, II, or III) in the National Collegiate Athletic Association (NCAA) or in the National Association of Intercollegiate Athletics (NAIA), don't be surprised at receiving a lot of calls from coaches. Go to www.NCAA.org and www.NAIA.cstv.com to learn more about the guidelines that apply to your recruitment situation.

- Be attentive to deadlines and special instructions involving required auditions or portfolios. Provide clear captions and descriptions. Late and/or incomplete submissions can be the "kiss of death" at this level of competition.

- Choose your best work. Where possible, show work that reveals the range of your talent set. Give the observer a sense of the possibilities.

- Use professional equipment if possible. This may mean you need to plan in advance. Make sure you factor that time into your preparation schedule.

- Ask your coach, director, instructor, or adviser to submit a personal assessment of your talent and potential to his counterpart at the colleges to which you apply.

- Home videos can be cute but, unless they address a specific talent, they are not likely to be viewed. Newspaper clippings and copies of certificates are nice but not terribly helpful.

- When you visit campuses, make sure you carve out time to meet with the people who run the programs in which you are interested.

- If you are an athletic recruit at the NCAA Division I level, make sure you register with the NCAA Clearinghouse that helps to determine your academic eligibility.

Athletic Recruitment

If you are a competitive athlete, one of the most exciting letters you can receive early in your college search is the one that informs you that XYZ would like you to suit up and compete for them. Before you get too excited, though, take a minute to think about this. On what basis was this letter written? When did the coach see you play? What does she know about your grades?

The fact is the coach probably doesn't know much if anything about you at all. Sorry to burst your bubble, but it is common practice for coaches to buy lists of names from referral services. This is the beginning of a long process of information gathering and talent assessment on the part of the coaches. As they do this, they constantly cull through the names to determine which players might be viable recruits. That is what the letter is all about. The coach is beginning to learn about you—and thousands of other prospects.

Between the Lines

Don't Exaggerate!

When college coaches first get in touch with you, they will probably ask you to complete and return player profile forms. The forms will ask for information such as height, weight, position, events, GPA, standardized test scores and, possibly, times in the 40 yard dash and bench press stats. While there is a natural tendency among athletes to exaggerate their stats (that's why coaches want to see film), padded numbers will catch up with you at some point. It's better to be honest with the coach from the outset and not risk certain embarrassment later!

While this sort of attention may be flattering, you need to keep it all in perspective. For example, the coach won't necessarily hold the ticket to your admission. In each case, you will need to demonstrate that you can compete in that institution's classroom if you want to be able to compete on its athletic fields. The fact that a coach likes you and wants you in her program doesn't mean that she can get you in if you are not on the right playing field academically.

You also need to keep in mind that coaches tend to act in their own self-interest. The "love" they express for you today can be gone tomorrow as they cast an ever-widening net in which they hope to find the best talent. Until they've seen every prospective athlete possible—or they run out of time—they will treat each recruit as if she is special. Then, they are often forced to make critical judgments about who will fit best in the program and who can get in without (the coach) having to give up too

much political capital. You may well possess a special talent that is valued—until the coach is able to land another recruit whom she likes better or finds out your chances of admission are not that great.

It is worth mentioning here that most athletes who continue their playing careers in college are not scholarship supported. For the most part, they attend NAIA or NCAA Division II or Division III schools. At the NCAA Division III level, colleges are not allowed to give any special preference to athletes in the financial aid process. While such programs are not scholarship supported, that doesn't mean they don't like to win and won't try to get the best talent possible. You might be surprised by the number of playing fields that are still available to you.

Chapter 9

Hotspots and Hooks

Calibration

The approaching application season is bound to raise apprehensions about the schools that are emerging on your short list. "Do I have enough schools?" "They seem awfully selective—what if I don't get in?" "How will I know if I'm applying to the right places?" Despite your best efforts to find colleges that fit you well—places at which you would be on the right playing field—the growing uncertainty about the imminent competition is unsettling.

The good news is you have tools at your disposal that can be helpful in assessing your chances. In addition to calculating the odds based on your credentials and the selectivity of the colleges that interest you (Chapter 3), you can apply what you have just learned about the Agendas to calibrate further—to see how closely you might fit at these schools. You do this by taking an analytical look at how your credentials will appear on the application through the eyes of the admission officer.

If your application can be likened to a personal statement (not THE personal statement!), you need to consider how those who read it will find and interpret the information you present. The first instinct of an admission officer is to skim the application for an indication of what you are saying about yourself and, more specifically, for key themes that might set you apart from the competition. Such information can give the reader a strong sense of your competitiveness or a bias that must be validated through the balance of the review.

Between the Lines

The "Big Hook"

Most admission officers start with the academic record in reviewing credentials. An experienced reader can tell within seconds whether you will be competitive. Your record not only puts you on the "playing field," but a superior transcript can be a signal to the admission committee to keep an eye on you for possible scholarship consideration (if scholarships are offered). If, on the other hand, your record is comparatively modest, the review will be short.

Let's refer to the places on your application that are skimmed as "hotspots." Depending on the application form, there might be eight to ten hotspots that an admission officer might check quickly—often in less than 2 minutes—in search of key information that might establish a bias in favor of your credentials. The key information might be called a "hook."

A hook is a good thing. In the mind of the reader, it is the credential that pulls your application out of the pack. It distinguishes you from the rest of the competition. In fact, it should put you in the top 10 percent of a college's applicants with regard to that hotspot. In most instances, the hooks that emerge are consistent with the themes you attempted to establish throughout your application. Among other things, a "hook" could be your gift, the diversity you represent to a particular college or the extraordinary academic record you have compiled.

When everything else is equal, hooks make the difference in an application. Think about your credentials within the context of the Agenda and the Hidden Agenda—"what colleges want." How will the personal statement *that is your application* speak to the admission committee? Remember the "What do we get?" question. Where do the "hooks" emerge? If your hook(s) is highly valued by a college, it can

offset areas of weakness or inconsistency to give you a competitive advantage.

Locating the Hotspots

The following are hotspots on most applications that admission officers are likely to skim in their initial reviews of your credential. Based on what you know of the colleges on your short list, think about where your credential might fit. Keep in mind the selectivity of each school and evidence you have seen that the school will value you for the credential in question. Something that is a hook at one school might not be as highly valued at another.

Home Address Where you live has an impact on your view of the world. If your life experience *is considerably removed from the mainstream* of a college you are considering, then you may have a hook. (Your address can work *against* you if you apply to an out-of-state public university.)

Definite Hook___   Not Sure___   No Hook___

Potential Major If you have a genuine interest (as demonstrated on your transcript and/or in your activities) in an academic program that is underpopulated on a college campus, you may have an advantage in the selection process.

Definite Hook___   Not Sure___   No Hook___

Candidate for Financial Aid? You will be asked *on most applications for admission* whether you will be a candidate for financial aid. Saying "yes" should not hurt you. Colleges that discriminate based on demonstrated need will wait to see hard evidence that you actually need assistance. On the other hand, saying "no" because you are not likely to *need* financial aid in any of your four years means that a potential obstacle is eliminated. In effect, you are "free"—the college can consider enrolling you without having to spend any of its financial aid. The fact that you are "free" is a potential hook in many competitive environments.

Definite Hook___   Not Sure___   No Hook___

Ethnic Background An indication that you come from an ethnic minority background can be very important to an institution that is trying to maintain a diverse community on its campus. Evidence that you will share

your cultural heritage, though, may be required to establish a hook as you ascend the Pyramid of Selectivity.

Definite Hook___   Not Sure___   No Hook___

Family Background The fact that you are related to someone who attends or attended a college may give you an advantage. Key legacy relationships are parents, siblings, and grandparents. While the legacy factor is often a tie-breaker, its importance diminishes as you consider institutions at or near the top of the Pyramid.

Definite Hook___   Not Sure___   No Hook___

Academic Honors/Extracurricular Activities This is where you get to present your talents and accomplishments. What stands out? Where is the evidence of your passions—your gifts? A gift that is highly valued by a college can carry the day in a tight admission scenario.

Definite Hook___   Not Sure___   No Hook___

Personal Statement The Personal Statement or essay is a unique opportunity to create a hook. If you are a gifted writer or have a compelling story to tell, consider crafting an essay that will grab the attention of readers on the admission committee.

Definite Hook___   Not Sure___   No Hook___

Transcript The transcript is a snapshot that effectively captures your academic performance on one page. Meeting expectations will put you in the competition. *Exceeding* expectations may give you a hook. What does your academic "snapshot" say about you?

Definite Hook___   Not Sure___   No Hook___

Standardized Tests Colleges that value test scores in their deliberations will be impressed by scores that are in the top quartile for their entering students.

Definite Hook___   Not Sure___   No Hook___

There is no formula to be applied in interpreting the results of your self-assessment other than basic logic. The Pyramid of Selectivity, though, is a useful point of reference as the degree to which a college is selective determines the relative strength of the credentials you are submitting. Nine hotspots have been identified here. The farther up the Pyramid you aspire,

the more important it is that you present multiple, well-developed hooks—and that your transcript and testing profile are among them.

The View from 30,000 Feet

In getting your arms around the hotspots and your potential hooks, you might need to step back and gain perspective. This is particularly true if you find yourself living on auto-pilot—constantly scrambling from point "A" to point "B" without much reflection. When this happens, it is easy to forget what you are doing and why.

It is important, then to periodically challenge your assumptions with regard to the college application process. Why are you interested in a college? What makes you so sure that it is the best place for you? How do you know that your credential will be a hook? Why should they admit you? If you don't ask yourself questions like these, you will fail to grasp the urgency that is needed for the purposeful preparation of your application. As a result, the credentials that emerge from your daily routine may resemble nothing more than a collection of random facts that lack energy, focus, and direction. That may not be a problem in admission environments that are relatively open. As you consider colleges that are more selective, though, you need to present a credential that comes to life—that breathes a passion and excitement reflective of who you are and what you want to become.

In order to gain a better perspective on these questions, it might be helpful to go to "30,000 feet" for a look around. At 30,000 feet, you have a vantage point that gives you a sense of the big picture. Your life becomes part of a much larger panorama. How do you see it unfolding? What patterns do you see in your thought processes? What do you care about more than anything? How are you acting upon that passion? Answers to these questions will help ensure your placement on the right playing fields as you apply to college and will give you direction as your prepare your credentials.

Chapter 10

When "Stuff" Happens

"My computer crashed."

"The book I needed to finish my research wasn't in the library . . ."

"The dog ate my homework!"

Do you ever find yourself in a situation where you can't produce desired results for reasons that are obviously beyond your control? You know, everything would have been fine if only your little sister hadn't spilled her drink on your paper. Or you were making great progress on your project until a passing storm knocked out the electricity. When stuff like this happens, you're left with a helpless feeling when it comes to trying to finish your work.

When "stuff" happens, you also tend to lose your focus. Distracted by the circumstances, you might not be able to produce the kind of results that you would normally expect of yourself. In most instances, you make the best of the situation and move on. These developments might ruin

your day but not your life. Your ability to make the best of such situations, to "react to setbacks," is one of the things about which your teachers will comment in their letters of recommendation for you.

Occasionally, stuff happens that alters your ability to perform and achieve on a much larger scale. For example, you might be injured or experience an extended illness. Suddenly you can't respond to your assignments the way you normally would. Or maybe your family moves and you change schools. Worse yet, you might be faced with the loss of someone close to you. When stuff like this happens, it takes you out of your rhythm—in life and in the classroom. You lose focus and find it difficult to carry on as you would like.

Understanding the "Blips"

Now, let's fast forward to the application process. Think about how such developments might be reflected on your college application and high school transcript. Despite evidence of strong achievement overall, your record might include grades that are lower than usual, incompletes or course selections that might not represent those that you would like to have taken. Given your overall academic profile, these developments would seem to be anomalous. "Blips" on your record, they do not represent the true picture of what you are capable of doing.

We talked before about how admission officers try to understand your performance contextually. The important contexts for them are the environments in which you live and learn. Not only are these contexts instructive in a general sense, but when "stuff" happens that alters your program or performance, admission officers need to understand what has been going on. The "blips" on your record will raise questions. Is something going on in your life—perhaps beyond your control—that affects your ability to perform? Or are you simply unfocused, disinterested, and lazy?

Ideally, quick detective work on the part of the reader will reveal compelling answers. She'll read notes from your interview explaining that your grades dipped when you missed three weeks of school due to an emergency appendectomy. Or she'll read your counselor's explanation that you don't have an honors science class in your senior year because it conflicted with the orchestra schedule and you wanted to finish your high

school career as first chair in the trumpet section. This type of information fills important gaps in the reader's understanding of your performance and can help move your credentials through a tight admission process.

Between the Lines

Tell Your Story

The further up the Pyramid of Selectivity you aspire, the greater the likelihood that admission officers will regard anomalies in your performance as a reason to deny your application. When "stuff" happens that affects your program or performance, you have a story to tell. Your ability to get the message across to admission officers may determine your success as an applicant.

Absent any strong clues or clear explanations, though, admission officers are left to guess about the reality of the situation. That's not good. While many schools will be forgiving in such situations, you can't count on the good will of admission officers to help you in every case. Folks at highly selective places tend to be far less charitable in their assessments. Rather than trying to piece together the possibility that there are good reasons for these anomalies, they will be more inclined to mark your file for denial and move on.

If there is a story to be told, it's up to *you* to make sure the circumstances that have had a bearing on your performance are appropriately documented. You know what is at stake. Don't assume that someone will do it for you or that the admission committee will somehow figure it out. You need to address such situations in personal statements, interviews, and brief attachments to your application.

You also need to make sure that the mitigating factors are known to the people who will write on your behalf. In addition to validating the information you report, they (your advisers, counselors, and teachers) can coach you in finding solutions that reveal your story in the admission process. This can be especially helpful if the circumstances are awkward, painful, or difficult to discuss. These folks can't help you, though, unless you let them. You must take the initiative.

Stories About You

Not all stories are tales of woe. Is it possible, for example, that you have experienced circumstances in life that define "who" you have become? In

talking with a young woman who had been placed on the Wait List at my school, I was surprised to learn that her family had been exiled politically during a violent overthrow in their home country, a fact she had neglected to share in her application. She was an infant at the time of the turmoil and wanted her application to be a reflection of her accomplishments rather than the celebrity of her family's situation. While this was a noble ambition, she had failed to consider the impact of her family's circumstance on *who* she had become. She had a story to tell and, fortunately, was able to convey it before it was too late in her application process.

Another student who understood his story all too well is the young man who arrived in my office from the streets of New York City. Homeless but not helpless, he was determined not only to survive but become an agent of change. His story of survival was vivid and compelling—enough to overcome academic credentials that would not otherwise have warranted a second glance. He told his story and found an opportunity. He recently received a Ph.D. and is now an educator dedicated to serving his community.

Between the Lines

More Background Please!
In seeking to diversify their campuses, admission officers often look beyond the checkmarks that identify ethnicity to learn how your background has affected your personal development. In doing so, they might ask: "Where is the evidence that she will share her cultural heritage and experience with anyone on our campus?" Let the reader know how you are connected to your roots. The absence of any indication that you are deeply in touch with your cultural heritage means that you may have missed an opportunity to tell an important story.

As you prepare your application for admission, remember that you are the product of many influences and experiences in life. Take stock of all this information—your family, your ethnicity, your community, and your values. Understand how it has helped shape you. Then, consider the importance of the story that is emerging from this confluence of factors—the story that is you.

Dealing with Discipline

Sometimes "stuff" happens that results in a change in your status at school. For example, you may have faced disciplinary action because you were at a party where underage drinking took place. Regardless of your role or participation, your school took action by issuing suspensions for all involved. Now, you have to deal with the consequences of a disciplinary action on your record.

Such a situation is very difficult to say the least. You wish it would go away yet it looms like a dark cloud over everything you do—especially the college process. You worry endlessly. Will colleges find out? How will they react? Will I ever be able to get into a "good" college?

The truth is it's hard to tell on all accounts. While there is a degree of compassion and forgiveness in every admission process, the extent to which it is exercised is often related to the manner in which the information is conveyed. If you ignore the situation hoping it will go away, you take a big risk. It might indeed go away—or it can just as easily blow up in your face if it surfaces independently. When the latter happens, the prospects for positive outcomes are not good.

Generally speaking, if admission officers are inclined toward forgiveness it is because you have erred on the side of self-disclosure and contrition. You have come forward with your side of the story. As is the case with most other aspects of your college application, ownership can go a long way in paving the way to positive outcomes. Dealing with discipline is no exception. While it might be "easier said than done," you give yourself a chance to regain the respect of those who will sit in judgment of your application. Even then, of course, there are no guarantees.

In the end, ask yourself: "Does my application help the reader understand the circumstances that affected my performance—or is it an illusion?" The people who read your application will be sensitive to evidence that you dealt with difficult or challenging issues (and how you overcame them). Moreover, you have a much better chance of "clearing the record" by dealing with adversity head-on rather than by leaving things to chance.

As you come to grips with your story, consider the opportunities to get it out there. Explanations for things that have happened in your life, whether they are good or bad, will not materialize out of thin air. It is your responsibility to tell the story. You must own it.

Take Action in Telling Your Story

The following are opportunities for you to tell your story.

Personal Interview—Take advantage of the opportunity to tell your story person to person. The interviewer's notes will be added to your application file where they can provide valuable contextual understanding of your performance and perspectives. Such a meeting also gives your interviewer an opportunity to put a name with a face—and to be your advocate later in the process.

Personal Statement—Use the space provided on the application or attach a second statement that addresses your circumstances.

Letters of Recommendation—Make sure that the people who write on your behalf can speak knowledgeably about you. Give them what they need to know in order to help them tell your story.

Outside (of School) Recommendations—In establishing points of difference or distinction in an application, it is often useful to involve people from the community who provide a perspective that validates your experience. For example, a letter from a private music teacher who attests to your diligent preparation, your ability to perform under pressure, and your determination to compete at a certain level will cast your private music study in more substantive light. Similarly, the coordinator of a local homeless shelter can testify to your selflessness and generosity. Recommendations such as these tell another story as they bear witness to who you are and what you have to give.

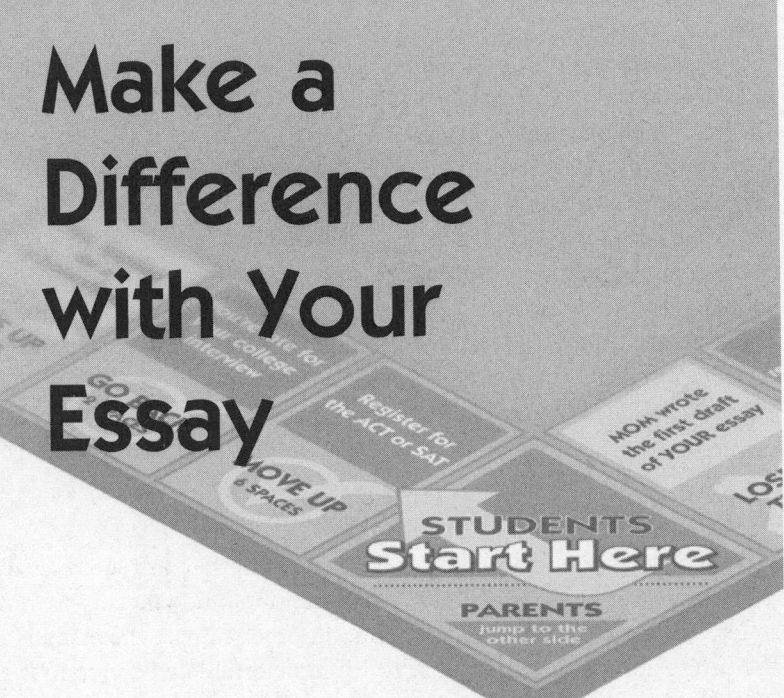

Chapter 11

Make a Difference with Your Essay

A Possible Hook

The personal statement (a.k.a. college essay) is arguably the most difficult assignment you will face in the next few years. Along with standardized test taking, it will probably rank among your least favorite things to do! After all, you are supposed to say something profound about yourself (in 500 words or less!) that will impress absolute strangers—strangers who have the power to determine your educational future.

The prospect of having to fill the space with something meaningful can be paralyzing to say the least. After all, what do you say? What do they want to see? How can you set yourself apart? The empty space just stares at you. You know you've got to come up with something, but what? How?

As you apply to college, the essay is your best opportunity to make a statement about *who* you are—in the "here and now." Think about it. Your academic record is exactly that—a matter of record. You can't go back and change courses or substitute new grades. Your scores are, well,

your scores. There isn't much you can do to change them, either, until the next time you sit for the test. And your extracurricular profile or resume is also well established—a representation of things that have already taken place in your life.

The college essay, however, is an opportunity to reveal a different side or dimension of you that has yet to be explored. You may even see in the essay an opportunity to create a "hook" that might set you apart from the competition. If that is the case, all you need to do is wrap your arms around the assignment and get it done. See the possibility and run with it!

This chapter will take a look at how you can use the essay assignment to make a good impression or create a "hook." We will not discuss specific topics or examples of what has worked for previous applicants. Rather, the objective here is to help you think about the essay—why it is required and how admission committees use it—so you are able to produce an essay that will work for you.

What Colleges Want

Have you ever wondered why colleges even bother to require essays? As you mull over the possibilities, you develop some clues as to how you might approach the assignment. Among other things, the essay is one of the filters admission officers use to, first, determine who can do the work and, then, distinguish among strong candidates. The latter is especially true at colleges that can afford to be picky. The harder it is to get into a college, the greater the expectation that you will deliver a message that is imaginative and highly insightful.

At the most fundamental level, admission officers look for evidence of *technical merit* in your writing. They want to see if you can write—have you mastered the basics of grammar, syntax, punctuation, and structure? If you haven't mastered the basics, you will have trouble functioning in most college classrooms.

Even more important, college professors want to see evidence that you can think critically and write *well*. Do you possess the confidence to take risks with your ideas and perspectives? Can you step outside of the "box?" How are you at sorting out complex subject matter? Are you able to make critical distinctions? What are your sensitivities to social and political issues? Can you make and defend a thesis? Can you craft a persuasive argument? Are you able to paint a picture with words that gives the reader insight if not absolute clarity into your soul?

Your ability to think critically and use your developed technical skills to articulate a range of thoughts and ideas in an essay on a college application is indicative of your capacity to communicate in an intellectual environment. When you write well, your work also conveys a message, creates an image, or makes an argument that engages the reader. This is vital to the success of anything you write. Think about it. You might feel like your ideas are flowing, but if they are not reaching the reader they are like a radio signal that is never received—lost in space. You need to be mindful, then, of the agendas of the audiences to which you are writing if you want your "signal" to be received.

Between the Lines

The Eye of the Beholder

How often have you heard, "beauty is in the eye of the beholder"? It's true. Each of us sees things differently. As a result, you need to be prepared for a range of responses from those who come in contact with your writing. Scary as it may seem, the success of your essay may well be determined by the predisposition of the person who reads it!

This is where the Pyramid of Selectivity can provide guidance. Whereas less selective colleges are not as discriminating in their assessments of essays—they may not even require them—colleges that make fine distinctions among excellent candidates are very sensitive to both the style and content of the presentation. The questions they ask on their applications are intended to probe your thought processes in search of unique perspectives. At the most selective of these schools, hundreds of great essays are passed over each year in favor of a few that happen to capture the reader's imagination.

The Audience

If an objective of the essay is to establish a relationship between the author and the audience, then it might be a good idea to develop a broader understanding of who is in the audience. On a given day, your audience could be any of a number of folks sitting on the admission committee. It could be a retired high school teacher or counselor who is reviewing credentials on a part-time basis. Perhaps it is a member of the faculty, or a "green dean" (recent graduate on the admission staff) who is

relatively new to the process. It might even be a veteran member of the admission staff.

Your audience is made up of people who are trained to evaluate applicants in a manner consistent with the overall selection criteria for the university in question. While most admission committees go to great lengths to achieve consistency across the board, readers will invariably yield to their own biases as they read essays. Some are sticklers for detail and watch to see if you have followed directions. Others want to see how you have *interpreted* the directions. Some like to be entertained.

Regardless, the folks who are likely to read your application and your essay are incredibly focused. Every day during the credential review is a race against time with thousands of essays to read and decisions to make in shaping the new class. To keep pace with the volume (and avoid more weekend work than is necessary in the dead of winter), each reader needs to get through as many as fifty applications, each with multiple essays, by the end of each day.

Much as readers might want to read every word of your essay, they aren't always afforded that luxury. They need to see if you can write and, if you so, how you are using the space to convey compelling messages. Because they are often pushed for time, they might check the first and last paragraphs to make sure you have the fundamentals down and then skim the content quickly to see if anything "pops" or grabs their attention. If not, they will acknowledge the technical merit and move on. On the other hand, if you are able to pique their curiosity, they will slow down and read further.

Your objective, then, is to get the readers to venture beyond the first paragraph to the second—and the third—and so on. Draw them in—get them to slow down *and read the whole thing*. Get them excited about you! If they find themselves investing more time in reading your essay and learning about you than they had anticipated, then you have a chance to win. Better yet, you want your essay to be the one that the readers insist on passing around for everyone to see—it's that good!

Keys to Approaching a College Essay

It should be clear that the blank page beneath the essay assignment is your opportunity to step up with a difference-maker—to be creative, to fill your "canvas" with a message that says "take me!" Such essays don't just materialize out of thin air, though. They require careful thought and

preparation. As you contemplate the various essay prompts you encounter, consider the following keys to developing your essays:

1. Relax
2. Choose a topic about which you are an expert
3. Invest in the development of a strong message

Relax

The biggest hurdle to developing an effective essay is anxiety. It's that inner voice that says "I can't."

Between the Lines

It's Up to You
There are no "magic bullet" essays—no ready-made solutions. For better or worse, this one is on you. The choice of an essay topic is intensely personal. Nobody can do it for you.

There are lots of reasons why you might feel that way about the college essay. Given what is at stake, that is understandable. You may not be an accomplished writer. You don't feel like you have the kind of vocabulary that will impress college admission officers. Or you don't have a clue about what to say!

The first thing you need to do is relax. There is no sense beating yourself up because you *feel* inadequate to the task. Rather, feel good about who you are—and feel good about your ability to talk with strangers. When you talk (or in this case, write) naturally, your voice emerges. That's important because your voice is like your DNA. Whether it is spoken or written, it establishes your identity. Once you have established your voice, you can say just about anything. You may not feel comfortable with your voice, but it is real and holds the potential to deliver powerful messages.

So, relax. Don't try to be someone or something you are not. Stay within yourself. Leave the big words to those who use them all the time. The same is true of complex literary devices. If they work for you, fine. If not, don't go there. It is not the words you use, but the way you put them together to get your message across that will make the greatest difference. I have encountered as many powerful, poignant, and persuasive essays written with "dime store" words as there are essays written with thesaurus words.

Choose a Topic About Which You Are an Expert

If you are like many students, the choice of a topic is a huge stumbling block as you contemplate your college essays. The spirit may be willing but you just get stuck as you try to come up with something catchy or clever. On some applications, the university will give you an essay prompt or a selection of prompts from which you can choose. In most instances, though, you'll be on your own.

Between the Lines

Demonstrate "Fit"

Many colleges use the essay to address their own issues of "fit." They want to see how you measure up with the norm for their academic and social environments. For example, some questions might probe the development of your moral and ethical perspectives. Others measure your awareness of and sensitivity to a range of social issues. In these cases, the essay becomes a litmus test to see how much you have thought about the issues or values that are important to the colleges in question.

That said, don't make this exercise any more difficult than it needs to be. There is no sense in lying awake at night waiting for the next great essay topic to hit you. Don't buy your own copy of the "69 Best College Essays." Those topics have already been taken and you will only frustrate yourself further by filling your head with someone else's ideas. And, if you are reading this chapter with the expectation that I will be delivering topic ideas on a silver platter, it isn't going to happen.

In order to do a good job, you need to work from your areas of expertise. "But I'm not an expert about anything," you might say. That's not entirely true. It is probably safe to say that nobody knows more about you—than you! That said, choose a topic or theme that enables you to work to your strengths—your areas of expertise—and start with the expertise that rests in your knowledge of *you*. Go beyond the facts of your life. Instead, take an editorial perspective—on just about anything. Tell the reader *why* an issue is important to you, *why* you have made choices in life, *why* you care.

When you answer the "why" questions, you do two things. First, you give voice to a perspective and establish ownership. You are no longer reporting an event, but you are interpreting its impact in the first person. Perhaps more important, though, you reveal a side of yourself that can't be observed anywhere else on the application. When you address the *why*

question with regard to a topic, you open a window into yourself through which the reader can discover otherwise-unseen dimensions of your personality and character that set you apart from your peers.

As you tap into the "why" questions, you will discover a rich reservoir of content that is waiting to be revealed. You will be reminded of what is important to you. By reacquainting yourself with these feelings and perspectives, you are able to find focus and give shape to messages that add definition to your life experience. The topic you choose, then, creates a channel through which you will communicate these messages to your readers.

Topic Tips

- Consider the message first. What is it that you want or need to get across to your audience? How can you work within the essay prompts to deliver a revealing message?

- Don't get hung up on titles. While the title can be a catalyst for you as you develop the message, trying to come up with something truly clever or inspirational before the message has been crafted is like putting the "cart before the horse." A good message will provide lots of title opportunities.

- Resist the temptation to write about pets, last-minute sports heroics, favorite grandparents, or hot news items—*unless* such topics are integral to meaningful "why" messages.

- Be creative with the essay prompt. Think out of the box. Many colleges value students who demonstrate a willingness to take risks.

- Think about how you can use different literary techniques to get your message across to the reader. Do metaphors work for you? What will work for them?

- Remember, the essay or personal statement should be exactly that—a personal statement. What does your message say about you? How does it tell your story?

Invest in the Development of a Strong Message

The next step is to get it done. While very few essays keep students out of a college, very few will get them in. Writing a good or "good enough" essay is easy. If your strategy is to put something together quickly, something that is good enough to satisfy the requirement—so the essay is done and you don't have to worry about it anymore—then so be it. Just remember, "good enough" won't provide the hook that gets you into a college.

On the other hand, putting together a phenomenal essay—an essay that can provide a hook for you—requires a serious investment. If you want a busy reader to slow down and digest everything you have to

say—if you want a good essay to become great—you need to commit yourself to a thoughtful process of writing and editing. It's your call, though. You need to decide what all of this is worth to you.

If you write the first and last draft of a college essay the night before it is due, you deny yourself the perspective that would otherwise have been derived from time and distance. While there is little doubt that you can knock out an essay that will satisfy the requirement, that's all it will do. The truly special essay—the one that might actually help you get you into the college—never emerges.

Between the Lines

Time as an Editorial Tool
In developing a first-rate essay, you need to give yourself ample time to draft and edit the concept. After all, time is a powerful editorial tool. It affords you a measure of perspective. When time is on your side, you can step back from your work and see it from different angles. And you can give it to someone else for another opinion—if you have time.

You have to decide the direction you want to take with the essay. When you consider the essay's potential impact as well as the disposition of the people reading it, you might err on the side of giving the assignment some extra time. If you want them to read past the first paragraph, you must give them a reason to do so. It's a pretty safe bet that an essay thrown together at the last minute won't inspire much interest. The following *Six-Step Approach to Developing a College Essay* is intended to give you direction as you prepare your college essays.

Six-Step Approach to Developing a College Essay

Step One. Get Organized and Gather Information (spring of junior year)

- Start a journal. Keep track of thoughts and discussions in which you find yourself articulating strong opinions.

- Begin to make note of the various "why" messages that help to define you. For example, the fact that you have been able to travel extensively is wonderful. *Why* has that been important to you and how has it had an impact on your development?

- Reflect on your life experiences to identify factors that have had a

bearing on who you have become and understand *why* that is the case.

- Write an essay to yourself entitled "*Why I Want to Go to College.*" Don't worry about making it perfect or showing it to anybody. It will be good practice, though.

Step Two. Distill the Information (summer prior to senior year)

- Collect applications from the schools on your short list. Create a spreadsheet that includes the name of each school, the essays required, and the deadlines for each.

- Refer to your journal to see if and where your various entries match up with essay prompts. Make note of these possibilities on your spreadsheet.

- From this spreadsheet, select the essay prompt that you suspect will be the most challenging and begin to mull over different approaches to the assignment. You might as well tackle this one first rather than putting it off until crunch time.

Step Three. First Draft (August prior to senior year)

- Speed-write a rough draft of an essay in response to the challenging prompt as well as any others. Use your journal notes and related reflections as the basis for the content you are developing.

- Don't try to be perfect. It's more important to commit some ideas to paper than it is to write the perfect essay the first time out. Do the same for other essay prompts. Save your drafts. Don't look at them again for at least two weeks.

- Continue to record thoughts and discussions in your journal.

Step Four. Review and Edit (Early September of senior year)

- Get out the drafts you wrote in August. Edit them critically but don't worry about making them perfect. Read them out loud. Listen to your words. Are they conveying the desired messages? Are they telling the stories that need to be told? Put these revised drafts away again for at least two weeks.

Step Five. Solicit Feedback (Late September of senior year)

- Get your essay drafts out again. Edit them. (Each time you edit your own work, it will look different and you will find new opportunities to strengthen the presentation of your messages.) Reduce the number

of words by 10 percent. This type of disciplined review will force you to tighten your overall structure.

- Ask one of your parents, a teacher, or a friend to review your drafts. This is a *read and react* session only! *Don't look for or accept written feedback*. Rather, listen to the conversation. What are you learning through the exchange that *you* can incorporate into your essay to make it better? Process what you have heard. Then, edit accordingly and put the draft away—again for at least two weeks.

- If time allows, repeat the process with another family member or friend.

Step Six. Final Edit (October of senior year)

- Retrieve your revised drafts one more time. Read them critically. Reduce the word counts by another 10 percent. You'll be amazed at how easy this is and how much better your drafts become as a result! Run them through spell check, grammar check, and any other "check" you can find!

- If you are typing or writing the essays long-hand, be careful to review your work for accuracy and legibility. When admission officers find themselves struggling to read your submission, they will lose interest and move on.

- If you are using the same essay for several schools, make sure that any customizing you have done in the body of the essay is true to each school that will receive it.

- Print the essays according to the specifications provided on each school's application form.

Final Thoughts

In order to produce a good essay, you have to look in the mirror—and then be prepared to talk about what you see. Look carefully. What you see is what colleges want to know about. They want to know what makes the person. They want to know who you are and how you view yourself.

The risk-reward element with the essay is very high, especially if you aspire to colleges near the top of the Pyramid of Selectivity. It might seem like the odds are already against you, so why not take a chance with your presentation in the essay? A "safe" essay might satisfy the requirement, but it won't get you in. In order to win, you must make yourself vulnerable. That isn't easy.

Ten Essay Writing Tips

1. **Give yourself time to do a good job.** Allowing yourself time on a project enables you to stand back from your work, see it from different angles and make it better.

2. **Invest in the drafting process.** Don't worry about making the first attempt perfect. Just let an idea flow. After you have written it, put it away—for two weeks. The more often you are able to repeat this process, the greater your opportunity to develop something special with your essay

3. **Don't try to be something you are not.** Colleges like authenticity. They want to see the real you.

4. **Be careful about pet stories, or accounts of a dear, departed relative, or your efforts in delivering the big play in the championship game.** These well-worn topics are not good vehicles for delivering fresh perspective and insight.

5. **Don't be redundant.** If you use your essay to talk about things that are already covered on your application, you have wasted the space.

6. **Eliminate distractions.** Readers are not going to spend time with essays that are hard to read. Run spell check—and grammar check—on your finished essay. If you are writing your essay by hand, make sure your writing is easily legible.

7. **When you think you are finished with your essay, read it again—out loud.** Better yet, read it to someone else. This will force you to slow down and consider how every word sounds. If you find yourself pausing or hesitating, highlight the passage so you can go back and fix it. Listen for rhythm. How do the words work together to convey your idea to the reader? Do they flow? Where do you need to add or edit punctuation? When you proof your work silently, you tend to read through it quickly and are not as apt to discriminate where you should.

8. **While it is possible to use the essay written for one college or scholarship competition to satisfy the requirements of another, it is not advisable.** Colleges have reasons for posing the questions they do. As they make fine distinctions between excellent candidates, admission officers are eager to see how you interpret *their* questions. It's much better to write thoughtfully— and well—in response to their question than to use an essay written for a different college. The latter will have a "done over" look that suggests the author is looking for shortcuts—an impression you do not want to give.

9. **Be careful about becoming involved with essay editing services.** If the rationale behind the assignment is to give you an opportunity to reveal the real "you," then the essays for hire will be awkwardly transparent.

10. **Be original.** The application and the essay are about you. Believe it or not, admission officers are pretty good at spotting essays that are not entirely authentic. The last thing you want is for an admission committee to question your integrity.

Chapter 12

Time to Apply: Get It Done!

Win the Battle with Procrastination!

One of the biggest stumbling blocks in the college application process is the application itself. You've done everything else—the thinking, talking, and planning. There is nothing left to do but complete the application! Much as that might seem like a "no-brainer," when it comes to actually filling out the forms, a lot of students can't seem to "find the time." As important as the pending competition for admission might be, there always seems to be a good reason why completing the application is put off to another day.

If you are like many other teenagers, this is a familiar scenario. Procrastination, or the ability to put things off until they really need to be done, is a strategic element of your survival plan, so no worries there. After all, why stress out on a project any more than is necessary—especially when you know you can do your best work under pressure? Why should your college applications be any different?

Well, you might consider the consequences. For example, waiting until the application deadline means that you are in a hurry and you are stressed. As a result, you won't have much patience for questions on the application that require reflective thought. You won't be as likely to tidy up grammar and spelling—and you certainly won't be inclined to ask anyone to look over your work.

So, what are you left with? Typos? Grammatical mistakes? Poorly developed ideas? Errors of omission—and the very strong impression that you, the candidate, didn't care enough to invest time and effort in preparing your application? Remember, to the reader your application is you. Do you want to risk presenting yourself in a bad light that might cause an admission officer to lose interest?

Between the Lines

Possible Academic Interest or Major

Many universities admit students by degree program. When that is the case, the academic discipline you list under "possible major" will determine the program for which you are being considered. It will also determine the competitive pool into which your credentials will be placed. As a result, you need to be clear in your own mind about what you want to do. And remember, it's okay to be undecided (the designation will be liberal arts or general studies at most universities).

As you prepare your application, then, do the little things well. Be thoughtful in your approach. Invest in yourself. When everything else is equal, you want the reader of your application to come away feeling: "Wow—we *need* to take this one!" The balance of this chapter is devoted to helping you work through some of the troublesome and potentially annoying details of the process. So, take a deep breath and get ready to tackle your applications!

The Application Form

As you assemble applications for the colleges to which you are applying, you will discover that, under the colorful wrappers, they are very similar. They are forms on which you record all the good stuff we have been discussing. Each will require three types of information:

Biographical Data

This is background information about you and your family. In addition, you will need to provide data regarding your possible major, the schools you have attended, and the standardized tests you have taken and will take.

Subjective

Most applications include at least one essay question. The more selective colleges will present a battery of questions, including a few mini-essays. Scholarship programs may require you to submit additional essays in response to specific prompts. Make sure each essay is directed to the appropriate office or program.

Extracurricular

Each application will provide space for you to present your activities and achievements. Unless otherwise indicated, list only the experiences that cover your high school years. If space is limited, focus on the most meaningful of your involvements. Be sure to demonstrate the depth of your involvement and any leadership opportunities that materialized. Out-of-school activities that are important to you should be noted as well.

Be attentive to the various forms and deadlines associated with your applications. Some colleges use a two-part application. Submit Part I or the "preapplication" as soon as possible. Many schools will use Part I to collect the biographic information and establish a collection point into which additional application materials can be filed. After you have submitted Part I, don't forget the deadline for Part II! Your application won't be complete without it. Other supplemental forms include Early Decision statements (requiring signatures for activation), scholarship applications, and forms certifying your intent and/or eligibility to apply without standardized tests.

Letters of Recommendation

Most applications include recommendation forms to be completed by teachers and counselors. Be sure to give these folks plenty of time in advance of deadlines. After all, you are asking them to do you a big favor! You can be helpful by making sure they have the necessary information and insight about you to write well-balanced letters. Let them know when

the letters are due and make sure they have the appropriate preaddressed, prestamped envelopes.

Students often wonder whether they will get to see their letters of recommendation. The answer should be "no." When you ask someone to write on your behalf, you will be asked to waive your right of access to that letter. Do it. It is vital that your recommenders be able to provide a complete and balanced perspective without having to worry about how you will react to what they have written.

If your recommenders are concerned about being secondguessed in any way, they will be less inclined to share the kind of information that is useful to admission officers in the credential

Between the Lines

"The Thicker the File, the 'Thicker' the Student!"
Resist the temptation to seek letters of recommendation from important people in the community who can say nice things about you. Before asking for extra recommendations, ask yourself: "What is it that this person can say about me that my teachers and counselor will not have already said?" If the individual can shed personal insight into the way you approach your work, interact with others, or react to setbacks, the letter might be helpful.

review. So, give them some space and a lot of trust. The people you have chosen for this task are your strongest supporters and want to see you do well.

Outside (of School) Recommendations

In establishing points of distinction in an application, it's often useful to involve people from the community who provide perspectives that validate your experience. For example, a letter from a private music teacher who attests to your diligent preparation, ability to perform under pressure, and determination to compete at a certain level will cast your private music study in more substantive light. Similarly, the coordinator of a local homeless shelter can testify to your selflessness and generosity. Recommendations such as these bear witness to who you are and what you have to give.

Apply: Online or the Old Fashioned Way

Many colleges offer the option of online applications. Some even waive the application fee if you apply online. The ease and efficiency of the online options are undeniable. However, you should pay attention to the following details if you choose to go that route. The responsibility for submitting an on-time and complete application is yours.

Between the Lines

Snail-mail or E-mail?

"Should I submit the application over the Internet or is it better to print out and send a hard copy?" This is a frequent question of students who are able to access online applications. The answer: "It really shouldn't matter." Unless the school strongly advises you one way or the other, use the form with which you are most comfortable.

- Follow the directions carefully. Know when to "save" and when to "send."

- Review a hard copy of your application before submitting it. While many HTML input screens are designed to accommodate endless entries, there are limits to what will display in the PDF output. An entry that is too long will be truncated.

- Before you send it, print a copy for your files.

- Don't wait until the last minute to submit your application. That is when the volume is peaking and the risk of system failures is the greatest.

- Don't be surprised to receive a post card saying that your application is incomplete. There may be a brief time lag as all the materials coming from different sources (the Web, your school, your references, "mail in" supplements) are compiled into one file.

- Call or e-mail the college within two weeks to make sure it received your online application if you have not otherwise received an acknowledgment. If you get a notice that something is missing, check to see that you have sent it and then give the notice to your counselor so she can determine if there really is a problem.

- If you are paying by credit card, you should submit your application early enough to allow for the payment to reach the admission office

in timely fashion. Without a recorded fee, many colleges will not process applications.

- When paying by check for an online application, use the voucher provided with the application. Be sure to include your full name and address and reference the date the online application was sent.

While online applications are very convenient for both you and the colleges processing them, be careful that an online application doesn't obscure your level of interest in a given college. By encouraging the online application, colleges are also artificially inflating the size of their applicant pool. Since the number of students to be admitted remains fairly constant, this makes them appear to be more selective. If you apply online, make sure your interest in that college is well established otherwise.

The Common Application

Perhaps the most popular online application is the Common Application. The Common Application is accepted by 300 colleges and universities around the country as their own—even though they may print and distribute an application under a separate cover. The beauty of the Common Application is that it can be completed one time and copied any number of times to be sent to member institutions.

If you choose this application, make sure that you secure and complete any supplemental forms required by the colleges to which you are applying. For more information or to complete the Common Application online, go to: www.commonapp.org.

Common Application Tips

- The Common Application is a viable option for member institutions on your short list. Don't get carried away, though. Some students see the Common Application as an easy opportunity to "test the water" at a larger number of schools without having to complete additional applications. Submitting applications in this manner is frivolous and irresponsible. It feeds the notion among admission officers that there are larger numbers of "ghost applications" in their applicant pools and distracts you from focusing on the places that have emerged as the best "fit" for you.

- Make sure you demonstrate interest. This might sound like a broken record, but you can't afford to have a college regard you as a "low-yield" prospect because its only contact with you is the Common Application you submitted.

- Make sure you know the deadlines and requirements for the colleges and universities to which you will apply. Even though they may share the same form, each school may have slightly different requirements for completing the application.

Starting the Financial Aid Process

Just about the time you are putting the wraps on your applications for admission, you'll need to turn your attention to how you will finance your college education. This is an important conversation for you to have with your parents. In all likelihood, they are very sensitive to the cost yet they want you to have the opportunity for a college education and will do whatever they can to support you.

If you and your parents believe that you will need financial assistance, the first thing you need to do is complete the Free Application for Federal Student Aid (FAFSA) in order to become eligible for federal assistance (various student loans and Pell Grants). Many colleges will also use this application to determine your eligibility for the funds they administer. Others will require you to complete the College Scholarship Service (CSS) PROFILE and/or applications of their own.

Between the Lines

Owning the Expense

Colleges assume that the responsibility for paying the bill rests with the student's family. Once you turn 18, however, the bills will bear your name. So will the grades and other official correspondence. Ready or not, you are about to be the proud owner of all of the college experience! In all likelihood, you will receive financial assistance from your family, your college, and from the government. But making it happen is ultimately your responsibility. The more engaged you can be in the funding side of things, the greater will be your appreciation for what you have as a student.

You can complete a FAFSA online at www.fafsa.ed.gov after January 1. You and your parents do not need to wait until taxes are filed. Rather, you can file based on estimated financials for the most recently completed tax year prior to your high school graduation. It is better to act sooner than later to get the process under way (and remember to apply for a PIN at the FAFSA Web site). Regardless, be attentive to deadlines. Don't wait until you know where you have been admitted to initiate a financial aid application. By then, the money may be gone.

While some families are able to afford all of the expense that is associated with attending college, others must rely on funding from the colleges themselves as well as scholarship assistance provided by outside sources. Colleges will typically inform you of the need- and merit-based

options that they have to offer. Be attentive to deadlines in pursuing these opportunities.

Scam Watch

If you are like most high school seniors, you've probably heard from companies offering to help you maximize your financial aid and scholarship potential. Be careful. While some of these advisers are qualified and well prepared to help families develop an effective plan for managing their resources in support of college costs, others are not. They will simply give you information you could easily find on the Internet or through one of the colleges to which you are applying—and you'll end up paying for it! The National Association for College Admission Counseling has a page on its Web site that allows you to access scholarship scam information. For more information, go to: www.nacac.com/preventscams.html

Additional Thoughts About Completing Your Applications

- Fill it out. Neither your mother nor your father is going to college. They shouldn't be "doing you a favor" by filling out the application. Despite their assurances that it's "not a problem," they "have more time to work on it than you do," and "besides, I can type faster"—don't let them do it! This is *your* process.

- It is your responsibility to know and follow your high school's procedures for getting transcripts, grade reports, and recommendations to your colleges. Make sure you take that responsibility seriously.

- Give your counselor a list of the colleges to which you will be applying along with the respective application deadlines.

- Develop a spreadsheet to track the various forms required by each college and their deadline. Post it someplace where you will see it every day.

- Take time to create a "master file" spreadsheet that includes all the data that might be included on an application (from social security number to your parents' middle names to the dates on which you sat for the SAT/ACT). Doing the research once will save you time and energy as you begin to fill out your applications.

- Create a resume that includes your extracurricular activities and

honors/awards. List the involvements that are most important to you first. This resume will be helpful as you develop the theme for your essay. You might also share it with the people who will write on your behalf so they can have the benefit of the full scope of your high school experience in front of them as they write.

- Note opportunities to submit portfolios or tapes of your performance and deadlines for these submissions. Call at least six weeks in advance to schedule auditions if they are offered.

- Complete a draft of your application (print it out) that you can review prior to sitting down to do the final version. Make sure you have all the information you need in the right places. Read the mini-essays out loud. How do they sound? You want this application to be ready for "prime time" when you start to fill out the final version.

- Give the teachers and counselors who will write letters of recommendation the time they need to give careful thought to the manner in which they endorse your candidacy. Make sure they have the necessary forms and envelopes as well as dates for when the materials are due.

- Take the time to do a good job on the essays.

- Make sure you have a handle on your testing record. Know which tests are required as well as those you have taken and those that you will take (and when). As you prepare your application, it's imperative that you have either satisfied the minimal testing requirements for each school or you can demonstrate how/when you will. Arrange to have your scores from tests taken in your senior year sent to the colleges of your choice as soon as possible.

Chapter 13

Playing the Early Decision Card

"To ED or Not to ED?"

Or, more specifically, "Will I have a better chance of getting in if I apply Early Decision?" That seems to be the question for many students as they try to calculate the best approach to their top choice colleges. If a first choice is emerging from your short list of colleges, this question may be weighing on your mind as well.

The Early Decision or ED option has become very popular among students as they seek to improve their chances of admission in what are bound to be tight competitions. Students who choose to apply ED are prepared to forego potential opportunities at other institutions in favor of an early—and binding—commitment to one. If they are dead certain of that commitment, choosing to apply ED can make a difference. Many also see a successful ED application as the ticket out of an application process than can drag on interminably throughout the senior year.

This is serious stuff, though. ED embodies a commitment—kind of like taking the "big step" in a relationship. Before moving forward, you

need to be absolutely, beyond-a-shadow-of-a-doubt-certain you are ready. There are lots of factors to consider. "What if they don't take me?" "What if I get in but they don't give me the financial aid I need?" "Can I change my mind if a better offer comes along later?" "How can I be sure I will feel the same way about the school six months from now?"

Between the Lines

The Early Decision Commitment
Early Decision (ED) is an application option that enables you to apply for admission and receive a decision in advance of the regular admission process. In order to apply ED, you must declare your intent to enroll if accepted. Should you be accepted, you also promise to immediately withdraw any other applications for regular admission that you may have submitted to other colleges.

As you will see in the coming pages, there are no guarantees when considering the ED option. Just as clearly, Early Decision is not for everyone. The balance of this chapter will give you greater insight into the "early" programs that are bound to come across your radar screen so you can be better prepared to make the right call when the time comes.

Important Note: Colleges that don't face as much pressure to be selective will consider students for admission on a rolling basis. In Rolling Admission scenarios, admission committees make decisions on the applications as they come in, and will continue to do so until their classes are full.

Behind the Scenes with "Early" Programs

Colleges' tendencies with regard to ED have changed dramatically over the years. Originally an application option extended by elite institutions to their best candidates, ED has become the perfect marriage between *institutions* with complex enrollment agendas and *students* on the competitive bubble who are eager to improve their chances of admission at those schools. Let's take a closer look at how and why colleges utilize their ED programs.

The admission process is an opportunity for colleges to manage enrollment—to maintain or improve levels of selectivity while enrolling just the right number of students. When the number of applicants far exceeds the number of places to be filled, institutions must calculate closely the number of students to be admitted or run the risk of missing

badly on their enrollments. One way they can reduce this risk is by accepting students in smaller increments (with staggered deadlines) that allow them to monitor the yield-on-offers more closely. At many places, the first such increment is the Early Decision or, in some cases, Early Action program.

A secondary benefit to the process of incrementally admitting and enrolling the class is that admission officers are able to keep a handle on selectivity (a.k.a. admit ratio) and yield. You'll recall that two of their objectives are to become more selective (limit the number of offers made) while improving the yield (percentage of

Between the Lines

Don't Confuse the "Rates"

Be careful not to confuse yield rates with your chances of getting in. The yield rate is a statistic used by institutions to predict the number of students to be admitted in a given competition. Your chances of getting in are reflected in the admit ratio or selectivity. Except for a handful of institutions at the top of the Pyramid, admit ratios for ED tend to be much higher than for Regular Decision admission.

accepted students who enroll). Let's take a look at how they do that within the context of the "Doors of Enrollment."

DOORS OF ENROLLMENT

As selective institutions contemplate their enrollments, they expect to enroll students incrementally through three different phases or "doors" of the selection process. Those doors are:

Early Decision

Regular Decision

Wait List

Early Decision is the door used by students who are eager to commit themselves to a college. If admitted, they will enroll. Early Decision is the first opportunity for admission officers to begin accepting students into the new class.

The *Regular Decision* door is the one through which most students enter. Even if they have favorite colleges, Regular Decision applicants want to see how all of their applications fare before making an enrollment commitment. The Regular Decision process can take several months to complete given the volume of applicants involved.

At many selective institutions, qualified students who are not admitted through the Regular Decision door may be offered places on a *Wait List.* Given the pressure on colleges to manage the admit ratio and yield rates carefully—and the abundance of strong candidates who are not admitted initially—colleges and universities tend to actively engage their Wait Lists as they complete their enrollments. Traffic through the Wait List door is heaviest from late April through May of the senior year.

Keep in mind that colleges want to improve their yields whenever possible. A higher yield is not only evidence of its popularity but also it enables the college to lower its admit ratio and increase its selectivity. Now, let's look at the yield rates a college might expect on offers of admission in each phase of the admission process. Among those accepted through each "door," what percentage is likely to enroll? The following are close approximations of yield rates you might expect to find at institutions that are selective.

	Early Decision	Regular Decision	Wait List
Typical Yield	very high (95-98%)	low (18-22%)	high (65-75%)

Does any of these yield rates surprise you? You would expect the Early Decision yield to be high, theoretically 100 percent, given the presumed commitment of ED applicants. By comparison, the Regular Decision yield is quite low. When you think about it, though, that is to be expected as most Regular Decision candidates are likely to find acceptances at numerous schools. The odds that such a student will enroll are relatively low. On the other hand, Wait List yield rates tend to be rather high as Wait List offers are generally directed at students who are likely to accept them.

The more ED candidates in a given enrollment formula, the less a college must depend on enrolling low-yield Regular Decision candidates. As a result, Early Decision would seem a "win-win" situation for a school that is managing its enrollment strategically. For every ED enrollment a college realizes, it can reduce by as many as 5 or 6 the number of students to be admitted in the Regular Decision process. Is it any surprise, then, that ED is the door through which colleges want to drive as many enrollments as possible?

For example, let's suppose that XYZ College is able to increase by 50 the number of ED enrollments it realized from one year to the next. That would reduce by 50 the number of students to be enrolled—and by

250 the number of students to be accepted—through Regular Decision. As a result, the yield goes up and the admit ratio goes down. XYZ College appears to have become much more selective.

Early Decision, Round Two

Now that you see the strategic value to colleges of a phased enrollment program, it shouldn't surprise you to learn that many offer multiple "rounds" of Early Decision. In other words, if you have discovered a first-choice college *after* its posted deadline for Early Decision applications, look further. It may offer an opportunity for you to apply ED in Round Two of its deliberations.

Deadlines for ED Round Two applications or conversions—you

Between the Lines

Know What You Are Getting Into
While Early Decision Round Two may seem like a great idea, it can be a trap for students who are exhausted by the process and simply want to get it over with. You are suddenly confronted with what seems to be a no-brainer: apply ED now and improve your chances of getting in. Tempting as this may be, don't abandon your priorities and the sense of "fit" that emerged from your earlier thoughts about college. Your choice must make you happy for the next four years.

can "convert" the application you already submitted for Regular Decision to Early Decision—range from the middle of January to the middle of February. Some colleges will informally accept ED Round Two applications right up to the beginning of March. It is their intent to enroll as many students through ED as possible in order to reduce the number of candidates to be admitted through Regular Decision.

Note, however, that the same standards of commitment articulated for ED Round One apply to ED Round Two. While the odds might be in your favor, the expectations remain the same. If admitted, you will be expected to withdraw your other applications and enroll. If you are still struggling to figure out how you will manage college costs, don't pursue ED Round Two until you have resolved those concerns with the financial aid office.

Early Action

Whereas Early Decision programs are contractual in nature, Early Action (EA) programs offer a bit more flexibility. When you apply EA, you are expressing strong interest in that school. In return, the school will take

action on your application earlier in the process. *However*, you are not committed to enroll if admitted, and you are not obligated to withdraw the applications you have submitted to other colleges. This gives you the advantage of knowing the outcome at your first-choice college without having to commit until the deadline for Regular Decision enrollment.

Some EA schools offer a version of Early Action that is called "Single Choice Early Action." This means that a student choosing to apply Early Action

Between the Lines

The Hidden Agenda and ED/EA Options
In addition to managing enrollments, colleges and universities have a strategic interest in promoting ED/EA options. The outcomes, higher yields and lower admit ratios, contribute to stronger rankings in guidebooks.

may do so at only one institution. Make sure you are familiar with the rules and deadlines for applications at each of the schools on your list.

From an institutional point of view, EA is another opportunity to incrementally enroll the class from a large group of applicants. Because EA does not involve a commitment, the yield will be somewhat lower than the yield for ED. Schools that have used EA over time, though, will be able to forecast yields on such offers that can be as high as 70 to 80 percent.

For more information about the advantages and disadvantages of ED/EA, as well as a directory of the 378 colleges and universities that offer ED/EA options, visit the Web site for the National Association for College Admission Counseling (NACAC) at www.nacac.com/earlyadmission.html.

Making Early Decision Work for You

While we have determined that the odds do favor the ED applicant, do NOT apply ED—unless the college in question has passed the "certainty" test. Is it *truly* the very best "fit" for you? Too often, students start their college searches believing they "need to find an Early Decision school." This is not a good idea! If you become obsessed with finding an ED school, you will lose your focus on your more fundamental priorities and, possibly, end up at a place that is ill-fitted to your needs.

The best-case scenarios for ED involve schools that emerge from a systematic search process in which you have exhausted any reasonable

doubt about the level of your commitment. When you find such a place, the next step is to try it on. Put it to the test. If a place can pass the "certainty test," then you might have something.

Early Decision applicants are admitted, denied, or deferred. In the case of deferral, the application is set aside to be reviewed again with the regular decision candidates. Generally speaking, though, an admission committee will admit you ED if it believes you would be on the "playing field" as a regular decision candidate. If you *do* apply "early" somewhere, it makes sense to cover yourself by having regular applications to other colleges ready in the event that your Early Decision application is unsuccessful.

Between the Lines

The Certainty Test

Before applying ED, spend 24 hours on that school's campus. Attend classes, talk to professors, sleep in the residence halls, and hang out with the students. In short, immerse yourself in the campus culture. Then put your passion to the test. Repeat the experience at the school that is your second choice. If, after all this, the first school remains your first choice, then ED makes sense.

Most ED/EA programs operate on deadlines well ahead of those established for regular decision, typically ranging from November 1 to December 1. Decisions are usually mailed within thirty to forty-five days of the deadline. Colleges that offer a second round of ED usually post deadlines that fall between January 15 and February 15.

ED and Financial Aid

The availability of financial assistance for ED candidates varies from school to school. Some prefer not to award financial aid until they have seen applications from all of the candidates who need assistance. In that case, your application may be deferred in order for it to be considered later with the regular decision candidates. Others may award aid to admitted ED candidates in much the same manner as they would regular decision candidates. Yet others may admit you and offer less aid because of your presumed commitment ("He'll come regardless of what we give him."). If you are considering an Early Decision application and the availability of aid is a factor for your family, you might ask the college's financial aid office to give you an "early read" of your likely financial obligation if you are admitted.

One at a Time!

According to the rules for Early Decision, you may be an active ED applicant at only one college. In return, that college will give you a decision within thirty days. If you are deferred or denied, then you become a "free agent." You are released from any commitment to that school and are free to apply ED to another school (presumably under an ED Round Two plan).

Occasionally, students are tempted to submit more than one ED application *at a time*. Don't do it! Such an indiscretion would be a violation of the moral and ethical commitment you are making. Besides, it's not uncommon for colleges and universities to share lists of accepted students. More than one student has had all of his applications tossed out by the schools involved upon the discovery of such chicanery.

When an ED Application Comes Up Short

Ideally, your ED application will result in good news—you'll get in! When that happens, the implications are clear. You've won a place in the class! You submit your enrollment deposit and proceed to embrace (and enjoy) the balance of your senior year without the ongoing distraction of the application process.

On the other hand, the envelope you receive may not bear the news you wanted to hear. You could be deferred or denied. As difficult as it might seem, a denial letter can "cut both ways." The disappointment is obvious and you understandably feel a sense of betrayal. On the other hand, you know the outcome sooner than later. Assuming ED was your best chance of getting in, the news wasn't going to be any better later in the winter as a Regular Decision candidate.

If there is any good news about a letter of denial, it is that you are free to refocus your efforts at a time when other application options are still available to you. That's why keeping other applications ready during the time when you are an ED candidate at your first-choice school is a good idea. It affords you a measure of insurance in the event that things don't work out.

A letter of deferral, though, is something of a mixed blessing. While you have not been accepted, the admission committee found enough merit in your application that it decided to place your credentials into the competition for Regular Decision admission. It is putting off a final decision until later.

The good news is you are afforded more time to compete with new grades, score reports, and personal achievements that might materialize

during the winter of your senior year. As you do this, though, you are released from your commitment to enroll and can pursue other applications, including ED possibilities at another college. The bad news is you are looking at the prospect of having to compete for another two to three months without any certainty of the outcomes. And don't get your hopes up. As a deferred candidate, the odds of gaining admission are generally less than the odds for regular decision candidates who have not come through ED. If the admission committee had been sold on the strength of your application, it would have taken you as an ED candidate.

If you are to have any chance as a deferred candidate (at your ED college) through regular admission, you need to make sure your file is as current as possible. Improvement in grades will make the greatest impact. Additional letters of recommendation are helpful only to the extent that they add *new* insight into your performance. In all likelihood, the admission committee will wrap-up its decision making by the third week of March. Any information they don't have by then won't be considered.

A constructive exercise for you to consider in the aftermath of an ED deferral or denial is to reassess your other college options for "fit." Is it possible that, in your excitement over applying ED to one college, you overlooked another place that might be even better for you? The bottom line: you *will* be able to pursue (with distinction) your academic and career goals through many excellent colleges and universities. If ED doesn't work out, perhaps the best thing you can do is chalk up your experience as instructive—and then move on.

Early Decision "Do's and Don'ts"

- Do visit multiple college campuses before choosing to apply ED. Stay overnight at several. Give yourself a good perspective from which to choose appropriately.

- Don't apply ED to more than one school at a time.

- Do ask for an "early read" of your financial aid application before you apply ED if you have concerns about affording that college's costs.

- Don't apply ED if you feel it's important to compare financial aid offers.

- Do make sure that you are "in love" with a school before applying ED. It might be the place you call "home" for the next four years.

- Don't apply ED simply to "beat the odds." Chances are you might get in—and then find yourself in an unhappy situation at a school that really isn't for you.

- Do understand what the institution's rules are with regard to ED/EA submissions.

- Don't succumb to the temptation to let the other applications you submitted "ride" after you have been admitted ED somewhere. Not only is it unethical, but the chances are good that you will get caught—and lose all of your enrollments!

While You Wait

Behind Closed Doors

You are now a college applicant. It's mid-winter of your senior year. Your applications have been submitted and all you can do is wait for the admission decisions. After months of mail, campus visits, interviews, e-mail exchanges, and phone conversations, the chatter from the colleges has all but disappeared. The silence is deafening.

Life goes on as the senior year holds plenty of distractions of its own. You can't help but wonder, though, what is going on behind the "closed doors" of the admission process. It is natural to be curious. After all, it's only your future that's at stake! So, what *does* happen to your application when it reaches the admission office? Who reads it? What will they think? How will they decide? When will you hear? Surprisingly, the answers aren't that simple.

While you wait and wonder, the admission "wheels" are turning as applications are processed and the credential review begins. It's a crazy scene. The mailroom and data entry areas alone are humming with

nonstop activity as applications arrive. Once it is fully assembled, the typical application includes about 18 pages. Multiply that by the number of students applying to gain an appreciation for the sheer volume of paper and data that must be processed.

Another way to think about this scenario is to imagine dumping the contents of a 5,000-piece jigsaw puzzle on your dining room table. Just as the puzzle pieces need to be sorted, grouped, and tested for "fit," the elements of applications from thousands of students need to be gathered, collated, and processed *before* they can be evaluated for "fit."

Once assembled, the applications are passed on to the admission committee where the credential review will take place. From November through the middle of March, the admission committee is engaged in the search for the right pieces to each part of the puzzle that, once assembled, will be the new entering class. After months of intensive review and debate, the puzzle starts to take shape. With a strategic tweak here and there in the final days of this four-month marathon, the puzzle starts to take shape. The committee has done its job and the letters are ready to mail.

This chapter will take you through the different stages of the "marathon." While there is little you can actually do during this period— other than remain focused in the classroom and continue to do great things in the world—you might take comfort in having some idea as to what is happening behind closed doors.

Enrollment Planning

The selection process starts with a plan shaped at the highest levels of an institution that is surprisingly simple in its basic expectations, yet remarkably complex in its execution. At its core, the plan is to meet new enrollment goals and improve all the qualitative measures that are typically used to compare institutions publicly. The enrollment of a new class also affords a college the opportunity to immediately replace the tuition revenue it loses as students graduate. As a result, the number of new students required is generally fixed based on the need to generate revenue. The plan starts with this number and builds upward. The Enrollment Model for XYZ College gives us the opportunity to follow the logic of the plan as it unfolds in the early stages.

Enrollment Model
"XYZ College"
8,000 Applicants
50% Selectivity/Admit Percentage
4,000 Acceptances
25% Yield
1,000 Enrolled

With an enrollment goal of 1,000, enrollment managers (a.k.a. admission officers) at XYZ are guided by the yield on acceptances in past years as they predict the current year yield within a percentage point or two. You can see from the model that the overall yield rate at XYZ is historically about 25 percent of those admitted. In order to enroll 1,000 students, XYZ must admit 4,000. Or so it would seem.

In the last chapter, we talked about the "Doors of Enrollment"—each of which had a different yield rate attached to it. Imagine that the Enrollment Model at XYZ can be broken out to reflect the enrollment goals and yield rates attached to each of those "doors."

Expanded Enrollment Model
"XYZ College"

	Early Decision	Regular Decision	Wait List	
Applications	600	7,400	—	
	70%	*47%*	—	Admit Ratio
Acceptances	420	3,473	107	
	90%	*15%*	*75%*	Yield
Enrolled	399	521	80	

You can begin to see the complexity. The numbers on the original model actually reflect the final outcomes from each phase of the enrollment process. The yield percentages taken from the "Expanded Enrollment Model" are those used for planning purposes. Note that the totals for applicants, acceptances, and enrollments each match the numbers on the original model.

The expanded model also illustrates how the "Doors of Admission" can be used strategically to influence the overall selectivity and yield. Assuming a goal of 1,000 new students and a desire to improve selectivity and yield, XYZ can tinker at the edges of its enrollment model to achieve each objective of the plan. By taking more "high yield" students through Early Decision and from the Wait List, XYZ can reduce the number of students to be admitted through Regular Decision.

Adding to the complexity of the plan at many places, particularly universities, is the need to use expanded enrollment models *for each college and degree program* that must manage its own respective enrollments. For example, the college of arts and sciences at a university will have an expanded enrollment model that looks much different from the model for the college of engineering or the college of business.

Unfortunately, statistics that are published for an institution often represent the overall enrollment experience and can obscure the realities of the various programs within it. That's why you need to understand the competition for admission at the college or degree program you want *within* the university you are considering. The reality of the competitiveness for the engineering program may be far different (much more selective) than the overall selectivity of the university might suggest. As you can see, the selection process is an essential tool in achieving enrollment goals. It can also be used to manipulate selectivity and yield outcomes.

Between the Lines

The "File with Your Name on It"
The moment you express an interest in an institution, a data file is created that has your name on it. Every subsequent contact you have with that college results in a new entry in that data file. The file becomes an electronic collection point for your application materials and serves as a tracking device for your contacts with the college throughout the process.

Layered on top of the selection process is the task of determining how financial aid might be utilized to secure the class and achieve strategic outcomes. Who will get the merit scholarships if they are offered and how will the need-based financial aid be administered? A private institution the size of XYZ might be able to commit $10 million to the exercise. While that may seem like a lot of money—and it is—it won't be enough to cover the financial need of every worthy candidate. In order to get the most out of their financial aid dollars, then, admission officers will discriminate among strong candidates in favor of those whom they value most.

The enrollment "plan," then, defines the ground rules that determine how your credentials will be evaluated and, ultimately, valued. Before a single application is reviewed, XYZ has "set the bar" academically for the coming competition and articulated the parameters of its

"Hidden Agenda." This information is quickly absorbed into the consciousness of those who review your credentials and guides them throughout their deliberations. By the middle of March, the plan objectives will be sharply in focus as admission officers put the finishing touches on the class.

A File Is Developed

Before the plan can materialize, though, admission offices must receive, process, and prepare the applications submitted by students they have been recruiting. The true "behind the scenes" work starts in September with the arrival of the first application materials and continues until the last decision is made. Actual processing procedures vary across colleges and universities depending on applicant volumes, levels of selectivity, and institutional agendas. Generally speaking, though, admission office staff will check your application packet upon arrival to determine its contents and then match it against existing files for any materials that might have been received in advance of your application. Information that arrives later will be routed directly to your application.

At most schools, the receipt of an application form along with the required application fee (or fee waiver) is sufficient for the admission office to officially count your application and "activate" your file. Before an active file can be reviewed, though, the admission staff must make certain that all required application materials are in the file. Electronically submitted applications are either printed out into hard copy files for distribution to the admission committee or prepared for review online. With credentials assembled, the detective work can begin.

Detective Work

Faced with a mountain of applications—and with a plan in hand—admission officers can go to work. Their job: Get the best class possible that meets the specifications of the plan. In doing so, they will sort through the applicants, one at a time, to determine who is on the academic playing field and then choose, from among that group, the brightest and most uniquely talented. When admission officers get to your application, their detective work will prompt them to:

- Scope out the scene—develop a basic familiarity with you and your background. Who are you? Where do you come from? What do you want to do? The part of the application you filled out provides this introduction.

- Look for evidence that you can do the work—are you on the "playing field?" A quick look at your transcript, essays, letters of recommendation, and test results will tell them whether you have what it takes to get the job done in the classroom.

- Determine "what they get" if they admit you. What is your gift—your talent, your perspective? How would it fit into the community they are trying to build?

- Decide whether they want to invest in your enrollment. They've seen all the good stuff in your application. Now, they must attach a value to your potential enrollment. This is when they make the critical distinction between everyone who is on the playing field and those who will be invited into the class.

If this sounds familiar, it should. In subtle and not so subtle ways, elements of the "agenda" and "hidden agenda" guide readers as they sort through candidates and credentials. It is more art than science. While there is a certain degree of calculation involved with determining who is on the "playing field," the decision making rests heavily on judgments made by the admission officers.

As a result, the selection process is shrouded in mystery at most schools. As application deadlines come and go you will hear a lot of speculation among your friends about who should "get in" and at which schools. While the consensus may seem clear, the reality of the outcomes may prove to be far different. Committees need time and space away from this type of speculation to apply their respective agendas in sorting through the qualified candidates.

The Pyramid of Selectivity offers perspective here. Admission outcomes are fairly predictable at schools that accept more than half of their applicants. The picture is much less clear, though, at places farther up the Pyramid. Admission officers must be at their sleuthing best at these schools in order to make incredibly fine distinctions between candidates. They are just as often looking for reasons *not to admit* a student as they are looking for the "hooks" or nuances of talent, character, or experience that cause a candidate to rise above the rest. The more selective the school, the greater is the pressure to make such distinctions.

The Committee at Work

The manner in which admission committees engage in their "detective work" varies greatly across institutions. While the "committee" might literally be a room full of readers debating credentials, it is more likely to be a collection of individuals reading independently—sometimes at home. Or

it might be the programmed wisdom of the computer that determines the fate of your application.

The review of your credentials—the detective work—starts with your transcript. Readers note the strength of your academic program and look for patterns of achievement. "How are you performing in your current environment?" "Do you demonstrate the capacity to do the work at the next level?" "What does your senior year performance say about your determination to finish well?" Assuming you are on the "playing field," they want to see how your performance sets you apart from the competition.

Next, they look at interviews, essays, and extracurricular activities (noting any "hooks" or points of distinction along the way)

Between the Lines

The Context of Your Learning Environment

The context of your current learning environment is very important to the admission committee's understanding of your performance. Readers want to know as much as possible about your school (rigor of the courses offered, competition in the classroom, and successes of past graduates) and how you are using the opportunities available to you to grow academically. And, yes, admission officers are pretty savvy regarding the differences between high schools!

for clues that you might possess unusual talents or perspectives. In a very short period of time, they develop a bias—a sense of what you have to offer and where you fit in the competition. Before long, they get to the question, "What do we get by admitting this student?"

Assuming the bias is favorable, the readers quickly scan letters of recommendation for validation of the information on your application. These letters convey critical elements of your story and provide an added dimension of understanding to the circumstances surrounding your performance.

It is not uncommon for at least 2 readers to independently review a set of credentials. If they agree in their assessments, a decision might be reached. If they disagree, your application goes to either a third reader or a committee that makes the decision. Candidates at opposite ends of the competitive spectrum are sorted rather quickly and easily. Those failing to make it onto the playing field are processed for denial letters while the clearly superior candidates are marked for possible scholarship. The real

and ongoing competition exists among those who remain on the bubble in the middle.

At universities that consider applicants according to the respective college or degree program for which they have applied, credentials are reviewed within the context of the enrollment plans for those programs. Many specialty programs will spend time evaluating credentials (auditions, portfolios, SAT Subject Tests) that serve as filters on top of the normal academic requirements. In such instances, you need to show that you are on the "playing field" academically *and* that you are among the most proficient in the areas in which you want to study. This is especially true of the competition for admission to conservatories and art schools.

The deliberations and detective work continue through the winter until all of the applications have been read. That's when things get interesting as admission officers begin to make refinements to the class they are assembling.

TINKERING WITH THE CLASS

Far from finished, they must now reconcile the priorities of the enrollment "plan" with the qualities of the class that is beginning to take shape. This is when the tinkering takes place—when the music director makes her pitch for another cellist in the orchestra, the theater coach argues for a couple of students who were impressive in their auditions, or the basketball coach makes an impassioned plea for the 6'8" kid who can score 20 points a game and play defense. The Alumni Office pushes for "legacy" applicants and the admission committee makes sure it has given due consideration to compelling candidates from disadvantaged backgrounds

It is also a time when a review of mid-year grades—yes, grades are reviewed well into March of your senior year—will cause some head scratching among the readers. More than a few excellent applicants make the mistake of "checking out" early from the classroom. Little do they know how close they got—that the admission committee was all set to admit them until the mid-year grades arrived!

In particular, March is when the "hidden agenda" lives large in the selection process. Yield-savvy colleges read between the lines of your application to determine the seriousness of your interest—"Will she come if we take her?" Without clear evidence of your interest in the university, your application is unceremoniously moved to the Wait List.

And don't forget the money factor. It is at this point that admission officers determine the value they want to attach to candidates. The "What do we get?" question becomes part of a larger discussion around the question, "Is this someone in whom we want to make a monetary

investment?" This line of questioning is particularly germane if there are concerns that admitting everyone on the tentative acceptance list will result in an over-expenditure of financial aid funds. Applicants most vulnerable at this stage of the game are those on the competitive "bubble." Rather than risk putting their financial aid budgets in the "red," enrollment managers will quietly move candidates on the bubble to the Wait List for possible consideration later if there is any money left over.

After a college arrives at the number of acceptances it needs in order to accomplish its enrollment plan, any juggling that takes place to accommodate candidates who are "moved up" due to special circumstances will necessarily force the removal of others to the Wait List. Some candidates are "moved down" due to less-than-stellar senior year performances. Others on the "bubble" simply fall short because they lack advocates at a time when advocates can make all the difference.

The Wait List

While the focus seems to be on whom to admit and why, the Wait List quietly emerges as an important player in the credential review process. Long regarded by applicants as a "polite denial," the Wait List is an important reserve of talented students on the competitive "bubble." Initially established by admission committees to provide insurance in the event that actual enrollments came up short, the Wait List is now a "door" through which colleges can enroll talented, high-yield students. If you present good but not great credentials, you might find yourself on a college's Wait List.

In the end, most selective colleges offer the opportunity for active Wait List status to a large number of candidates. Those who remain "active" on the Wait List have a reasonable chance of getting in *if they are patient*. Because the opportunity for Wait List movement depends on available places in the class, enrollment managers will proceed strategically in making their offers. While most schools go to the Wait List from late April into the middle of May, it is not uncommon for places to call students from the Wait List well into the summer.

Chapter 15

The Envelope, Please

The "Thick Envelope"

It is the objective of anyone who has ever applied to college. It's what you have worked hard to achieve for years—the prize, the "brass ring" of the college admission process. The source of great anticipation and the inspiration for wild celebration, it arrives in a "thick envelope."

Wherever you are in the process—Early Decision, regular decision, or beyond—"it" is the long-awaited "good news" and the thick envelope is what you want. The mail "watch" will be an obsession at your house until the thick envelope finally arrives. You know its contents and you can't wait to open it. The news you have been waiting for is finally in your hands—a happy ending to a long and arduous process. "Congratulations, we are pleased to offer you a place in the class . . ." the letter begins. There is more and you might read on, but that first sentence says it all. You've done it! *You're in*! You've survived the admission gauntlet and won the opportunity to enroll.

Hopefully, you will have similar experiences with each of the colleges to which you applied. While the odds are not with you in that regard—that you will get in everywhere—you are likely to find some measure of success if you have been diligent about putting yourself on the right playing fields. Let's take a look at some of the scenarios you will likely encounter as the mail arrives at your house.

The Mailman Cometh

After months of waiting, usually around the middle of March, you will begin to get envelopes in the mail or you receive word that decisions have been posted on the Internet. As the decisions trickle in, they are greeted with a predictable range of emotions.

Between the Lines

Stay Focused

As the good news begins to arrive, your life will change as colleges roll out the "red carpet." You'll be invited to parties in your honor. Prominent alumni will call to wish you well. Some schools will even offer to fly you to their campuses for the weekend. In the midst of all the ego food being tossed your way, however, you need to stay focused. Do your own detective work and remain true to your priorities. Much of the stuff that goes on in the weeks prior to your enrollment decision is staged for your benefit.

The thick envelopes bear the good news and you are immediately relieved to know that your accomplishments have been recognized. The years of hard work paid off not only in an offer of admission, but also, perhaps, a scholarship or acceptance into an "honors" program or preferred housing options. You also find satisfaction in finally knowing you will have a new address in the fall. You may have to figure out, though, *where* that will be if you receive more than one acceptance. One thing is certain—you're moving on!

Some letters in thin envelopes may be short and to the point as they politely inform you that "due to the extremely competitive nature of the applicant pool, we are unable to offer you admission." Ouch! While you knew in the back of your mind this could happen, seeing it in print still hurts. You knew the odds but had worked hard to prove yourself. Maybe, just maybe . . . and, just like that, it's over.

Keep your chin up. Outcomes such as this are not a reflection on you or your family. This is *not* a matter of a university saying, "We don't like you." You are *not* a failure. You are a good person with a lot to give and much to accomplish. You gave it your best shot, but that school

wanted something different. If you aimed high with your college applications and fell short, you are in good company! You should still have quality options, though—places that will value and embrace you—*if you have done a good job of finding the best college "fit" for you.*

Then, there are the letters that bear the curious message, "We are pleased to offer you a place on the Wait List." It's certainly a mixed message. You can't find the word "congratulations" anywhere, yet they are "pleased to offer you"—what? Your instincts say that if you are not "in" you must be out. Rejected. You quickly convince yourself that it is just a polite denial letter.

In reality, the Wait List offer is a "definite maybe." Whether you knew it or not, you were on the "bubble" at such schools. When it came time for the admission committee to make very fine distinctions between strong candidates, you came up short. Rather than outright denying you, such an institution has decided to keep you in reserve because it is concerned about the yield on its regular offers of admission. In offering you a place on the Wait List, it is really saying, "We might not get the number of enrollments we need from the initial round of acceptances. If that proves to be the case, then stay tuned." While such an explanation does not feel very reassuring as you read it for the first time, you may well have options before this whole thing is over. Hang in there.

A variation on this theme involves an invitation for you to start in the *second semester*, after requiring you to participate in other off-campus programming during the first semester. This is a strategy employed by colleges to create yet another, albeit invisible, "door" of enrollment. You must understand, though, that you are not being offered admission for the fall semester and, in most cases, will not be given the opportunity to enroll in the fall even if the Wait List becomes active. If such a scenario is agreeable to you, go for it. It may represent your best chance of getting into that school.

Finally, you might receive an offer of admission that is contingent upon your participation in a remedial program over the summer. If a college likes what you have to offer (it is excited by the way you answered the "what do we get" question!) but is concerned about the degree to which you are *prepared* to find success, it might refer you to a series of pre-enrollment courses designed to bolster your academic and study skills. While it would seem that the college values you and is investing in your success, you need to be realistic in your assessment of the situation and make sure *you* are prepared to do what is necessary to make good on the opportunity.

You're In! What Next?

By the time all of the mail is open and the admission decisions are in, you should have options. Quality options. There might be two or three—or, if you're lucky, half a dozen. Now in control of the final phase of decision making, you need to recheck your priorities. What was important when you constructed your list of colleges? Has anything changed? Why? The answers to these questions will be your compass as you wade through decision making in the coming weeks.

The elements of a good college fit apply now more than ever as well. Even the "best" college (by acclaim) won't help you reach your goals if getting through is likely to be a struggle academically. Choose wisely. Stay within your ability to comfortably embrace the academic programs and achieve the educational goals you set for yourself.

Checklist for Decision Making

Using your priorities as a guide, take another look at the colleges that accepted you. You have until the end of April to choose one of them. Return to their campuses where you can immerse yourself in the sights, sounds, and overall culture of the places. How do they feel to you? In doing so, try to accomplish the following:

- Spend a weeknight in a residence hall, eat at least two meals in the dining facilities, and go to two classes in different disciplines, including an introductory first-year class.

- Talk with a faculty member as well as the appropriate preprofessional adviser from the academic department that interests you.

- If you are a recruited athlete, visit with the coach as well as members of the team.

- If you have academic support needs, talk with the person on campus who coordinates the Special Needs Support Center or the Writing Center.

- If you have financial concerns, make an appointment with the financial aid office. Take copies of your application as well as any relevant tax returns for reference.

- Hang out. Watch people. Listen to them talk. Ask them what they think about campus life, politics, sports, religion, or whatever is important to you.

- Inquire about safety information, crime statistics, and campus escort programs.

- Use good judgment as you explore the social scene. Know your limits.

In other words, take in as much as possible. Most students who emerge from this process acknowledge that much of the decision making comes down to a gut feeling. Make sure the college you choose fits well and feels good before you commit yourself.

The Wait List: Another Opportunity to Win

Competing for admission from the Wait List is like playing in a contest that has gone into overtime. If you assume the game is lost, you can't win. If you keep playing—hard and smart—you may have a good chance. Take heart. Most of the selective colleges in the country will admit students from the Wait List every year in numbers ranging from half a dozen to well over 100.

Information about Wait List status and movement is closely guarded. Colleges are sensitive to negative inferences that are made about the need to go to the Wait List and prefer to be discreet about the extent of their reliance on it for enrollment. Here is what you need to know in order to give yourself a competitive edge.

Between the Lines

Success from the Wait List
Make sure that the school knows it is your first choice. Visit. Send new grades. Give them new insight into your performance. Stay on their radar screen. If there has been a question about financial aid, be clear about what your family can afford. Your need for assistance could well be a determining factor.

1. Wait Lists will be active because colleges are constantly gambling that their yield on initial offers will be better than expected. They are usually wrong.

2. Colleges target their offers of admission from the Wait List. They don't want to admit any more students than absolutely necessary. Contrary to popular belief, most Wait Lists are not usually ranked numerically.

3. Be sure to provide evidence of your potential hooks. Colleges redefine their needs as they go to the Wait List. They may have plenty of tuba players, but need an oboist. They may need to balance their gender mix. They may need students who won't require financial assistance.

4. Admission committees constantly search for new information upon which they can base an acceptance. Provide new (and improved) grades, a letter of recommendation from a senior year teacher, new financial information, and evidence of recent accomplishments that might not have appeared on your initial application.

5. Stay on the radar screens of the schools that have placed you on the Wait List. Make sure they know you are available and ready to accept an offer of admission. Continue to show your interest without becoming a pest.

6. Don't allow yourself to become so preoccupied with the Wait List situation that you lose track of your more immediate options. You don't want to talk yourself out of another school that you really like.

Should the call—it might literally be a telephone call—come offering you a place in the class from the Wait List, be ready. You may not be given much time to respond. If you have already deposited at another school but want to accept the offer of admission from the Wait List, you will forfeit the earlier deposit.

What If I Don't Want to Go to the Colleges That Accept Me?

Let's consider the possibility that, despite your best efforts, you may find you are not admitted to any of your top-choice colleges. You got into a couple of your "safety" schools, but they don't hold the same luster that is associated with the places that turned you down. As "back-ups" they we were fine—perhaps because you didn't think you would ever really have to consider them. Besides, now that your friends have been admitted to some of the places that turned you down, the schools you are left with may not seem nearly so exciting. If this is the case, what do you do?

If you find yourself in such a situation, reassess the options you *do* have. They weren't so bad when you decided to apply. Rediscover them and find out why. They may not carry the same cache as the places that turned you down, but the academic opportunities they present are probably every bit as good as those you would have found at the other schools.

If this line of logic doesn't work or you find that your priorities have shifted substantially, you might apply somewhere else as a late applicant. This is easier said than done, though, as most schools are reluctant to entertain late applications from students with whom they have little or no history. Your best chance in this instance is to find a college or university with an active Wait List and hope it will see your credentials as competitive. This is not likely to be the case, though, at places that are as selective as those that turned you down earlier.

Another alternative is to take the year after high school "off." Don't go anywhere. Instead, get a job. Travel. Get involved in community service. In short, take the opportunity to write a new and different chapter in your life. A "gap year" of this sort can be very healthy and productive to your personal development *if you use it well*. Besides, you are then afforded the opportunity to reapply a year later. I have yet to hear of an institution that doesn't see this as a positive development.

What About Financial Aid?

Between the Lines

Closing the Sale

From a business perspective, May 1 is the day when colleges expect to "close the sale." Imagine the financial impact on a dealership when it sells a new car. Now, multiply that by 100 or 1,000 or even 10,000! This is the impact that the Candidates' Reply Date has on a college or university. Needless to say, this is a high-stakes, high-anxiety time for everyone on college campuses.

If you applied for financial aid, sit down with your parents to compare the various financial aid awards or "packages" you have received. Your first two questions should be: "How much do we need to come up with out of pocket and can we manage it?" The next question must be considered within the context of each college: "Will my experience as a student and the likely outcomes (earning potential) merit this level of financial exposure?" In other words, *what is the value proposition for you in attending that school*?

Ideally, each college would respond to you with the same financial aid. That is not likely to be the case, though, because schools work with different pricing scenarios. For example, you may receive substantial assistance at a high-priced private college but not be eligible for much assistance at a lower priced, state-supported university. Or two private institutions that appear similar to you might provide financial aid awards that are very different in terms of the amount your family is expected to contribute as well as the composition (scholarship, loan) of the awards themselves. Remember, each institution will direct its resources toward the students it values most.

The End Game (Candidates' Reply Date)

After months, if not years, of planning and preparation, the admission process rushes to an end late in your senior year. You have little more than a month to ponder your next steps before a decision must be made. All that remains is a final determination of the college or university you will call home. The deadline for that decision is May 1.

On the flip side, May 1 (the Candidates' Reply Date) is the source of great anticipation on most college campuses. It's the date

Between the Lines

Choose ONE

You can enroll at only one college. If you are fortunate to have several attractive options, you may find it difficult to make a final decision. That's natural. Resist the temptation to submit enrollment deposits to more than one college so you can make the decision later. Not only is that unethical, but it could result in your forfeiting your options.

by which admitted students are expected to declare their intentions. While you are sorting out your final decision, colleges are sweating out their final enrollments. The "Candidates' Reply Date" will provide insight into the strength and character of their new classes and, if the enrollment plan works, May 1 will secure the operating budgets for the coming year.

Enrollment managers will actually begin to watch the mail on a daily basis in the middle of April in order to chart the growth of the class. Each new enrollment deposit is added to the base established by the Early Decision "class." The total is compared with enrollments on the same date in previous years. Any hint of a shortfall will result in a call to the Wait List. At selective colleges, it is not uncommon for 75 percent of the regular decision enrollments to arrive in the last five days of April! Few dates in the life of an institution are watched more closely than May 1.

As May 1 approaches, then, the implications are clear for everyone. The date represents the end-point of the process for you and is the last day you can post your enrollment deposit. It might not seem fair that you don't have more time to deliberate, but this is it. You need to decide. If your deposit arrives late, it will be the first to be returned if the college receives *more* enrollments than anticipated.

As soon as you have done what you need to do to check out your options, look inwardly to find your final direction. What does your gut

tell you? Sort through the smokescreen of the "sales pitches." Forget how you think your family or friends will react to the school that you choose. Your future happiness and success are at stake. Go with what works for you. You're now on your way!

Epilogue

Like most adventures, the college search and selection process will be over before you know it. Despite entering your life rather innocently ("Just think, you'll be going to college in a few years"), it soon morphs into an expectation of daunting proportions—"If you want to get ahead in life, you need to get into the best school possible!" Whether college is a rite of passage or you are the first in your family to pursue a college education, the swirling caldron of expectation and uncertainty that engulfs you can be just as maddening as it is exciting.

It might be easier said than done, but try to block out all of the extraneous stuff—the emotional ups and downs that your peers experience, the anxious questioning that comes from your parents, and the curiosity of well-wishers in the community. There'll be more than enough drama going around, and you don't have to be part of it. Instead, be yourself. Do your thing, whatever *it* is, as well as you can. And stay true to the vision you have for yourself.

Most of all, don't take yourself or the process too seriously. Otherwise, it can devour you! Relax. Smile. Know that the future of the world doesn't rest on the outcome of your college applications. You won't be branded a success or a failure *unless you allow that to happen*. The simple truth is that the success you experience in life has little to do with where you go to college and much more to do with how you take advantage of the experience while you are there.

Finally, if you go into this process expecting that the outcomes will be fair and logical—that you will get what you deserve—you'll be greatly disappointed. At the end of the day, colleges and universities will admit whomever they want for reasons that are only important to them. This is especially true of the more selective institutions. Why? Because they can. It is incredibly important that you find colleges that fit you well. By putting yourself on the right playing field, you greatly reduce your vulnerability to what can otherwise be an arbitrary selection process. Moving forward, then, make sure that you:

- Know Yourself
- Make Good Choices
- Do What You Love; Love What You Do
- Sprint to the Finish

Know Yourself. As we discussed throughout the early chapters of the book, this whole process is all about you—not your parents, your teachers, or your best friends. It's certainly *not* about the colleges! Remain centered on *who* you are, *what* you need, and *how* you function most comfortably. Don't allow yourself to be distracted by the agendas of others. Find the college that fits you best and you'll have the rest of your life to find emotional satisfaction.

Make Good Choices. The application you submit to colleges represents the body of your work over four years of high school. As a result, the decisions you make on a daily basis—not just about the big stuff like course selections and after-school involvements but the amount of time you spend on your homework or in editing a paper—will have a bearing on how you compete for admission at colleges that can be selective. So make good choices in the classroom and in life. Put yourself in a position to compete.

Do What You Love; Love What You Do. Your capacity to contribute to the quality of life on a given campus helps to define your value to that institution. Find your gifts, your passions. Cultivate them, nurture them, and allow them to grow so that when the inevitable question is asked, "What do we get if we admit him?" the answer will be readily apparent.

Sprint to the Finish! Think of your high school experience as being analogous to the mile race (four times around the track). If you have ever run the race, you know that you must complete each lap in order to be in a position to post a good result. Being in command of the race at the end of the third lap (junior year), though, does not guarantee victory. You may feel good about where you are relative to the competition, but you have yet to win anything! The senior year is the "gun lap." It is when the race is won. So, regardless of where you are at the end of your junior year, take control. Seize the opportunity to make a race of it in the senior year by sprinting to the finish!

Finally, embrace the opportunity that lies before you. Don't let the inevitable stresses of the admission process diminish your excitement for what you will achieve in college and beyond. Regardless of where you end up spending your college years, you'll be fine. All the best for a happy and productive college experience!